The Relevance of the Prophets

The Relevance
of the Prophets

R. B. Y. SCOTT

Department of Religion, Princeton University

REVISED EDITION

MACMILLAN PUBLISHING CO., INC.
New York
COLLIER MACMILLAN PUBLISHERS
London

To The Memory of My Father
JOHN McPHERSON SCOTT, D.D.
A faithful minister of the Word of God

Library of Congress Catalog Card Number: 68-17519

Revised Edition, Sixth Printing 1978

Macmillan Publishing Co., Inc.
866 Third Avenue
New York, N.Y. 10022
Collier Macmillan Canada Ltd.

PRINTED IN THE UNITED STATES OF AMERICA

CONTENTS

ABBREVIATIONS

AV   — King James or Authorized Version

ANEP — *The Ancient Near East in Pictures*, ed. J. B. Pritchard, 1954

ANET — *Ancient Near Eastern Texts*, ed. J. B. Pritchard, 2nd ed., 1955

ET   — *Expository Times*

EVV   — English Versions, where these differ from the Hebrew Bible in the numbering of chapters and verses

JAOS — *Journal of the American Oriental Society*

JBL   — *Journal of Biblical Literature*

RSV   — Revised Standard Version

VT   — *Vetus Testamentum*

ZAW — *Zeitschrift für die alttestamentliche Wissenschaft*

ABBREVIATIONS FOR BOOKS OF THE BIBLE

Gen.	Genesis	Prov.	Proverbs	Zech.	Zechariah
Ex.	Exodus	Is.	Isaiah	Mal.	Malachi
Lev.	Leviticus	Jer.	Jeremiah	Macc.	Maccabees
Num.	Numbers	Lam.	Lamentations	Mt.	Matthew
Deut.	Deuteronomy	Ezek.	Ezekiel	Mark	Mark
Josh.	Joshua	Dan.	Daniel	Lk.	Luke
Jg.	Judges	Hos.	Hosea	Jn.	John
Ru.	Ruth	Jl.	Joel	Acts	Acts
Sam.	Samuel	Am.	Amos	Cor.	Corinthians
Kg.	Kings	Mic.	Micah	Gal.	Galatians
Chr.	Chronicles	Nah.	Nahum	Tim.	Timothy
Jb.	Job	Hab.	Habakkuk	Heb.	Hebrews
Ps.	Psalms	Zeph.	Zephaniah	Rev.	Revelation
		Hag.	Haggai		

PREFACE TO THE REVISED EDITION

The author is grateful that this modest volume has proved useful to many people and has continued in print for more than twenty years. In the interval much scholarly work has been done on the Hebrew prophets, so that for a new edition it has been necessary to revise the text throughout and to re-write parts of it. It remains a modest treatment of a great subject.

Appreciation must be expressed for the stimulus received from friends and colleagues in learned societies in this country, in Canada and in Europe, notably Professor Gerhard von Rad, Professor H. H. Rowley, and the members of the Biblical Colloquium. From my graduate students I have learned more than they have learned from me.

R. B. Y. SCOTT

Department of Religion,
Princeton University
July, 1967

PREFACE TO THE ORIGINAL EDITION

The writing of this book has followed upon a suggestion by my friend Professor Gregory Vlastos that a book on the Hebrew prophets was needed which would show their importance for religion today, and especially for the responsibility of religion in the struggle for justice, freedom and human solidarity. As long ago as in August, 1937, a series of lectures under the title of this volume was given at the Summer School for Clergy at MacDonald College, Quebec, and the discussion follows the outline and to some extent incorporates the substance of those lectures. The book may indeed bear the marks of having been composed at intervals in a busy life over a considerable period of time.

This interpretation of prophetic religion and its bearing on our problems is addressed to ministers and laymen who are not afraid of serious critical study of the Bible, but who are not particularly interested in the more technical discussions which lead professional students of the Bible to their conclusions. The result of critical study is not to destroy but to clarify the spiritual value and moral authority of the Scriptures. The writer has attempted to state in positive terms the meaning and worth of the Hebrew prophetic writings, and to indicate their profound importance as a feature of our religious heritage which has the constant freshness of a perennial stream.

There is little, if anything, in what follows, which will be new to Old Testament scholars and teachers. The writer hopes, however, that the arrangement and treatment of the material is sufficiently distinctive to warrant its inclusion among the books on Prophecy referred to in seminary class rooms and consulted in libraries.

I wish to acknowledge the interest and help of my colleagues Principal G. G. D. Kilpatrick and Mr. Robert George, who have read the entire manuscript, and also of my colleague Professor Gerald Cragg and my former teachers Dr. Richard Davidson and Professor W. A. Irwin who have given me the benefit of their criticism of individual chapters. Without the constant help and encouragement of my wife the book would never have been completed.

R. B. Y. Scott

Divinity Hall,
Montreal
January, 1944

I

WHAT IS PROPHECY?

For the purposes of this study "prophecy" is taken to mean the work of the Hebrew prophets whose literary records are found within the pages of the Old Testament. Hebrew prophecy was and is not altogether unique, but it remains incomparable in its spiritual quality and permanent significance for religion. "The prophets" *par excellence* are the prophets of Israel, and their words are the standard of prophecy, even though they come to us in the language of a remote and antique world. Indeed, it is only by strong imaginative effort, and then imperfectly, that we can recapture the feeling of that moment when first a prophet spoke to his contemporaries the word God had given him to speak.

One of the gains of the intensive Biblical studies of the last century and a half, together with the rescue from oblivion of remarkable remains of the civilizations which surrounded and antedated Israel, is this recognition that the prophets are primarily figures of the past. Their message—or what survives of it—was addressed to men of their own day, in the conditions and circumstances under which they lived, and in language which only men of their own nation and time could fully understand. It abounds in figures of speech and contemporary allusions which to us are obscure; not (as some imagine) because prophecy is a tongue of esoteric mystery, but mainly because our knowledge of that ancient time is so far from complete.

The prophets were men of Israel and spokesmen of Israel's God to the nation of which they were members. They would have been astonished to learn that their words would be preserved in written form for many centuries, and be read aloud in places of worship in this unimaginable modern world—in new tongues indeed, but with local and temporal setting unaltered. They would have been dismayed to hear that some in this latter day would fail to distinguish the living Word from its incidental setting; that instead of recognizing in their prophecies the timeless message of God to mind and conscience, they would use them as a soothsayer's manual for predicting the future. For the relevance of the prophets' message for us must lie in some other realm than that of the soothsaying and divination which the prophets themselves so sternly denounced. "He has forsaken his people, the house of Jacob," says Isaiah, "*because* they are filled with diviners from the east, and practise soothsaying like the Philistines."[1]

PROPHECY AND PREDICTION NOT IDENTICAL

In popular usage today "prophecy" is roughly synonymous with "prediction of the future." The Greek word *prophētēs* means "one who speaks on behalf of someone else," in this case for God. Prediction is, in fact, *one* of the dictionary meanings of the word. Some Christians believe ardently—and many others vaguely—that the Bible foretells the course of events in the present and future ages, so that a skilled interpreter can learn from its pages the secrets of history as yet unwritten. Teachers who claim this skill find ready followers among the uncritical, who are led on by native curiosity and the fascination of the mysterious to fancy that they can pass the forbidden door and gaze on the designs of the Most High. There are many of these, indeed, whose Christian graces compensate somewhat for their bizarre ideas and unconscious superstition. But such a use of the prophetic scriptures is actually a revival of the ancient heathen practice of divining the future, heedless of the rebuke: "It is not for you

[1] Is. 2:6.

to know times and seasons which the Father hath set within his own authority."[2] A sense of the critical nature of the times in which they live leads men to select their own age as the beginning of the End, the goal of all history. But the wars and rumours of wars, the increase of knowledge, apostasy and worldliness to which they point as signs of the End could with equal or greater reason have been pointed to by men of many earlier periods.

That this did happen is the record of history. Millennarian speculation has appeared from time to time within the Christian community from its earliest days for the very good reason that it is suggested by certain eschatological and apocalyptic passages in Scripture. Ignatius, Polycarp, Justin and Irenaeus in the second century A.D. believed that they were living in the last times. In the third century Hippolytus declared that the end would come five hundred years after the birth of Christ. In the fourth century Lactantius taught that the Judgment was at hand, as Otto of Freising was to do eight hundred years later. The end of the first millennium of the Christian era was expected by some to be the end of the world. Shortly before 1260 A.D. Joachim of Flora in "The Eternal Gospel" set that year for the inauguration of the new Age of the Spirit. Militz of Kromeriz similarly fixed on the years 1365–1367, and in the Reformation period Hoffman the Anabaptist set the date 1533. In more recent times but with equal futility Guinness in "Light for the Last Days" (1886) picked the year 1930; Russell in "Millennial Dawn" (1907) the year 1914; and Bell Dawson in "The Time Is At Hand" (1926) the year 1934.[3]

If the Biblical passages on which these writers have based their predictions are examined, it will be found that they are taken chiefly from Daniel and Revelation, together with sections of the first three Gospels and the Epistles where similar language and ideas are found. On the other hand, there is scarcely any reference (except for brief Messianic passages) to the collection of prophetic books which forms

---

[2] Acts 1:7.
[3] On this section see S. J. Case: *The Millennial Hope*, 1918, from which some of the above examples are quoted.

the second of the three divisions of the Hebrew Bible which is our Old Testament. Yet it is this division which contains the books of the three "major" prophets, Isaiah, Jeremiah and Ezekiel, as well as "the Book of the Twelve," i.e., the twelve "Minor" or shorter prophetic books. The book of Daniel in the Hebrew Bible is not included in the collection entitled "The Prophets"; it is in the third division known as "The Writings," a more miscellaneous collection.

PROPHECY TO BE DISTINGUISHED FROM APOCALYPTIC LITERATURE

The fact is that Daniel and Revelation are not prophetic writings in the original sense at all. They belong, together with the other similar writings mentioned above, to a distinct type known as "apocalyptic" or "revelation" literature which began to be written by the Jews when the voice of prophecy proper faltered and fell silent. "Apocalyptic" has some features in common with prophecy. In fact, as Rowley says, it is "the child of prophecy . . . the re-adaptation of the ideas and aspirations of earlier days to a new situation. . . . Its message is represented as something to be kept from general knowledge, and to be handed down in secret,"[4]—as in Dan. 12:9, "The words are shut up and sealed until the time of the end." It is derived largely from older prophetic material, and indeed may be said to be a late and specialized form of written prophecy dealing in a new way with a single prophetic theme—the consummation of history. But it cannot simply be equated with prophecy, as such, and used to the exclusion of the older and greater prophetic books. It is a distinct phenomenon.

What strikes the eye at once in comparing these apocalyptic writings with prophetic books such as Isaiah and Jeremiah is the constant use in the former of visionary symbolism, beasts of fantastic form, horns and bowls and trumpets; signs in the heavens, a woman arrayed with the sun and crowned with stars, a man riding on the clouds, "the Ancient of Days" seated upon a throne surrounded by a

[4] H. H. Rowley, *The Relevance of Apocalyptic*, 1944, pp. 13–14.

heavenly multitude. As such things could not be visible to the eye of flesh, they are said to have been disclosed in a dream or vision. Usually an angelic being is introduced to interpret to the seer the sights and sounds of the vision.

The apocalyptic books have been called "tracts for bad times" because they seem to have been written to provide, for people suffering adversity and persecution, the consolation of a great hope in the God who works behind the scenes of history. Most of them are dominated by the conviction that evil is increasing, and is approaching a climax which will bring the catastrophic intervention of God and the end of the age. This breaking-in of the supernatural into the natural order marks the dualism which is characteristic of apocalyptic writing, and which is explicitly expressed in IV Ezra 7:50: "The Most High hath not made one world (or, age) but two." The seer is enabled in vision to look on at what is happening in that heavenly world, the counterpart of what happens in *this* world; the successive appearance of weird creatures and the battles of angelic champions determine the history of the earthly kingdoms they represent.[5] Events here and there are interlocked, and on the basis of the vision the apocalyptic writer proceeds to predict the future course of events.

Apocalyptic, in one sense, is mythology—a pictorial and narrative representation of a reality lying beyond sense experience. It is a mythology, not of the origins of all things (like Genesis 1–3), but of the End. Present events are felt to be rushing to a climax in which the moral enigmas of life will be resolved through the direct intervention of God himself.

Another characteristic of this type of literature, differentiating it from prophecy proper, is its fictitious ascription commonly to the authorship of some ancient sage or prophet. In Ezek. 14:14 Daniel is named along with Noah and Job as a traditionally righteous man, although, on the conservative dating of the books which bear their names, he and Ezekiel would have been contemporaries. The Bible knows nothing of the modern notions of literary property and plagia-

---

[5] Cf. Dan. 7 and 10:13–21.

rism. In fact, developed literatures such as the Law, the Psalms and
Proverbs are ascribed to authors traditionally associated only with
their beginnings. Similarly with apocalyptic literature, it was an
accepted literary device to ascribe the book to some ancient worthy.
This literature began to be written after the time of Ezra when the
period of inspiration was held to have ended,[6] and a new writer, in
order to secure a hearing, had to assume the role of a known prophet
or patriarch of olden time. The deception was more apparent than
real.

Another consequence of the scribal teaching that the period of
inspiration had closed was a new interest in the predictions contained in existing prophecy. If they had not been and apparently
could not be literally fulfilled, then they must be explained sym-
bolically. The "seventy years" of Babylonian servitude in Jeremiah
25:11, 12 becomes in Daniel 9:2, 24 "seventy *weeks of years*," in
order to bring the "accomplishing of the desolations of Jerusalem"
down approximately to the Maccabaean period for which the author
was writing. Thus the calculation of times and seasons began, and
with it a scheme of predetermined future history.

Apocalyptic, then, is a dualistic "mythology of the End" which
succeeded spoken and written prophecy in pre-Christian Judaism. It
is not the same thing as prophecy. But it is historically and religiously
important in its own right, because it affirmed deep convictions as to
the meaning of successive crises in relation to the transcendant End
of history. The distinction is most necessary, because of the confusion
between the two on the part of those who take apocalyptic as representative prophecy, to the neglect of books like Amos, Hosea and
Jeremiah.

PREDICTION AND DIVINATION

While the predictive element in apocalyptic is much greater than
in true prophecy, numerous predictions are to be found also in the

---

[6] Cf. Josephus, *Against Apion*, I, 8(40); 1 Macc. 9:27; Lk. 9:8.

words of the great prophets. The example given above from Jeremiah is one of the most explicit. To say that prophecy and prediction are not identical is not to deny the existence and importance of *a predictive element* in the former. How then can it be said that modern prognosticators are following wandering fires when they calculate on the basis of Scripture the dates of future events? The answer is, first, that they have mistaken apocalyptic for prophecy; and second, that they are using the Bible (in some degree at least) as a soothsayer's manual and an instrument of divination.

Divination, says Professor Rose,[7] is a practice resulting not alone from human curiosity as to the future, but also from the inability of the undeveloped mind to comprehend a negative argument which rules out definitely what has seemed possible. There is also involved a vague idea of the uniformity of nature. Divination is almost universally practised by peoples at the lower levels of culture, and became a specialized art among the nations of the ancient world, including Israel. Unusual sights, as of a bird acting strangely, or occasional involuntary human actions like sneezing, were taken as signs of calamity because at some time they had been followed by calamity. Natural portents such as eclipses and earthquakes were both unusual and terrifying. Dreams and presentiments came apparently unbidden to the mind. What could they mean? The dreamer might dream again (he usually does) and establish a reputation as a seer. Another who professed to discern the meaning of a message written in the starry heavens could gain a hearing from the uncritical. The curious markings on the liver of a sacrificed animal could be read as the secret script of a god. Men devised ordeals and games of chance, the outcome of which, not being humanly determined, was ascribed to supernatural agency and interpreted accordingly. Persons in abnormal mental states were believed to be spirit-possessed, and their strange cries were taken as a divine message to be translated by skilled men (as at Delphi).

[7] In *Hastings' Encyclopedia of Religion and Ethics*, vol. iv, 1912 art. "Divination."

There was much of this sort of thing in early Israel. Joseph is said to have had a cup by which he "divined" (by observing the shapes assumed by wine dregs or by oil poured on water).[8] Gideon asked for the omen of a dry fleece on wet ground and of wet fleece on dry ground.[9] David heard the sound of the marching of an unseen army in the swaying of balsam trees.[10] The ephod and the sacred lots Urim and Thummim were instruments of divination in official use by the priesthood, and it was only when Yahweh[11] answered Saul "neither by dreams, nor by Urim, nor by the prophets" that the king resorted to necromancy at Endor.[12] A later Judaean king, Ahaz, set aside a special altar "to enquire by."[13]

These examples show that such practices were familiar in Israel down to the prophetic period. But they were expressly repudiated by the prophets themselves as being alien to the genius and spirit of their religion. This is made emphatic also in Deuteronomy, the re-codification under prophetic influence of older laws. "There shall not be found with thee any one that . . . useth divination, one that practiseth augury, or an enchanter, or a sorcerer, or a charmer, or a consulter with a familiar spirit (i.e., a spiritualistic medium), or a wizard, or a necromancer. For whosoever doeth these things is an abomination unto Yahweh. . . . (But) I will raise them up a prophet from among their brethren, like unto thee (i.e., Moses); and I will put my words in his mouth."[14] Nothing could be plainer than that prophecy in the tradition and manner of Moses is something utterly different from these various methods of prying into the future, which

[8] Gen. 44:5.
[9] Jg. 6:36 ff.
[10] 2 Sam. 5:24.
[11] "Yahweh" is probably the original form of the name "Jehovah." The latter is not a Hebrew word but a hybrid form combining the consonants of "Yahweh" or "Jahveh" with the vowels of "Adonai" meaning "Lord," as an indication that the latter was for reasons of reverence to be pronounced in place of the former. The form "Jehovah" came into use only in the Middle Ages, through failure to recognize how it came to stand in the Hebrew text of the Old Testament.
[12] 1 Sam. 28:6.
[13] 2 Kg. 16:15.
[14] Deut. 18:10–12, 18.

are denounced as heathen practices, presumptuous and wrong. The prophet has no such secret lore and mantic skill. He can speak only when God gives him a word, and then he cannot choose but speak. "The Lord Yahweh hath spoken," cries Amos; "who can but prophesy?"[15] But unlike the apocalyptist he gives no time-schedule for his predictions of doom.

THE PREDICTIVE ELEMENT IN PROPHECY

What has just been said refers primarily to the classical prophetic period which opened about the middle of the eighth century B.C. The earlier stages of Hebrew prophecy, as will be seen in the next chapter, were more closely associated with soothsaying and spirit possession. The great prophets shook off all but a few traces of these early associations, but there remains in their prophecy an element of prediction which it is important to distinguish from the prognostications of the soothsayers and diviners.

We may take as examples Amos and Isaiah, both of whom made predictions which were fulfilled. With awful insistence and in lurid colors Amos pictured the imminent overthrow by earthquake and conquest of a society corroded by injustice. Within two years[16] there followed one of the most memorable of Palestine's earthquakes, and less than a generation later invasion by the Assyrians had brought to an end the political existence of the Northern kingdom of Israel. Isaiah, in the crisis of the Syro-Ephraimite attack in 735–734 B.C., assured the Judaean king Ahaz that before a child shortly to be born had outgrown his infancy, the threat to Judah would have vanished; before another infant was able to say "mother" and "father," the allied foes of Judah would have been despoiled by the Assyrians.[17] These predictions were fulfilled, apparently within a year. Again,

---

[15] Am. 3:8; ct. Dan. 12:11–12.
[16] This is the point of the accusative of duration in Am. 1:1: "*during* the two years before the earthquake"; cf. T. J. Meek in J.A.O.S., vol. 61, pp. 62–63. There is a further reference to the same earthquake in Zech. 14:5.
[17] Is. 7:10–16; 8:3, 4.

when Jerusalem was threatened by the forces of Sennacherib in 701–700 B.C., Isaiah assured King Hezekiah that the city would not be taken. Once more the forecast was justified by the event.[18]

These examples are typical, and it is to be noted of what sort they are. The prophets foretell doom in the one case and deliverance in the other—a doom or deliverance which is to befall the people whom the prophet is addressing. More important, they will experience it as an immediate consequence of their moral and spiritual condition at the moment when the prophet speaks. "If you are willing and obedient, you shall eat the good of the land; but if you refuse and rebel, you shall be devoured by the sword" (Is. 1:19–20). The margins of present time (so to speak) are extended to include a near future which is vitally and morally related to that present.

Such predictions are not glimpses of a predetermined future which is shortly to pass through the present moment into the past, like a motion-picture film passing the lens of the projector. The future is not so mechanically determined. What is about to happen is *the necessary consequence of a moral situation*; at the same time it will be the concrete realization of the prophetic "Word" which expresses in relation to that situation the righteous will of Yahweh. When God is about to act, he makes known his purpose: "Surely the Lord Yahweh will do nothing without revealing his plan to his servants the prophets."[19] These predictions are integrally related to the spiritual situation of those who hear them; furthermore, they are morally conditioned by that fact. "You have not returned unto me, says Yahweh, . . . *therefore* thus will I do unto you, O Israel."[20] "Take heed, and be quiet, fear not. (But) if you do not believe, you shall surely not be established."[21]

This moral conditioning and immediate reference explains how a prophetic forecast, far from being inevitably fulfilled with literal

[18] Is. 37:33 ff.
[19] Am. 3:7.
[20] Am. 4:10, 12.
[21] Is. 7:4, 7.

exactness, can be modified or withdrawn altogether. Isaiah declares categorically that Hezekiah is about to die, but later conveys word to him of his reprieve. Yahweh shows to Amos visions of an approaching locust plague and of a great fire, but heeds the prophet's plea for pity: "Yahweh repented (or, was sorry) concerning this; 'It shall not happen,' said Yahweh."[22] God retains the full freedom of an active will; he cannot be tied down by any pre-announcement of events or chart of dates.[23] But his freedom is neither capricious nor arbitrary. Its limitations are the requirements of his own nature—justice, mercy and truth: "he remains faithful, for he cannot be untrue to himself."[24] "The prophetic promise proclaims at its deepest level not a coming *something*, after the manner of the fortune-teller, but *he* (*sic*) who comes."[25]

As a consequence of what has just been said, we may see how some prophetic predictions could remain unfulfilled, while others were fulfilled in essence though not literally. For example, though Isaiah 17:1 declares that Damascus will become a heap of ruins, it remains a populous city to this day. In Ezekiel 26:7–14 we are told that Yahweh will "make a bare rock" of the city of Tyre by the hand of Nebuchadrezzar, whereas in a later chapter (29:17–20) it is acknowledged that Nebuchadrezzar's siege of Tyre had been unsuccessful, and it is said that Yahweh will give him the land of Egypt in compensation. More interesting still is Micah's declaration: "Zion shall be ploughed like a field, and Jerusalem shall become ruins," when taken with the explanation given a century later in Jerusalem itself that the contrition of Hezekiah had led Yahweh to change his mind.[26]

Another point to be remembered is that these predictions are usually clothed in the language of poetic imagery and hyperbole

---

[22] Is. 38:1–6; Am. 7:1–6.
[23] Cf. Jer. 18:6–10.
[24] Moffatt's translation of 2 Tim. 2:13.
[25] W. Zimmerli, in *Essays on O.T. Hermeneutics*, ed. C. Westermann and J. L. Mays, 1963, p. 105.
[26] Cf. Mic. 3:9–12 and Jer. 26:17–19.

which no one but the most prosaic literalist could insist on taking
as exact description. Take for example the familiar "It shall come to
pass in the latter days that the mountain of Yahweh's house shall be
established *on the top of the mountains.*"[27] How far from such stony
literalism is Jesus' understanding of the way in which ancient prophecies are to be fulfilled comes out in his comment on John the Baptist:
"If you care to believe it, he is the Elijah who is to come."[28] Many
Jews expected, on the basis of the prediction in Malachi 4:5, 6,
Elijah's actual return to earth. But it will hardly be contended that
Jesus taught re-incarnation. Thus for Jesus the fulfilment of the
prediction was on a deeper level of meaning, as when he said on
another occasion that Moses had written of *him*.[29]

Nevertheless, two passages in the Deuteronomic law do refer to the
fulfilment of prophecy as a criterion of its genuineness. Deuteronomy
18:22 says: "When a prophet speaks in the name of Yahweh, if the
thing does not follow nor come to pass, that is a thing which Yahweh
has not spoken: the prophet has spoken it presumptuously."[30] In
Deuteronomy 13:1–3 the test is carried further: "If there should arise
in the midst of you a prophet . . . and he should give you a sign or
a wonder *and the sign or wonder comes to pass* in connection with
which he spoke to you, saying 'Let us follow other gods . . .'; you
shall not listen to the words of that prophet . . . , for Yahweh your
God is testing you to know whether you love Yahweh your God with
all your heart." In other words, failure of a prediction may serve as a
negative test, but its fulfilment is no guarantee of genuineness if the
substance of the prophet's message departs from the basic religious
tenets of Yahwism. True prophecy would turn men from evil.[31]
Nothing could be clearer than that the essence of prophecy is not
prediction but the declaration of religious truth.

[27] Is. 2:2.
[28] Moffatt's translation of Mt. 11:14. That is, the role of Elijah the forerunner has been filled by John.
[29] Jn. 5:46.
[30] Cf. Jer. 28:9.
[31] Cf. Jer. 23:21–22.

SPOKESMEN OF CRISIS

The prophets of Israel were thus no mere prognosticators; they were spokesmen of a living Word from God. Their frequent references to the future, and especially to the immediate future, result from their sense of the spiritual importance and moral urgency of the present. They were certain of what Yahweh was about to do *because of* that present spiritual situation, which included not only men's attitudes but the *fact* of God's presence. They spoke in the atmosphere of moments which were critical for men because Yahweh's righteous will was present, and his claims were pressing. In this connection the prophet is to be distinguished from the priest, on the one hand, and from the "Wisdom" teacher, on the other.[32] The priest ministered in terms of the eternal and changeless to that in man's life which was constant or recurrent. The "wise man" distilled in his teaching the essence of common and long experience. The message of the prophet was differently related to the temporal setting of life. Time, as man knows it, has two aspects: it goes on, passing in ceaseless movement; the generations rise and pass away. But some present moments stand out from all the others. The hour strikes; the moment of decision and supreme experience comes. In that moment there is something more than one drop of time glimpsed as time's stream passes over the brink of the waterfall. It can be a *great* moment, charged with eternal issues determining destiny. There and then the Eternal stands revealed, claiming and challenging. The prophet, not the priest or the teacher, is the voice of God in that moment. He is the spokesman who can articulate the meaning of an eternal order and a Divine reality. He discloses the moral crisis in which men stand unheeding. He declares which is the way of life and which the way of death, and calls for decision.

An illustration may be found in chapters 7 and 26 of the Book of Jeremiah, where we have two accounts of Jeremiah's message on one

[32] On these three groups as the accepted spiritual guides of the community, cf. Jer. 18:18.

particular occasion. The setting is the gateway of the Jerusalem temple, where the crowds are gathered for a religious festival. The prophet is opposed by priests and people when he declares that this house shall be destroyed like the ancient sanctuary at Shiloh, because Israel has come to identify essential religion with the round of services according to the festival calendar, rather than with ever new responses to the ethical claims of God.

The prophets were primarily *preachers* in the highest sense of that term, rather than teachers or prognosticators. The epigram which describes them as "forthtellers rather than foretellers" makes a useful if not a completely accurate distinction. They *did* make predictions, but these often were only incidental to their message. Their relevance today is therefore not that they foresaw the course of events in the modern world. They do not speak *of* our age but *to* it, because our age also is critical and the issues at stake are spiritual and moral. If we can see beyond the local and temporal setting of their Word as spoken to men of that ancient world, we shall find that it is spoken to us too.

THE RELEVANCE OF THE PROPHETS

To use the word "crisis" with the glibness which is all too common dulls its edge. It may seem foolish for men, who of necessity cannot view their situation in historical perspective, to speak of it as being charged with issues of unusual gravity. But in point of fact every time is to the men who live then critical, for in it they are called to judge, decide and act. Their own is the one crisis which they are called upon to face. The prophets of Israel can disclose the reality and nature of our crisis when speaking of their own. They face us again with the responsibility of decision in response to God. Their prophecies express their moral certainty and spiritual understanding of *what will be* because of *what is*, because Yahweh and no other god is *Lord*.

Thus the prophets' message is relevant today in a deeper and truer sense than if they had foretold our story like a gypsy telling fortunes.

They are the contemporaries of every generation because the truth they declare is permanently valid. What they say has the timeless quality and compelling power of authentic spiritual utterance. The more we read their words, the more we are impressed with their self-lessness and fearlessness, their rich humanity and poetic genius, their spiritual insight and authority. There is nothing in the pre-Christian world and its rich and varied civilizations that is comparable with the great succession of Hebrew prophets. No explanation of them is sufficient which does not recognize that through them the Eternal God was carrying out his purpose for the spiritual creation and redemption of mankind.

It will help us today to discover what were the conditions of the tremendous spiritual vitality of the prophetic movements. The prophets were men who had given themselves with complete abandon to the service of the God whom they knew in their own lives, and through the religious experience of their people. "Yahweh *took me* from following the flock," said Amos simply, of his call to the ministry.[33] "Here am I. Send me" was Isaiah's prompt response to the call of Yahweh for someone to bear his message.[34] Through whole-hearted allegiance to the God of the fathers came a deeper understanding of the meaning for the present time of what was essential in the ancestral faith. Through moral obedience to the known God came new knowledge of him, and in the recognition of his presence a fresh and fuller revelation of his nature and his purpose. These men were not consciously innovators. If something new emerged in them it was Yahweh's doing, not theirs.

Again, the great prophets without exception were tremendously concerned with social conditions and public issues as marking a *spiritual* crisis. They do not speak merely in general terms of sin and repentance, still less of the conventional discharge of religious obligations. They are specific and startling in their indictments. Ecclesiastical machinery was to them an encumbrance and its offices an offence

[33] Am. 7:15.
[34] Is. 6:8.

to God, if meanwhile the actual human situation and urgent moral issues were ignored. "When you stretch out your hands, I will hide my eyes from you; yes, when you make many prayers I will not listen; —your hands are covered with blood."[35] This was what Yahweh was saying while the temple services went on; but only Isaiah, not the other worshippers, heard him.

Another factor contributing to the prophets' spiritual power was their vivid awareness of the presence and activity in the turmoil of men's ordinary social life, of the God they worshipped in the sanctuary. Their supreme testimony was that the God who had met the fathers and had spoken to Moses was present and speaking just as really now. He was not a god only of mythological beginnings, nor a god like Baal Melkarth "musing, . . . or on a journey, or asleep." Rather, he was a God who was about to "*do* something in Israel at which both ears of everyone that hears it shall tingle."[36] The prophets recognized that God was at work in their contemporary world because they did not think of him only in traditional and conventional terms.

Again, we may learn from the prophets something as to the way in which religion may become the dynamic and its ethic the directive of social transformation. The vital religion they proclaimed and the moral standards they set forth so firmly came to have in time a profound influence on the spirit and ethos of the community, and eventually on its forms of worship and social laws. A new understanding of religion and its all-embracing ethical requirements was established because of their mission, though of course the mass of men fell short of full understanding and still farther short of its implications for conduct. Nevertheless, the religion of Israel and its culture were re-created through the mission of the prophets, as may be seen from the fact of their dominant influence later on the composition and collection of the Hebrew Bible. The utter transformation from the superstition and nature religion of the early kingdom, with its attend-

[35] Is. 1:15.
[36] 1 Kg. 18:27; 1 Sam. 3:11.

ant social conventions, to the flowering of Judaism at its best, is the measure of what, under God, the prophets of the eighth to sixth centuries B.C. accomplished.

Finally, we may learn from these ancient spokesmen of eternal truth that, as their God was not bound within the tradition of the past ages of Moses and David, so our God is not bound within the tradition of their age or of the first century A.D. He is the *living* God, at work not only in the souls of individuals today but present as the final arbiter in the struggles and confusion of our social life. Where the ruthless forces of this modern world bear down upon and crush the spirits of men and women, there God is present in power, the Vindicator of those for whom the odds are too great. For men and peoples who have vision and faith and moral earnestness God holds open his door—to a personal and corporate life that is noble and free. If in our pride and self-sufficiency we will not heed his Word and its demands, we shall find that today also his judgments are in the earth.

2

THE WORLD OF THE PROPHETS

The world in which prophecy came to flower in the eighth century B.C. was a meeting place of three different ways of life, the way of the herdsman, the way of the farmer and the way of the city-dweller. The Israelite tribes, prior to their conquest and settlement of Canaan, had been nomads or semi-nomads; a simple patriarchal society deriving its subsistence from flocks and herds, supplemented by minor crops raised at temporary halting-places. The conquest was a piecemeal process in the course of which the Israelites after a long struggle established themselves as the dominant class in what was largely a continuing Canaanite society. Unable at first to dominate the fertile plains where the Canaanites had fortified cities and chariotry, most of the newcomers established themselves in the sparsely settled hill country by clearing the forests.[1] They adopted the Canaanite language (which we now call "Hebrew"), fused Canaanite culture with their own traditions,[2] and became a settled, territorial people. Their economic life now was supported principally by the fruits of the field, of the orchard, the vineyard and the olive grove, with flocks and herds in second place.

[1] Cf. Jos. 17:14–18; Jg. 1:19–35; Y. A. Aharoni, *The Land of the Bible*, 1967, pp. 217–18.
[2] Aharoni, *op. cit.*, p. 219.

Towns and villages became the settled centers of tribes and clans, and a local attachment strengthened (though it also might rival) the old loyalty of kinship. "In practice, after the settlement, the village stood for the clan."[3]

With the advent of the monarchy, and especially with the reign of Solomon, the urban and commercial way of life was greatly developed, partly at the expense of the older pastoral and agricultural community. The social structure now became more centralized and autocratic, and the state emerged as a new entity within Israelite society. The court, the royal officials and the standing army were non-producers, and could only in part be supported from the tolls exacted on trade in transit through Palestine, and from the tribute of subject peoples. Heavy taxation and unpaid labor for the state began to drain the moderate wealth of the community.

Such far-reaching changes in social and economic conditions could not fail to affect profoundly the people's religious conditions and beliefs. For whatever may be the ultimate source and significance of a religion, it must be relevant to the actual conditions under which people live. Its patterns of belief and behavior necessarily reflect the social and economic structure in which it is an operating factor, just as, in turn, that structure is affected by the standards and goals of life hallowed by religion.

The social and economic tensions resulting from the cultural clash within Israelite society under the monarchy produced in turn religious tensions and reactions of permanent importance. The nomadic, pastoral, tribal element in tradition and society remained to the end very largely the classical, normative ideal of Israelite religion. The portraits of the patriarchs in Genesis idealize the nomadic pastoral way of life. The work of Moses is made the pivot of later Israel's historical theology, and the tradition affirms that Moses led Israel *out of* "civilized" Egypt *into* the wilderness, and that he ended his work outside settled territory. Prophets and

[3] R. de Vaux, *Ancient Israel*, 1961, p. 13.

psalmists hark back to that pre-Conquest period as supremely significant.[4] They evaluate the events of the Exodus and the Wanderings much as Christian theologians have evaluated the events of the life of Christ, and especially the Cross. Some of the prophets raise the cry "Back to Moses,"[5] as modern preachers have cried "Back to Christ." There were not wanting "fundamentalists" like the Rechabites who took this literally, and refused to build houses, to till the ground or to drink wine, because these were the ways of Canaan in the modern age.[6]

Thus the nomadic tribalism of the patriarchal and Mosaic traditions permanently affected the future course of religious development. That is not to say that later religious leaders (except for reactionaries like the Rechabites) desired to go back actually to wilderness conditions of life. Rather they would revert to those characteristic ideas and values which first became explicit in the creative period of religious origins, and which remained valid even though they had to be re-interpreted from time to time according to the necessities and genius of the age. If we are to understand the world of the prophets, we must see how there was superimposed upon this tribal and pastoral religious culture the successive agrarian and urban cultures of Canaan. Each way of life had its distinctive social, economic and religious characteristics, so that the situation was complex and conflict was inevitable.

THE CHARACTERISTICS OF PASTORAL SOCIETY

Early man lived chiefly by hunting. When he learned to domesticate animals his food supply became more assured, and consequently his life was prolonged and the family became established as a stable social group. As the size of the herds increased, families developed into clans and ultimately into tribes, moving with their flocks and herds in search of pasturage.

[4] E.g., Am. 5:25; Hos. 9:10; 11:1.
[5] 1 Kg. 19; Mic. 6:4, 5; Hos. 13:4.
[6] Jer. 35:6, 7.

Owing to the fact that the interior of Arabia is desert the inhabitants of that region have remained to a large degree wandering
pastoral peoples to the present day. From time to time incursions
have been made into the more fertile lands to the north and west,
Mesopotamia, Syria, Palestine and Lower Egypt, and there nomadic
tribes settled down among the earlier inhabitants to establish the
more stable societies made possible by the cultivation of field crops.
The ancestors of Israel belonged to the North Arabian desert, and
to that part of the "fertile crescent" that lay across the upper
reaches of the Euphrates. They invaded Canaan as nomadic tribes
in more than one wave, and centuries later their social and
ideological structure still bore the marks of their nomadic, pastoral
inheritance.

The fundamental fact about Semitic nomad society is the bond
of blood kinship. This vivid "family consciousness" pervades the
thinking and governs most of the activities of the social group.
Cain's question: "Am I my brother's keeper?" could arouse nothing but consternation. The family was not only the primary social
unit but the primary economic and religious unit as well. In the
patriarchal stories, as, for instance, in the prologue to Job, the
father's wealth gives subsistence to all the "father's house," and
the patriarch offers sacrifice on behalf of his family. The importance
of kinship and the pride of descent appear in the genealogies
which abound in the Old Testament, and which strike the Hebraic
note in the birth stories of Jesus in Matthew and Luke.[7] The
veneration of an ancestor's tomb[8] and the desire for a son to
perpetuate the family[9] are further illustrations of the importance
attached to blood relationship. The usual method of reckoning
descent was through the father, but traces remain of a matriarchal
system which may have been older (or peculiar to certain tribes).
Examples are the mother's naming of a child at birth[10] and the

[7] Mt. 1:1–17; Lk. 3:23–38.
[8] Gen. 35:20, cf. 1 Sam. 10:2.
[9] Gen. 15:2, 3; 1 Sam. 1.
[10] Gen. 29:32–35.

beena form of marriage,[11] where the wife remained in her father's household and the children belonged to his family.

This vivid sense of blood-brotherhood lies, too, behind that most characteristic of desert institutions, the practice of blood-revenge. When a man was slain, his clan was thereby injured. The clan blood had been shed and must be avenged upon the clan whose representative had committed the murder, and brought its guilt upon his kin.[12] As the community grew more civilized, a clear distinction was made between wilful and accidental homicide, and provision was made for an accused to find asylum from the enraged relatives until the circumstances of the case could be determined.[13] Guilt and punishment were restricted to the individual for the first time in the post-prophetic law of Deut. 24:16.

Society was a family of families. The closest approximation to our word "family" is the word translated "house," which meant in this connection an actual household, or a single group of three or four generations descended from a surviving male parent.[14] The clan comprised a group of these "fathers' houses" who felt a psychic unity because of claimed common descent from a more remote ancestor. This unity found expression especially in an emergency, as when "Gideon blew a trumpet; and Abiezer (the clan of his father Joash) was gathered together after him."[15] The tribe, too, was ideally a family, and the "twelve tribes" of Israel each claimed remote descent from one of the sons of Jacob. But that the tribe was sometimes only an artificial family we know from the composition of the tribe of Judah, which was formed by the alliance "by covenant" of distinct clans,[16] just as the "super-tribe" of Israel was formed by covenant federation, yet claimed Jacob as a common ancestor. The tribe may be defined as a group of clans

[11] Cf. Gen. 2:24; 31:43; Jg. 15:1.
[12] Gen. 4:23, 24; 2 Sam. 3:27; cf. 2:23. Cf. de Vaux, *op. cit.*, pp. 10–12.
[13] Deut. 4:41, 42; Ex. 21:13, 14.
[14] Gen. 7:1, 13; 46:5–7; 50:22, 23.
[15] Jg. 6:34. Cf. 6:11, and Num. 1:2.
[16] 1 Chr. 2, Jg. 1:11 ff. Cf. Aharoni, *op. cit.*, pp. 224–25.

claiming descent from a remote ancestor, sharing a common religion, and acknowledging a common authority.

The formation or enlargement of a tribe by federation into a larger artificial family brought into play the institution of the "covenant," which belongs in the same circle of kinship ideas. A covenant was more than an alliance: it was the intermingling and identification of one life with another. The Hebrew idiom "to *cut* a covenant" may refer to the slaying of a sacrificial victim, that its life might form a bond between the parties when its body was consumed at the covenant feast.[17] The deity was made a party to the covenant by the smearing of blood upon the altar before which the ceremony was enacted.[18] The "blood of the covenant" made men "blood-brothers," and established between them a community of souls as when "the soul of Jonathan was knit with the soul of David."[19]

Certain consequences of this family-tribal organization of society are to be noted. The first is that the economic wealth of the community was actually community wealth; though vested in the head of the family or clan, it was held in trust for all. Personal property was confined to personal items such as ornaments, dress and weapons, and there was no individual private property, as a rule, in the flocks and herds upon which the community as a whole depended for its existence. Thus, though by common consent some had privileges appropriate to their position as chiefs and leaders, there were no rich and no poor in the clan, except as the whole clan was rich or poor. Even slaves were members of the household.[20]

The seat of authority lay with the heads of families, and in the larger aggregation, the tribe, with a council of elders. These gave judgment in disputes according to the accepted morals and cus-

[17] Gen. 15:7–21; 31:44, 54.
[18] Ex. 24:5–8.
[19] 1 Sam. 18:1, 3.
[20] Ex. 20:17; Gen. 15:2, 4; 24:2.

toms of the tribe.[21] They had, however, no despotic power. The freedom of the desert and its untamed, wandering life, together with the strong sense of clan brotherhood, resulted in a strong and lasting love of liberty and equal justice.

In matters of religion we must distinguish between two distinct elements in Israel's inheritance from her nomadic past. There was, first, that which she held in common with other Semitic nomads, belief in spirits and demons, and in a deity who was in "blood-covenant" with the tribe. There may also have been belief in a supreme sky-god "El," recognized as the power behind all phenomena, in a lunar deity and in a goddess of fertility originally associated with oases. To this nomadic inheritance should certainly be traced such features of the later Hebrew cultus as the herdsman's sacrifice of the first-born of his flock, and the festivals of the lunar deity who guided desert wanderers through the coolness of the night, Pesach (or Passover) and New-moon.[22]

The second element of Israel's religious heritage from her desert days distinguished her from other Semitic peoples—the worship of the God Yahweh to whom Moses had introduced her.[23] Yahweh was a God whose power was manifested in storm and volcano and earthquake, and whose personal characteristics of righteousness and mercy made corresponding demands upon those within its covenant. He was personally concerned and active in the historic events which had befallen his people. The covenant with Yahweh established a community with the characteristics of a great family, with a common interest, a common life and a common will. Israel became ideally a "people" in the strict sense of the Hebrew word 'am, which means those who together form an entity, a whole, and whose members are united by "fellow-feeling" as brothers and

---

[21] Ex. 18:21–26; cf. 2 Sam. 13:12.

[22] Note also the association of "New-moon" and "Sabbath" as related festivals in Am. 8:5 and 2 Kg. 4:23.

[23] *How many*, and *which* tribes were parties to the *original* covenant is another question. We are concerned here with the later "pooled" traditions.

comrades. The harmonious operation of the covenant was "peace," and produced well-being, or "blessing." Under the terms of the covenant Yahweh promised "salvation" (i.e., prosperity, or victory) conditional upon Israel's loyalty to the moral and religious standards set by him, and upon faithfulness, responsiveness and obedience to himself. The traditions vary as to the particular obligations of this "covenant of obedience," as may be seen, for example, by comparing the several forms of the Decalogue found in Ex. 20, Deut. 5, Ex. 34, Lev. 19 and Deut. 27. But they are unanimous that the right to worship and serve Yahweh was conditional upon ethical obedience. As the later prophets and psalmists put it, "Will ye steal, murder and commit adultery, and swear falsely, and burn incense unto Baal, and walk after other gods that ye have not known, and come and stand before me in this house?" "Who shall ascend into the hill of Yahweh? And who shall stand in his holy place? He that hath clean hands, and a pure heart."[24]

SETTLED AGRARIAN SOCIETY

The conquest of Canaan by Israel was a process extending over several generations, and it was accomplished probably as much by peaceful penetration as by fire and sword.[25] With some exceptions like Hazor in the north, the tribes could not take the walled cities, but settled among, and in time dominated and absorbed the agrarian and urban Canaanites. As with the modern Arabs of Trans-Jordan,[26] neighboring clans and tribes would be at the same time in various stages between pastoral nomadism and settled agricultural life. To the end, especially in the less fertile southern part of the country, herds of sheep and goats continued to be an important economic factor.

By the time of David the cultivation of barley, flax and wheat, together with vineyards, orchards and olive groves, had opened a

[24] Jer. 7:9, 10; Ps. 24:3, 4.
[25] Cf. Jg. 1:16, 19, 21, 27–33.
[26] Cf. de Vaux, *op. cit.*, pp. 4–5.

new and richer economic life to the mass of Israelites. Methods of cultivation were primitive enough. When the stony ground had been sufficiently cleared, it was ploughed with the help of oxen and sown by men "weeping, bearing precious seed."[27] Reaping was a festive time, as men put the sickle to the standing grain, and bound it into sheaves. At the threshing-floor the grain was beaten out with a flail, or was crushed under a heavy sledge; it was then tossed into the wind with a "fan" or flat shovel, to blow away the chaff. The grain was eaten "parched," or was ground into flour. Grapes were grown in carefully cultivated vineyards,[28] and were crushed in a winepress hewn out of the rock, or were dried for use as raisins. Olives were crushed to obtain the oil used in cooking, and for anointing the person. Figs, pomegranates, dates and date honey added variety to the diet.

The cultivation of field crops, and of trees and vines was an art which had to be learned from the Canaanites. At the same time the Israelites learned from them to reverence the *baalim* (baals), the local manifestations of Baal, the rain-god whose favor was necessary to assure a crop. This was not obvious disloyalty to Yahweh, for "they *did not know* it was I who gave the grain, the wine and the oil."[29] Yahweh was God of the federation and people of Israel, the sole God of the political society and the national tradition. The gods of fields and vineyards were thought of as belonging to another sphere altogether. It was only when, in the time of Ahab and Elijah, the local manifestation of Baal the storm-god who was the city-god of Tyre, became Yahweh's rival in the *political* sphere, that irreconcilable conflict resulted. The familiar condemnation by the post-prophetic editor of Kings: "They built them high places and pillars and Asherim on every high hill and under every green tree"[30] assumes the conditions and judges by the standards of the

[27] Ps. 126:6. The custom originated in the weeping for the death of the fertility deity, symbolized by the burying of the seed. Cf. Ezek. 8:14 and 1 Cor. 15:36.
[28] Cf. Is. 5:1, 2.
[29] Hos. 2:8 (EVV).
[30] 1 Kg. 14:23.

seventh century. For Jacob himself was said to have set up one of these sacred pillars at Bethel, and Samuel had sacrificed at a local "high-place."[31]

The extent to which the later Israelite forms of worship were indebted to Canaanite precedents was very considerable. The three great annual festivals of the sacred calendar were harvest festivals: "Unleavened Bread" (with which Passover had come to be associated) at the beginning of the barley harvest, "Weeks" or "Harvest" seven weeks[32] later at the conclusion of the wheat harvest, and "Ingathering" or "Tabernacles," the vintage festival in the autumn. These feasts were of long standing in Canaan before the entrance of the Israelites, and even in the later Jewish ritual traces of a Canaanite religious background can be discerned. Moreover, the familiar varieties of sacrifice in the Old Testament, such as the peace-offering, the sin-offering, the meal-offering and the whole-burnt-offering were similar to features of the Canaanite cultus.[33] These things were taken over in early Yahwism because they were not in obvious conflict with its simple traditional cultus, but were felt to be supplements necessary to the new conditions of agrarian life.

Yet the moral dangers of the Baal worship were present from the beginning. Its primary object of securing the fertility of man and beast and land led to the association with the sanctuaries of "holy" prostitutes, both male and female. This, together with the riotous feasting and drinking that accompanied certain festivals, tended toward the deterioration of a people who had lived under the more austere moral code of the desert. The very multiplicity of the Baal shrines, and their association with the daily business of making a living rather than with occasional emergencies like war and pestilence, kept the Baal cults rather than Yahweh constantly

[31] Gen. 28:18, 22; 1 Sam. 9:12, 19, 22–25.
[32] At first approximately, later exactly seven weeks; cf. Ex. 23:14–16; Lev. 23: 15, 16.
[33] Cf. J. Gray, *The Legacy of Canaan*, 1957, pp. 140–152; H. Ringgren, *Israelite Religion*; 1966; p. 176.

in mind. Indeed, Yahweh himself came to be spoken of as a *Baal*, whose particular province was that his people should prosper and multiply and replenish the earth. Proper names compounded of "Yahweh" ("Jo-," or -"iah") and "Baal" were given to Israelite children: Gideon's second name was Jerubbaal; one of Saul's sons was called Ishbaal; and one of David's warriors was Bealiah, which means "Yahweh is my baal."[34]

"Baal" means literally "owner," "lord," or (in a derived use) "husband," since the wife was the husband's property and it was he who was responsible for her fertility. The word is used of property-owners, as in Jg. 19:22, 23, "the man who was owner of the house," and the familiar Is. 1:3, "the ox knoweth his possessor, and the ass his baal's crib." Job 31:38, 39 speaks of landowners as "the baals," and the laws of Ex. 24:14 and Deut. 15:2 use the same term of men capable of entering upon law-suits and of lending money. With the worship of the *baalim* who "owned" the fields and vineyards was associated a system of individual private ownership and an attitude to possessions quite alien to the nomadic tradition.

It is to be remembered that Israel proper was a minority of the total population, a minority which had established itself as the dominant class, while adopting much of the way of life long established in the land. As a result, we witness a radical social and cultural upheaval within the Israelite community itself. Nomadic tribes whose deity had been god *of the tribe* and their economic basis flocks and herds held as common property, now became a settled agrarian people, worshipping not only Yahweh but also gods *of the land* from which they now drew their principal subsistence. Yahweh was still the God who maintained the kin: the local shrines embodied the spirit of locality and property. The multiplicity of these local deities was obviously a dividing force, in contrast to the unifying influence of the sole God of the tribal federation, whose power was manifested in characteristic fashion

[34] Jg. 8:35; 1 Chr. 8:33; 12:5.

in the heroic episode recorded in the Song of Deborah.[35] But with
the passing of time there came a lessened emphasis on kinship, and
an increased emphasis on locality. The village became a new center
of loyalty beside the clan, though in most cases the two had
coincided at the beginning of the process.

With this came a new concept of property in land, stable and
permanent, as compared to property in herds that could be carried
off overnight by raiders. Israel asserted her claim to Canaan on the
basis of a religious tradition that Yahweh had promised the land
to the patriarchs and to Moses. It became the "land of the fathers,"
stamped with a mystic folk-relationship of blood and soil; the
vital source of the community's existence, giving "seed to the sower
and bread to the eater."

As the land of Israel was related to the psychic totality of the
people. so the family's land was bound up with the family's soul.
Naboth, the ordinary citizen, rejected with indignation the king's
suggestion that he might barter or sell his ancestral portion: "Yahweh forbid it me, that I should give the inheritance of my fathers
unto thee."[36] The laws of real property in the Old Testament were
designed to keep the land in the family, and to facilitate its recovery if lost. The law providing for redemption by the next-of-kin
(Lev. 25:25), the law providing for periodic cancellation of debts
(Deut. 15:1–3) and the so-called Jubilee law annulling all land
transfers at the end of fifty years[37] (even if the last-named seems
never to have been actually in effect)—all were designed to maintain
the sacred attachment of the family to its own soil. The owner held
the land as representative of his family; he had the usufruct only,
not the right of disposal. The principle at stake was fundamental
from the religious viewpoint: "The land shall not be sold in
perpetuity, for the land is mine, and ye are strangers and sojourners
with me."[38]

[35] Jg. 5.
[36] 1 Kg. 21:3.
[37] Lev. 25:8–17.
[38] Lev. 25:23.

URBAN COMMERCIAL SOCIETY

The third way of life which added to the complexities and tensions of Israelite society prior to the prophetic period, was that of the urban and commercial culture in which the spirit of Canaan found its most developed and characteristic expression. (Note that the word "Canaanite" is used in Prov. 31:24 as a synonym for "merchant.") This way of life began to make a considerable impact upon the Israelites in the reign of David, when three factors worked toward this end simultaneously. The first was the conquest of almost all the remaining Canaanite cities and their assimilation by Israel, together with their established customs. The second was the establishment by David of a capital city which, with its court and military forces, could not be supported from the soil in its immediate vicinity, but must draw upon the economic surplus of the whole land. The third was the initiation in David's reign of large-scale commercial relationships with the Phoenicians, or northern Canaanites.

The fruits of this beginning were reaped in the reign of Solomon, which effected an even greater social, economic, cultural and religious revolution than that which Israel experienced when she became a settled, rather than a nomadic, people. For with Solomon the free, kinship society came under a royal despotism, which was at the same time an oppressive form of monopoly state capitalism. By his policy of heavy taxation and the exaction of conscript labor, the king made slaves of the mass of his subjects, and their property became his property. He alone (except for his court favorites) profited by the new extension of foreign trade, the export of copper from Edom,[39] and probably also of Israelite tribesmen to serve as Egyptian mercenary soldiers.[40] The solemn warning put in the mouth of Samuel in the anti-monarchial and theocratic document

---

[39] Ancient copper mines have been found in the Arabah between the Dead Sea and the Gulf of Aqaba.
[40] Cf. Deut. 17:16; 1 Kg. 10:28.

in 1 Sam. gives us Solomon's policy drawn to the life: "He will take your sons, and appoint them unto him for his chariots, and to be his horsemen, . . . for captains of thousands and captains of fifties, and to plough his ground, and to reap his harvest, and to make his instruments of war; . . . and he will take your fields and your vineyards and your oliveyards . . . and give them to his courtiers; . . . and he will take the tenth of your flocks: and ye shall be his slaves."[41] As von Rad says, "the institution of the monarchy was a newcomer in Israel. Consequently . . . its relationship with the central tradition of the faith was strained from the outset."[42]

Though the northern tribes revolted against this oppression after Solomon's death, and attempted to establish a more democratic monarchy of their own, it was not long before there too the court became a center of ostentatious wealth and power. No compromise between absolutism and fraternal democracy could be worked out easily in the atmosphere of Canaan, where the example of divine right was set by local tradition and by the practice of surrounding nations. The clan brotherhood of Israel was rent permanently into the powerful and the oppressed, the rich and the poor. Once a people loses its organic relationship with its means of subsistence, the herds of the nomad, or the fields and vineyards of the farmer; once individual wealth and power become the accepted goal of endeavor within the community—poverty, injustice and social strife have come to stay.

In the nomadic period, as we have seen, economic production and distribution were both on a family basis of mutual service and common advantage, and any economic surplus went to increase the wealth of the clan as a whole. The economic process was so natural as to be largely unconscious. With the transition to agriculture, family land-holdings and village life, the family and its dependents shared in the more abundant provision made available.

[41] 1 Sam. 8:11–17.
[42] G. von Rad, *O.T. Theology*, 1962, vol. i, p. 40.

Again, any surplus was immediately distributed by increasing the family's possessions and amenities. (Exchange was effected by barter in the marketplace, or by the weighing of silver. Gold was used chiefly for ornamental purposes, and was rare before the time of Solomon. Coinage did not come into use till the Persian period.)

But with the establishment of the court and the determination of Solomon to ape the worldly glory of neighboring states, there began a concentration of wealth which drained off the economic surplus of the community, and left the mass of the people at or below the poverty line.[43] Vast quantities of food, goods and services were now taken for the upkeep of the royal establishment and the army, while the conscript labor which built chariot cities and embellished Jerusalem, left crops and herds untended. The importing of great new quantities of gold and silver (as in Europe when the tribute of the Spanish Main poured in) forced prices upward in a sudden inflation. Men were compelled to mortgage their lands, their persons or their children to pay the exactions demanded. The interest was usurious, and many free Israelites lost their land and became slaves, while those who had an initial advantage amassed lands and money. The human result of the working of such a system is aptly summed up in the words of Jesus: "Unto every one that hath shall be given, and he shall have abundance: but from him that hath not, even that which he hath shall be taken away."[44]

As the tribal worship of Yahweh had been the religion of the nomadic period, and as a mixture of Baal worship and Yahwism had prevailed in the early period of settlement in the land, so the urban and commercial developments had their religious parallels. These arose in the first place from the function undertaken in the cultus of all current monarchies by the semi-divine king, and in the second place, from the mutual acknowledgment of national deities which accompanied commercial and political alliances. Babylonian, Syrian and Egyptian gods had long had their shrines among

[43] Cf. de Vaux, *op. cit.*, pp. 72–73.
[44] Mt. 25:29.

as captives. The siege of Jerusalem was made memorable by the prophet Isaiah, and its deliverance ascribed to a miracle.

Toward the end of the seventh century, bled by two hundred years of war, and weakened further by barbarian raiders from the north, Assyria collapsed under the combined attacks of the Medes and the Chaldaeans. The latter people, who had established the seat of their power at Babylon, now engaged in a mortal struggle with Egypt for the reversion of the Assyrian world empire. Meanwhile Josiah of Judah had declared his independence in 621, by purging from the worship of Yahweh all traces of Assyrian and other alien influences. In 609 Josiah was killed by the Egyptians, apparently when resisting their transit through the country on the way to the Euphrates. A nominee of Pharaoh was placed upon the Judaean throne.[48] When, four years later, Egyptian ambitions were finally thwarted upon the battlefield of Carchemish, Judah became a vassal state of Babylon. But her allegiance wavered. A pro-Egyptian party was active in her internal politics, and the second of two revolts resulted in Nebuchadrezzar's destruction of Jerusalem in 587 B.C., the deportation of her leading citizens and the end of the Davidic monarchy.

POLITICAL HISTORY OF THE TWIN KINGDOMS

From David to the fall of Jerusalem one unbroken line of kings had ruled over Judah, whereas, in its separate history of about 212 years, the northern kingdom of Israel was ruled successively by kings of ten different families. It is true that the Judaean line once depended upon the slender thread of a baby's life, when, in the ninth century, the torrent of revolution characteristic of the northern kingdom overflowed into Judah.[49] But the thread held, and David's descendants sat upon his throne for eighteen generations.

Rehoboam of Judah, whose folly had broken David's kingdom in

[48] 2 Kg. 23:29–30, 34.
[49] 2 Kg. 11:1–3.

two, continued to regard the Israelites as rebels, and began hostilities which continued spasmodically for fifty years. The appeal of his grandson Asa to Damascus for help against the northern kingdom began a long series of wars between the Syrians and Israel, from which Judah derived little benefit. For the next Judaean king, Jehoshaphat, though ostensibly an ally, appears in the humiliating position of taking orders from the king of Israel to risk his life for the latter's protection upon the battlefield.[50] The son and grandson of Jehoshaphat married into the northern royal family, and it was an Israelite queen dowager who seized the Judaean throne when the kings of north and south were simultaneously assassinated by Jehu.[51]

The story of the north Israelite kingdom is a story of many assassinations. Only Omri and Jehu founded dynasties lasting longer than two generations, and no less than seven kings took the throne by murdering its occupant. The great Omri was the survivor of a murderous struggle among three contenders for a throne already stained with blood.

Omri may be called "the David of the north," for he laid the foundations of the northern kingdom's power. The Book of Kings gives him only one verse[52] (in addition to the annalistic formulae), because Jewish religious historians were not interested in the achievements of their rivals. But from extra-Biblical sources, as well as from what is incidentally recorded in the Old Testament, we may measure Omri's greatness. He is the first Israelite or Judaean king to be mentioned by name in foreign inscriptions, and Israel was still known as "the land of Omri" in the reign of Jehu, who took the throne from Omri's grandson. Like David, Omri showed astuteness and strategic insight when he founded a new capital, Samaria, on a site independent of tribal associations, of great natural strength, near the trade routes, yet isolated among

[50] 1 Kg. 22:30.
[51] 2 Kg. 8:26–27; 11:1–3.
[52] 1 Kg. 16:24.

the hills. Again like David, Omri fortified and beautified his capital, extended his power by foreign conquest, established close relationships with Tyre and ended the internecine struggle with the other people of Yahweh. In the eighth-century prophet Micah (6:16) there is a curious reference to "the statutes of Omri," apparently a law-code of the individualistic commercialism which now was displacing the ancient community economy of Israel's past.

Omri's son, Ahab, was no Solomon to his father's David. He was an abler king than Solomon, and a fit successor to Omri. The Book of Kings gives six chapters to his reign, because it was also the period of the prophet Elijah.[53] Israel now lay under the shadow of the Assyrian menace. Ahab's two notable battles with Damascus[54] probably resulted from an attempt by Damascus to force him to join the anti-Assyrian alliance. Eventually Ahab did so, and contributed the largest contingent of chariotry to the allied forces which confronted Shalmaneser III at Karkar. At home in peacetime Ahab gave himself to building cities, and an "ivory house" or palace which became famous, and from the remains of which carved ivory inlays have been recovered in modern times.[55]

The end of his reign finds Ahab again at war with Damascus. 1 Kg. 22 gives a circumstantial account of the battle to recover Ramoth Gilead, and of the stratagem by which Ahab hoped to have the Judaean king draw the enemy's fire, while he himself fought unnoticed in the ranks. But while man proposes, God disposes, and the historian cannot forbear to gloat over the end of Jezebel's husband and Elijah's enemy.[56]

The religious conflict between Ahab and Elijah had turned on the growing influence of the cult of Melkarth, the Tyrian Baal. This cult had been introduced by Jezebel, Ahab's queen, and daughter of the priest-king of Tyre, to the scandal of those who

[53] 1 Kg. 16:29–22:40.
[54] 1 Kg. 20.
[55] 1 Kg. 22:39; Am. 3:15; Ps. 45:8 (EVV). Cf. ANEP, nos. 129, 130.
[56] 1 Kg. 22:37–38.

prized the Yahwist tradition which had made Israel a nation. It was not wholly a doctrinal conflict, for Yahwism championed a way of life that was antagonistic to the new commercialism, the absolutism of kings and the class division of society. The judicial murder of Naboth by Jezebel, in order that the king might have his vineyard, went to the very roots of the Israelite's attachment to his family land. The old order of tribal tradition still persisted, and religious and economic customs were so entwined that revolt against the new forces, threatening traditional ways, came under the aegis of a sort of Puritan Yahwism. And "Puritan" is often not synonymous with meek and gentle.

Thus Elijah began a revolution in the name of the "old-time religion" which was to end in a welter of blood at Jezreel and Jerusalem. The church called upon the secular arm to purge the state, when Elisha provided for the anointing of Jehu ben Nimshi king over Israel.[57] If violence, battle, murder and sudden death could do Yahweh's work, Jehu was the man. The story of his wild ride to Jezreel and his slaughter of two kings and a queen, is one of the most vivid and horrendous in the Bible.[58] That was only the beginning. All royal princes of both houses, whom Jehu could find, were slain, and the worshippers of the Tyrian Baal slaughtered as they stood defenceless in their temple. Jehu excused his orgy of bloodshed by invoking the name of God; meeting the leader of the Puritan sect of the Rechabites, he gleefully called him to witness his "zeal for Yahweh."[59] Thus the dynasty of Omri came to its dreadful end.

Judah's king also had perished at Jehu's hand. But at Jerusalem Jehu was matched by one as ready and as brutal as himself, Athaliah the Queen Mother, daughter or half-sister[60] of Ahab. Seeing that her son the king was dead, she slew the Judaean royal family to

---

[57] 2 Kg. 9:1–10.
[58] 2 Kg. 9:16–37.
[59] 2 Kg. 10:15–17.
[60] Cf. J. Bright, A *History of Israel*, 1959, p. 222, fn. 41.

the last one (as she thought), and established herself on the throne. But her infant grandson was rescued and hidden, until, six years later, he was placed upon the throne by the Jerusalem priesthood and the Temple guard. Then Athaliah herself was slain, and her death was the signal for the completion in Judah of the revolt against the pretensions of Baal in the domain of Yahweh.

The blood poured out in this war of religions weakened both Israel and Judah for a generation. But with the almost contemporary accession of Jeroboam II in the north and of Azariah or Uzziah in the south (786–783 B.C.), there began two long reigns marked by prosperity and expansion, which may be called a "Victorian Age." The Book of Kings is again grudging in its information, saying of Jeroboam only that he was a great conqueror though unorthodox, and of Azariah that he was orthodox, but a leper. But in the contemporary and immediately subsequent prophecies of Amos and Hosea, Isaiah and Micah, we are given a vivid picture of material expansion and cultural development, elaborate buildings, splendid religious ceremonial. New wealth and luxuries stood in sharp relief against the new poverty which was their price. Like the Victorian age, it was a period which threw up strong personalities out of its manifold life: soldiers, administrators, merchant princes, writers and churchmen—most of them nameless. But, above all, it gave us the prophets, whose names live forever, spokesmen of a divinely sanctioned moral order, and of the Word of a Living God who is master of history and whose will is righteous.

The prophets spoke to this vain and worldly society a message of doom, and it was not long before the tragedy was played out. Within fourteen years of the death of Jeroboam, the Assyrians were ravaging Israel, and twelve years after this, Samaria had fallen and the land was an Assyrian province. A little later Judah was devasted by Sennacherib's armies, and though her dynasty, as we have seen, outlasted the Assyrian empire, it was soon to fall before their Babylonian successors.

3

ANTECEDENTS AND BEGINNINGS

Hebrew prophecy is the supreme element in what differentiated Israelite religion from other contemporary religions, and gave it a survival value they did not possess. Prophecy lies also at the heart of the Christian faith, for—whatever more one may say of Jesus—he was first called a *prophet*, "the prophet from Nazareth of Galilee."[1]

What is prophecy? The question cannot be answered simply in terms of cause and effect, of antecedents and environment; though prophecy when it came to its height retained features connecting it with antecedents which were something less than prophecy. But Amos and Hosea, Isaiah, and Jeremiah cannot be adequately explained in terms of development from these antecedents. Something new emerged in such men—a manifestation of spiritual power which brought them to an altogether different plane of religious experience and insight, and which gives them unique significance.

It is to these men that we must turn if we would know what prophecy is, to the traditions and writings in which their mind and spirit have been enshrined, and to the story of the people whose life and thought and faith they moulded. They were, as we have seen, not merely foretellers, though they did express upon occasion their moral certainty of what God was about to do. They were not moral philoso-

[1] Mt. 21:11.

phers, for they had no systematized scheme of the world, and their apprehension of reality was intuitive rather than rational. They might be called preachers, but not preachers "like the scribes" who were exponents of a revelation received from tradition; they themselves were media of a divine self-disclosure. They were mystics (in the best sense), but men of action and of the world as well; moralists as well as poets; social radicals because (again, in the best sense) they were religious conservatives; markedly individual, but representative of and identified with their people. They were spokesmen of God to their nation, and to men of all ages who will listen to their words. In very truth they were the servants and envoys of the Living God, instruments of his creative purpose in the realm of spirit. Many will be satisfied to describe them as men of unusual spiritual genius. But they themselves insisted that they were men upon whom Yahweh had laid his hand, and to "whom he had spoken in the ear."

But, for all its uniqueness of character and importance, we must remember that Hebrew prophecy appeared under the actual conditions of human life in this world. It had its real connections with a religious present and a religious past. God did not create it out of nothing. Prophecy was the answer of something at the heart of Israelite religion to the clamant call of humanity for a divine utterance. Within the Hebrew tradition there had been, and were, other ways of obtaining a divine response, ways that were common to many religions of that time and since. The gods were believed to speak through the priests or the priest-king, the augurs or the "holy men," the astrologers or the necromancers. Such ways of ascertaining the divine will were found also in the earlier stages and on the persisting lower levels of Israelite religion.

PRIESTLY DIVINERS AND SEERS

The law of Deut. 18:10 ff.[2] contrasts prophecy as the sole legitimate manner of learning the divine will, with the methods of the heathen. The significant distinction is that the latter are ways of

[2] See above, chap. 1, p. 8.

satisfying human inquisitiveness by invading and attempting to coerce
the world of spirits, whereas a prophet is "like unto Moses" in that
he speaks when bidden not by man but by Yahweh. Obviously, such
a law belongs to a period when prophecy has attained its full stature,
and the fact that it was necessary indicates that the old superstitions
still persisted. The story of Saul's stealthy visit to the necromancer
at Endor[3] shows that such practices were only driven underground
when they came under the official ban.

The three "official" methods said to have been tried by Saul without success were *dreams*, *Urim*, and *prophets*. The prophets referred
to were of a much more primitive type than Amos and Isaiah three
hundred years later, and, together with the other methods mentioned,
appear to have been directly associated with the various local temples.
It cannot be accidental that the Hebrew word for "priest"—*kohen*,
has as its counterpart in Arabic the word meaning "diviner." The
priest is the original "holy man." In Jg. 18:1–6 the migrating Danites
consult a local priest, precisely as Saul and his servant go to Samuel
the Seer to ask their way, in 1 Sam. 9:8–10. The answer to a question
put to the priest was obtained by the use of an *ephod*, which appears
to have been a sacred vestment with a pouch, out of which the
sacred lots called *Urim* and *Thummim* were cast. (The late priestly
regulations of Ex. 28 provide for an ephod of cloth, to be worn by
the high priest under a jewelled "breastplate of judgment" containing the Urim and Thummim.)

While there is no evidence that the early prophets made use of
these priestly instruments of divination, it is to be remembered how
closely they were associated with the priesthood. In the Pentateuch,
Moses is represented not only as a prophet, receiving and speaking
the word of Yahweh, but as a (priestly) Levite by birth, while Aaron,
the priest, is the recipient along with Moses of the word of Yahweh.[4]
Samuel, the first character in the post-conquest story of Israel to be
called a prophet, had ministered as Eli's assistant in the temple at

[3] 1 Sam. 28:6–25.
[4] Ex. 2:1 ff., 19:3–6; Num. 12:2.

Shiloh.[5] Elijah the prophet built an altar at Mount Carmel in the course of his contest with the prophets of Baal, and offered sacrifice.[6] In later times, Jeremiah is introduced as "of the priests that were in Anathoth," and Ezekiel as "the priest."[7]

The eventual distinction of the function of the prophets from that of the priests seems to have come about as follows. As the temple cultus became more elaborate, the work of its ministers became correspondingly specialized, and some among them who were specially favored or successful in the giving of oracles assumed this function more exclusively. For the answer of the sacred lots could be only yes or no (or, no answer): further elaboration[8] required someone who could "speak for Yahweh"[9] as one who was his confidant and could interpret his will. This is the meaning of Samuel's vision (or, strictly speaking, "audition"): Samuel hears what Yahweh is about to do; he is "established to be a prophet of Yahweh . . . for Yahweh revealed himself to Samuel in Shiloh *by the word* of Yahweh."[10] We should notice that the prophet here receives his inaugural revelation in a temple, as happened long afterwards in the case of Isaiah.[11] With the great prophets such a close connection with the cultus was exceptional; but that bodies of "official prophets" continued to be associated with the temple priesthood, is clear.[12]

Dreams, too, were modes of revelation at the sanctuary. Jacob's famous dream of the ladder set up from earth to heaven came to him at a holy "place" on which he had happened inadvertently, and which was later held to be the site of the Bethel temple. Solomon's equally famous dream in which Yahweh appeared and promised him the gift of wisdom, came to him at the "great high place" at Gibeon

[5] 1 Sam. 3.
[6] 1 Kg. 18:32 ff.
[7] Jer. 1:1; Ezek. 1:3.
[8] As in 2 Sam. 5:23, 24.
[9] See below, pp. 44–45, on the meaning of *"nabi'."*
[10] 1 Sam. 3:21.
[11] Is. 6:1.
[12] Jer. 26:8, 11, 16; Lam. 2:20; Zech. 7:2–7.

where he had gone to offer sacrifice.[13] It was customary to sleep in a temple or holy place in the hope of such a manifestation of the deity: this may be the explanation of Am. 2:8, "they lay themselves down beside every altar." One can see how those who had a reputation as good dreamers would be much sought after as interpreters of the divine. In Deut. 13:1 a "dreamer of dreams" is almost another name for a prophet, and Jer. 23:32 speaks of those who "prophesy lying dreams."

The title given to such men in the early period was "Seer." The first to be given the name is Samuel himself, in the older document where he is pictured, not as a national leader, but as a local clair-voyant priest who for a small fee would assist in the finding of lost animals.[14] Two points in the narrative may be specially noted: Yahweh "uncovers the ear" of Samuel, i.e., he manifests himself by audition rather than (or, as well as) by vision; and Samuel promises Saul a message "in the morning," i.e., after there has been opportunity for a further dream revelation in the course of the night.

The visions of the Seer came not only in dreams during sleep, but also in the "second sight" of the ecstatic trance. Of this state Balaam's self-description in Num. 24:15–16 is a classical example: as one "who hears the words of God, who shares the most High's knowledge, who has a vision of the Almighty, prostrate, but with his eyes open." This abnormal mental state was attributed to possession by the deity, and might be deliberately induced by fasting, music or the use of intoxi-cants.[15] Perhaps the distinction between the dreamer and the ecstatic explains the two different words translated "seer": *ro'eh*, used of Samuel, and (apparently) of Zadok the priest; and *hozeh*, used of "the prophet Gad, David's seer," and (contemptuously) of Amos.[16]

The word *nabi*, translated "prophet" in the Old Testament means

---

[13] Gen. 28:11–17; 1 Kg. 3:5 ff.
[14] 1 Sam. 9:5–8. Note the different picture of Samuel given in the later source, 1 Sam. 7:3–17.
[15] 1 Kg. 19:5–8: 2 Kg. 3:15; Mic. 2:11.
[16] 1 Sam. 9:9; 2 Sam. 15:27; 24:11; Am. 7:12.

"speaker" or "spokesman."[17] It corresponds to an Akkadian word meaning "one called" or "appointed"; in the Old Testament an appointed spokesman (of God), as is clear from Ex. 7:1; 4:14–16; 1 Kg. 22:14. An editorial note in 1 Sam. 9:9 explains that "he that is now called a Prophet was beforetime called a Seer"; i.e., the functions of the seers were taken over by the prophets. The original distinction seems to have been that the Seer gained his supernatural knowledge by skill in interpreting signs and omens, or by dreams or second-sight; whereas the Prophet spoke directly out of an immediate ecstatic consciousness of divine possession. But there is also a distinction made between a higher and a lower level among "prophets" (a distinction which time was to underline), between those who stood in the line of Moses and those who stood nearer to the old seers and ecstatics. In Num. 12:6–8 Yahweh says to Aaron and Miriam: "If either of you were a prophet, I Yahweh would make myself known unto him in a vision, I would speak with him in a dream. My servant Moses is not so; . . . with him do I speak mouth to mouth, plainly, and not in riddles."

ECSTATIC PROPHETS

The description of the state into which Balaam fell when he spoke a divine oracle, "prostrate, but with his eyes open," has an interesting parallel in the account given by an Egyptian traveller named Wen Amon of an experience he had about 1100 B.C. at Byblos in Syria. "As the prince of Byblos was sacrificing to his gods, the god seized one of his youths and made him possessed; he cried: Bring up the god. Amon is the one who has entered into him."[18] This story, in turn, recalls the behavior of Saul, when "the spirit of God came upon him also, and he 'prophesied' as he went along . . . and he also stripped off his clothes and he also 'prophesied' before Samuel,

[17] Cf. W. F. Albright, *From the Stone Age to Christianity*, 2nd ed., 1957, p. 303; J. Lindblom, *Prophecy in Ancient Israel*, 1962, p. 102.
[18] Cf. ANET, p. 26.

and fell down and lay naked all that day and all that night."[19] Many kinds of abnormal human behavior were ascribed by the Hebrews, as by other peoples, to spirit possession, and especially the religious frenzy which produced temporarily the wild actions and cries of madness.[20]

Saul's was not an individual experience, but a contagion received upon meeting a company of these dervish "prophets" whose "prophesying" was not in intelligible speech, but resembled rather the "speaking with tongues" in the Acts of the Apostles.[21] That this product of religious excitement and mass suggestion is a by-way and not the highroad of prophecy, was recognized by St. Paul,[22] and is clear from the history of the prophetic movement in the Old Testament. The phenomenon persists in some modern Christian and Moslem sects, and a most interesting account is given in Curzon's "Tales of Travel" of the author's experience with a dervish sect in Tunisia, whose behavior recalled to him the story of the prophets of Baal at Mount Carmel.[23] The repeated cult cry and the limping dance about the altar of Baal, were characteristic of this orgiastic form of religion, which the Israelites found in Canaan. Its ultimate origin has been traced to Thrace, whence it spread into Greece, and also into Asia Minor, Syria and Canaan.[24]

The peculiar form which this group religious excitement took in Israelite religion was the formation of bands of devotees known as "sons of the prophets." When one of these groups first appears in 1 Sam. 10:5, it is called a "string" or "band" of prophets; which may mean (picturesquely) that they were marching in single file, or (more probably) that they were a "bound" or "pledged" band. The analogy

---

[19] 1 Sam. 19:23, 24.
[20] Cf. 2 Kg. 9:4, 11; Jer. 29:26; Hos. 9:7. For an informative account of this phenomenon of ecstatic "prophecy" in ancient and modern times, cf. J. Lindblom, *op. cit.*, chap. 1.
[21] 1 Sam. 19:20 ff., cf. 10:5 ff., and Acts 2:1 ff.
[22] 1 Cor. 14:2–19.
[23] *The Drums of Kairwan*, pp. 23 ff.
[24] See E. A. Leslie: *Old Testament Religion*, 1936, pp. 116–118.

of other groups of Yahweh devotees, such as the Rechabites, and the immediate association of Saul with these "sons of the prophets" after he had been set apart to deliver Israel, suggest that they were a religio-patriotic movement, making use of the dervish technique in the militant service of Yahweh. The reference here to musical instruments indicates that they sought to arouse warlike fervor in themselves and others, somewhat after the fashion of a military band. We see also that they were leaving the high-place or sanctuary under the influence of the spirit, "prophesying" or shouting in frenzy. When Saul caught the contagion "God gave him another heart"; i.e., he became delirious (since in Hebrew usage the heart is the seat of the intelligence and will rather than of the emotions). Like the others, Saul "prophesies"—but the verb has no object. These "sons of the prophets" did not give intelligible oracles; they just "prophesied," like the Corinthian Christians whom St. Paul admonished that it would be better to speak five words with the understanding than ten thousand words in a tongue.[25] That a similar estimate of the worth of this religious frenzy was made even in Saul's time by the more critical members of the community, is evident from the proverb that became current about Saul's own behavior.[26]

There is a gap of two hundred years before these "sons of the prophets" are mentioned again in our records. By that time the prophetic guilds appear to have become settled monastic communities, living by mendicancy, or on fees for services rendered, or by the king's bounty. They erected community buildings, shared a common table (though some were married), and were under the "rule" of one they called "Master," such as Elijah or Elisha.[27] Their activities were conducted largely among the ignorant and superstitious mass of the people, who credited them with power to call fire from heaven, to vanish, to cure poisoned springs, to curse objects of their ill-will, to multiply food, to revive the dead, to heal leprosy and to make iron

[25] 1 Cor. 14:19.
[26] 1 Sam. 10:12; 19:24.
[27] 2 Kg. 6:1–2; 4:38; 4:1; 3:11; 2:3.

float.[28] These particular exploits are, indeed, ascribed to Elisha himself, but the Master's powers might be passed on to one of his followers, as with Elijah's mantle.[29] The stories reflect the popular conception of the sort of men the "sons of the prophets" were.

Analogous to these prophetic guilds are the large groups of prophets who appear acting in concert, at various points in the history of the twin kingdoms:[30] the hundred prophets of Yahweh hidden by Obadiah from Jezebel's fury, the eight hundred prophets of Baal and of the Asherah who ate at Jezebel's table, the four hundred prophets to whom Ahab appealed on the eve of battle, and the bodies of prophets associated with the priests at the covenant-making of Josiah, and later, in the accusation against Jeremiah.[31] "A sort of professional prophecy emerged, . . . bound to the interests of the State and the King."[32] As a rule these spoke with one voice. But exceptional men among them acted independently, and it was they and not the "madmen of the spirit" who stood in the line of Moses and were the ancestors of the great prophets of the classical period.

The difference was in moral character and spiritual insight, as is plain from the story of Micaiah,[33] and becomes plainer still in the distinction drawn by the classical prophets between themselves and those who prophesied only for a living. When Amaziah the priest taunts Amos with being a seer who prophesies in order to "eat bread," Amos denies that he has any connection with the professionals: "I was no (professional) prophet, nor a member of a prophetic guild . . . but Yahweh took me and said to me, Go, prophesy." Micah declares that "the prophets divine for money"; they "bite with their teeth and cry, Peace"; (i.e., they prophesy prosperity when their mouth is filled) "and whoso putteth not into their mouth, they

---

[28] 2 Kg. 1:10; 1 Kg. 18:12; 2 Kg. 2:16; 2:19–22; 2:24; 4:42–44; 4:32–37; 5:1 ff.; 6:6.
[29] 2 Kg. 2:8, 14.
[30] The guilds of professional prophets disappeared with the fall of Jerusalem.
[31] 1 Kg. 18:4; 18:19; 22:6; 2 Kg. 23:2; Jer. 26:7, 8, 11.
[32] C. Kuhl, *The Prophets of Israel*, 1960, p. 21.
[33] 1 Kg. 22:7 ff.

declare war against him." Isaiah knows too well "the prophet that teaches lies," and Jeremiah is opposed by prophets of prosperity of whom Yahweh says: "It is lies which the prophets prophesy in my name; I neither sent them, nor commissioned them, nor spoke to them; what they prophesy to you is a lying dream, an empty superstition, a deceptive invention of their own minds."[34]

CULTIC PROPHETS

"The original home of prophecy was the cult," says Clements, "and both in form and substance the preaching of the prophets was greatly affected by the life and worship of Israel's great sanctuaries." "There can be little doubt," adds Lindblom, "that prophets belonged to the permanent staff of the Jerusalem temple."[35] Repeated references are found to their prophesying in the Jerusalem temple and at other shrines,[36] as well as elsewhere. Priests and prophets are associated as temple personnel, and often are denounced together by the canonical prophets for abuse of their sacred offices.[37]

As already pointed out, the differentiation of function between priest and prophet was not original.[38] Prophets such as Samuel and Elijah offered sacrifice. On the other hand the priesthood was responsible not only for service at the altar and for divination through use of the sacred lots Urim and Thummim, but also for verbal *torah* or teaching on religious matters. This *torah* (as in the five Books of Moses that have inherited the designation) comprised both rulings on ceremonial matters as in Hag. 2:10–13, and instruction in the covenant tradition and in conduct befitting the people of Yahweh's

---

[34] Am. 7:14, 15; Mic. 3:11, 5; Jer. 14:14: the last passage is quoted from *The Complete Bible, an American Translation*, 1939.
[35] R. E. Clements, *Prophecy and Covenant*, 1965, pp. 7–8; J. Lindblom, *Prophecy in Ancient Israel*, 1962, p. 80. Cf. A. R. Johnson, *The Cultic Prophet in Ancient Israel*, 2nd ed., 1962, for a careful examination of this topic, with full bibliography.
[36] 1 Sam. 3:20–21; 1 Kg. 14:2; 18:20; Is. 6:1–13; Jer. 7:2; Am. 7:10–17.
[37] Is. 28:7–8; Jer. 23:11; 27:16; Mic. 3:11; Zech. 7:2–3.
[38] See pp. 42–43.

covenant.[39] The distinction between priest and prophet was not fully worked out before the setting up of the priest-ruled Temple state after the return from the exile, when the temple prophets were reduced to a subordinate status as members of the Levitical temple choirs.[40]

The question arises as to the relationships of the classical prophets with their colleagues on the temple staffs, particularly in view of the former's denigration of cultic worship as insufficient in itself apart from moral obedience to Yahweh.[41] It is evident from the stories of Amos' dispute with the priest-in-charge at Bethel, of Isaiah's vision when posted during worship so close to the temple proper that he could hear the vibration of the great doors in their sockets, and of Jeremiah's controversy with the priests and prophets in the Temple,[42] that all three might (and presumably often *did*) participate in conduct of worship along with other prophets. What set them apart was *what they said* when their turn came to speak. The priest of Bethel was outraged, not by Amos' presence, but by his daring to speak Yahweh's word against Israel, her sanctuaries and her king. Jeremiah's opponents were similarly outraged when he presumed to predict for the Jerusalem temple the fate that had long ago befallen Eli's and Samuel's temple at Shiloh. In Jer. 28 there is a later significant sequel to the story in chap. 26. A prophet Hananiah from Gibeon challenges Jeremiah by announcing as a Word from Yahweh the return of the first exiles within two years. He dramatizes his message by breaking the wooden yoke worn by Jeremiah to symbolize *his* word that all nations had been put by Yahweh under Babylon's yoke. In this case there was no protest by priests, prophets and congregation. What they wanted and expected from a prophet in the temple was re-assurance, just as Ahab had wanted prophetic support from his four hundred court prophets (1 Kings 22:1–28). Then, too,

---

[39] Deut. 26:1–11; 33:8–10; Mal. 2:4–11.
[40] As illustrated in the Chronicler's ascription to king David of the organization of the Temple worship and personnel as it existed in his own day (4th cent. B.C.); cf. 1 Chr. 25:1–5.
[41] Is. 1:10–17; Jer. 7:1–15; 21–28; Am. 5:21–26.
[42] Am. 7:10–17; Is. 6:1–4; Jer. 26:1–19, 24; 36:5–6.

a lone voice had been raised to set Yahweh's will to work against the wishes and vain hopes of men.

Further evidence for the participation of cultic prophets in the temple services comes from the Psalms. H. H. Rowley says that "it is undeniable that there are passages in the psalms which have the form of prophetic oracles."[43] The oracular style differs from the instructional manner of the priests' *torah*,[44]—"thou shalt. . ." The prophet proclaims Yahweh's will and Yahweh's answer in rhythmic and (literally) picturesque language. "He who sits enthroned in the heavens laughs, Yahweh has them in derision. . . . You shall break them as with an iron rod and dash them in pieces like a pottery vessel."[45] In Ps. 60 the supplication from the depths of national defeat in vv. 1–4 (EVV) is followed in vv. 6–8 by an oracular promise of Yahweh's aid, prefaced by the words—"God has spoken in his sanctuary." It is hard to see this as other than an oracle of *šālôm* or victory, of the kind against which Jeremiah protested.

In Pss. 12:5 (EVV) and 110:1 the prophets' messenger formula "says Yahweh" is actually used to introduce an oracle, and there are other references to the utterance of Yahweh's Word in worship.[46] So, in Ps. 50:1 "El, the God Yahweh, speaks and summons the earth . . ." is followed in v. 7 with the common oracular form of introduction—"Hear, O my people, and I will speak. . . ." That what follows is a prophetic oracle uttered in the course of a service of worship in the Temple can hardly be gainsaid.

NAZIRITES AND RECHABITES

The Nazirites and Rechabites must be considered here because, though they were not in any sense prophets, the Puritan Yahwism

---

[43] In his cautious treatment of "The Prophets and the Cult" in *Worship in Ancient Israel*, 1967, p. 161. While insisting that there is no proof of much of what Mowinckel says about the cult-prophets, Rowley agrees that his suggestions have "transformed and enriched" the study of the Psalter.
[44] Hag. 2:11–13; Lev. 19; Ps. 15. Cf. S. Mowinckel, *The Psalms in Israel's Worship*, vol. ii, 1962, p. 58.
[45] Ps. 2:4, 9.
[46] Pss. 81:5; 85:8; 95:7 (all in the verse numbering of EVV).

for which they stood gave them a special affinity with the main prophetic tradition. They maintained a constant championship of Israel's
connection with her nomadic past, and a standing protest against the
religion and culture of Canaan. The Nazirites were individuals who
had taken vows of a special sort; the Rechabites might be called
"a Nazirite family," for they were a clan which preserved nomadic
customs on religious grounds as a strict family tradition.

The word "Nazirite" means one "set apart" or "consecrated." The
Nazirite did not cut his hair, nor did he drink wine or liquor which
the artifice of man had corrupted for his own ends by fermentation.
He was particularly scrupulous to avoid contact with a corpse, or
whatever else might make him ritually unclean. In line with this
clinging to the natural and primitive was the Nazirite's rejection of
Canaanite culture, and his cherishing of the traditions of Israel's
nomadic past. As has been said, the principle seems to have been
"the farther from civilization, the nearer to God."

The part that was taken by these devotees as forerunners of the
prophets in the great struggle to preserve the distinctive tenets and
values of Yahwism, amid the dangers and seductions of Canaanite
life, is fairly clear. Both Samson, the typical lay hero of the struggle
against the Philistines, and Samuel, the prophetic and priestly leader
in the same struggle, were Nazirites.[47] Amos 2:11, 12 links the
Nazirites with the older prophets, as witnesses to the faith that was
so easily being forgotten under pressure from the Canaanite way of
life: "I raised up some of your sons as prophets, and some of your
young men as Nazirites . . . but you made the Nazirites drink wine,
and commanded the prophets, saying, Prophesy not." After this struggle lay far in the past, the priestly law of Num. 6 still provided in
detail for the making by individuals of a Nazirite vow; it had become
a form of self-offering for a special purpose and for a limited period,
rather than a lifelong dedication to the service of the religious
commonwealth.

[47] Jg. 13:5; 1 Sam. 1:11. The Qumran scroll 4QSam*a* in 1 Sam. 1:22 preserves
the reading, "I will make him a Nazirite forever."

The Rechabites, according to 1 Chr. 2:55, were a Kenite clan; a fact to be related to the special connections of the Kenites with the Mosaic origins of Yahwism.[48] They first came to the front as a body of protest and reaction in the ninth century B.C., in the course of Jehu's counter revolution in the name of "the old-time religion." Jehu, it will be remembered, greeted Jonadab ben Rechab as a fellow zealot.[49] In Jeremiah's time two centuries later, his descendants looked back with pride to this same Jonadab, and proclaimed as the strict rule of their family the rejection of the ways of agrarian and urban civilization, with which Baal worship was bound up: "They said, We will drink no wine, for Jonadab ben Rechab, our ancestor, charged us, saying, You shall drink no wine, neither you nor your sons forever: neither shall you build a house, nor sow seed, nor plant a vineyard, nor own any property; but all your days you shall live in tents."[50] The Rechabites, as a family, were dedicated to the nomad ideal of life and religion. It is probable that the founder, Jonadab, along with Elijah and Elisha, had played a leading part in the popular agitation of which Jehu's massacres were the outcome. When the prophet Micah storms against the city life of his day: "They build Zion with blood, and Jerusalem with iniquity," and when Hosea predicts that Yahweh will again make Israel to dwell in tents,[51] we see their affinity with the spirit of the *bᵉne Rechab*.

PROPHETIC MAKERS-OF-HISTORY

The later prophets recalled Israel to the God of the historic epoch which had made her a people with a distinctive religious and cultural tradition. They claimed to bear a torch kindled by Moses from the flames of Sinai, and passed from hand to hand by the prophetic leaders and makers-of-history throughout the generations. Moses, the creative genius of the beginnings, was called a prophet by later men

[48] Jg. 1:16; 4:11; Ex. 3:1; 8:12; Num. 10:29.
[49] 2 Kg. 10:15–17.
[50] Jer. 35:6–10.
[51] Mic. 3:10; Hos. 12:9.

of the prophetic lineage.[52] Deborah, a "prophetess," sounded the tocsin when the tribal federation was in mortal peril in the early days in Canaan.[53] Gideon, the deliverer from Midianite invasion—though not actually called a "prophet" in our sources—saw (the angel of) Yahweh face to face, and so received his commission to deliver Israel. Like other "judges" of Israel, such as Jephthah and Samson, Gideon was empowered by the spirit of Yahweh.[54] Samuel, last of the "judges," was foremost of the prophetic line which helped to create the national tradition. This line included Gad in the days of David, Ahijah in the time of Jeroboam, and culminated in the reign of Ahab with Elijah, whose hammer blows forged a renewed Israel upon the anvil of history.

Following in this national tradition, the great prophets made known the will of Yahweh, as they found it in the depths of their own inner life and writ large upon the face of history. But they did more. They felt their task to be the *making* as well as the interpretation of history, for they believed themselves to be instruments of the Maker and Master of history, in whose designs Israel had a peculiar place. Because they were morally certain of the will of Yahweh, they stood out boldly against the power of kings, the anathemas of priests, and the fury of mobs. More particularly, they detached themselves from the mass of professional prophets who sought to insure prosperity and victory by announcing these in the name of Yahweh, "saying, Peace, Peace, when there is no peace."[55] The "insurgent" prophets had something that could not be bought. They were a lonely succession of incorruptible men, often regarded by their contemporaries as heretics and traitors. They took their lives in their hands, and some of them did not escape.[56] Jesus

[52] Deut. 18:15, 18.
[53] Jg. 4:4–7.
[54] Jg. 6:34.
[55] Jer. 6:14. Note Johnson's translation—' "It's all right! It's all right!," when it is not all right.' A. R. Johnson, *The Cultic Prophet in Ancient Israel*, 2nd ed., 1962, p. 60, fn 6.
[56] E.g., the prophet Uriah; cf. Jer. 26:20–24.

knew what to expect, when he recalled the reputation of Jerusalem, "that killeth the prophets, and stoneth them that are sent unto her."

EMERGING ETHICAL PROPHECY

Already in the time of Saul and David certain individuals stand out who speak with the undoubted accent of the great prophets. Samuel himself, according to 1 Sam. 15:22, affirmed that obedience to the declared will of Yahweh is of greater importance in the sight of God than the proprieties of cultic service: "Hath Yahweh as great delight in burnt-offerings and sacrifices, as in obedience to the voice of Yahweh? Observe, to obey is better than sacrifice, and to hearken than the fat of rams." It is true that this quotation comes from a history of Samuel written about three hundred years after his day, so that its phraseology may have been influenced by the similar teachings then more common. But the determinative part played by Samuel as Yahweh's representative at the institution of the monarchy makes this sort of language entirely appropriate, and there is no good reason to doubt that we have here a sound tradition as to the substance of his prophetic teaching.[57]

The same may be said of other instances of the intervention from time to time in national affairs by prophetic champions of the religious ethic of Yahwism, men who have left no personal literary remains, but who are accorded a striking place in the national traditions. Nathan rebukes King David for a sin against one of his officers which was also a sin against the obligation of "mercy" within the covenant community, because—in the words which Nathan took from David's own mouth—"he had no pity."[58] The prophet Gad offers David a choice of punishments because of his census of the population for military or taxation purposes; this practice of civilization was sacrilegious from the traditional viewpoint

[57] O. Plöger, ZAW 63 (1951), pp. 157 ff., points to the coincidence of the loss of the ark (where Moses had received Yahweh's word) and the emergence of prophecy in Samuel.
[58] Cf. 2 Sam. 12:6, and its context.

that the increase and numbers of man and beast were the concern of deity alone.[59] Ahijah the Shilonite gives to Jeroboam a divine warrant for rebellion against the oppressive tyranny of the "civilized" King Solomon.[60] Jehu ben Hanani utters a doom against Baasha which recalls the language of Amos' doom of the second Jeroboam.[61] And Elijah challenges Ahab, both on the count of his primary loyalty to Yahweh, and on that of his conduct toward one of his subjects who is also his "neighbor" within the covenant.[62]

Thus we may observe, prior to the "writing prophets," the emergence of some of their characteristic teachings in a succession of men who kept alight the torch of Moses. The higher prophecy had already become the voice of Yahweh's moral demand upon the people of his covenant, and the requirement of ethical obedience was stressed as the central factor in Israel's distinctive religious heritage. Yahweh was seen to be actively concerned, both for the collective welfare and for the social behavior of his people. The function of his prophets was not to satisfy human inquisitiveness, but to declare his will; they spoke at the bidding of God rather than at the instigation of men. The initiative throughout was Yahweh's. The prophets saw Yahweh in the process of making history—the creator of the physical world which is the scene of events was himself an active participant in those events. The part he played was not the capricious intervention of a *deus ex machina*; it was the part to which he was committed by the requirements of his own nature, his consistent historic purpose, and the special relationship in which he stood to Israel.

Finally, these early prophets were independent spokesmen of Yahweh, independent, i.e., of the general mass of diviners and prophets so-called, and of the official cultus and its ministers. In their brave words to kings, we may see that they felt themselves

---

[59] 2 Sam. 24:1 says that the impulse to number the people came to David from Yahweh, but 1 Chr. 21:1 says the instigator was Satan.
[60] 1 Kg. 11:29 ff.
[61] 1 Kg. 16:1-4; Am. 7:9.
[62] 1 Kg. 18:16 ff.; 21:17 ff.

responsible only to the God of whose personal commission and command they were so sure. The word of Yahweh possessed them and found utterance through them. They were like the later Amos, who said, "The Lord Yahweh hath spoken; who can but prophesy?"[63]

SURVIVING TRACES OF PRIMITIVE PROPHECY

This survey of the antecedents and beginnings of prophecy would be incomplete without a brief reference to marks that remain in the classical prophets of the road by which prophecy came finally to supreme utterance. When Isaiah says that Yahweh spoke to him "with a pressure of the hand," and Jeremiah that "because of thy hand I have sat alone," when Ezekiel makes several references to "the hand of Yahweh" being upon him, we recall the ecstatic state in which Elijah was enabled to run from Carmel to Jezreel with "the hand (or ecstatic power) of Yahweh" upon him.[64] So Micah speaks of being "full of power . . . to declare unto Jacob his transgression."[65] It is in Ezekiel particularly that there are to be found clear indications of a trance state into which a prophet fell, at least occasionally, when he received a word from Yahweh: "As I sat in my house . . . the hand of the Lord Yahweh fell there upon me; . . . and he put forth the form of a hand, and took me by a lock of my hair, and the Spirit lifted me up between earth and heaven."[66]

Is. 6 is an outstanding example of the persistence of ecstatic vision and audition: "In the year that King Uzziah died, I saw Yahweh . . . and I heard the voice of Yahweh."[67] Amos has his visions or dreams, of which he says: "The Lord Yahweh showed me."[68] The comprehensive title of the book of Isaiah, which con-

[63] Am. 3:8.
[64] Is. 8:11; Jer. 15:17; Ezek. 1:3; 3:14; cf. 1 Kg. 18:46.
[65] Mic. 3:8.
[66] Ezek. 8:1, 3. These features of the picture of a prophet given us in the Book of Ezekiel are significant, whether we regard them as historical description or as an imaginative portrait.
[67] vv. 1, 8.
[68] Am. 7:1, 4, 7.

sists chiefly of poetic oracles, with some narrative, is nevertheless "the *vision* of Isaiah," and the books of Obadiah and Nahum have similar headings. That the word "vision" has here the attenuated sense of "prophetic oracle," is evident from the title of Habakkuk and the sub-title of Is. 2. The usage suggests that the substance of an oracle—with its emotional exaltation and rhythmic utterance— was perceived by the prophets with the actuality and certainty of the experience of sight.[69] It also connects the mystic inward vision of the prophets with the dreams and visions which men of former days had believed to be revelations of deity.

Wonder-working was essentially alien to the genius of ethical prophecy. It is a far cry from Gideon's sign of the fleece to Isaiah's sign of Immanuel. But the connection is there, and we may recall similar examples of events which are stated to be the pledge or the confirmation of prophecy.[70] Gideon's "sign" was a miraculous intervention in the natural order. Isaiah's "sign" was a significant but not a miraculous[71] happening, confidently predicted by the prophet as a sign-post on the road of the future which would mark the fulfilment of his word. The older type of sign is rejected as false magic by the literary prophet known as Second Isaiah: "I am Yahweh, that maketh all things . . . that frustrateth the signs of the soothsayers, and driveth diviners mad."[72] There is nothing in the teaching and lives of the prophets of the eighth and seventh centuries to correspond with the stories of Elisha's multiplying food, making an ax-head float, and raising the dead. They spoke words which bore the mark of their divine authority upon them, and had no need of the adventitious aid of magical powers. The signs they

[69] Cf. R. B. Y. Scott, "Isaiah XXI 1–10; The Inside of a Prophet's Mind," VT, II 3 (1952), pp. 278–81.
[70] Jg. 6:36–40; Is. 7:10–16. Cf. G. B. Gray, *Isaiah I*, pp. 121 ff.
[71] The crucial word in Is. 7:14 should be translated "maiden," not "virgin" for which there is a distinct Hebrew word not found in this passage. The *sign* is that, by the time a child shortly to be conceived is born, the mother will be able to name him "God-is-with-us" in celebration of the deliverance promised by Isaiah.
[72] Is. 44:24, 25.

offered were natural events, because the natural order was to them the scene of Yahweh's activity; the signs marked the working of his purpose on the plane of history. We may illustrate this by setting beside the above passage from Isaiah 7 another from Jeremiah: "And this shall be the *sign* unto you, saith Yahweh, that I will punish you in this place, that ye may know that my words shall surely stand against you for evil: observe,—I am about to deliver Pharaoh Hophra, King of Egypt, into the hand of his enemies."[73]

The classical prophets cannot be properly understood without some knowledge of their antecedents. Neither can they be sufficiently explained in terms of development from those antecedents. A difference in degree has become a difference in kind. They are linked to their surroundings and to the past because they belong to the real world. In relation to the central religious tradition of their people they are radically conservative. But *they* are new.

[73] Jer. 44:29, 30.

4

THE PROPHETIC SUCCESSION

One of the most significant things about Hebrew prophecy is its persistence in various forms throughout a great part of the religious history of Israel. There is an apostolic succession of prophetic voices for which the ancient world shows no parallel.[1] Otherwise we could not speak of this Israelite phenomenon as unique. The religions of Syria, Mesopotamia and Egypt had their prophets too.

The experience of the Egyptian traveller Wen Amon with an ecstatic prophet at Byblos has already been mentioned.[2] Parallels closer to the Hebrew prophets of the classical period have come to light on some of the thousands of clay tablets from the royal archives of the city of Mari on the Euphrates, dating from the eighteenth century B.C. On one of these a certain Malik-Dagan tells how, as he knelt in the temple of the god Dagan: "Dagan opened his mouth and spoke to me as follows . . . 'Now go! I have sent you! To king Zimri-lin you are to speak thus.'" (There follows a promise of aid in a particular situation.) This oracle received during worship in a temple and the commissioning a prophet to speak, recall the

---

[1] Cf. C. R. North in ET, vol. 47, p. 356: "Outside the Old Testament the figure most like the prophets is Zoroaster. But Zoroastrianism differed markedly from Judaism in that Zoroaster had no successor."
[2] See above, p. 45 ff.

circumstances of Isaiah's call to prophesy (Is. chap. 6). Another Mari oracle speaks of the past aid of the god Adad, just as Amos in 2:9–11 reminds Israel of what Yahweh has done for her. In still another tablet a prophetess brings to a royal official a message for the king: "The god Dagan has sent me. Send to my Lord (the king). Let him not be anxious." This reminds us that Huldah a prophetess gave a message to King Josiah, and of what Isaiah said to King Ahaz as Yahweh's word: "Take heed; be quiet (in mind); do not fear!"[3]

Coming down to a period more nearly contemporary with the Hebrew prophets, we have the inscription of Zakir, king of Hamat, who says that, in answer to his prayer in an emergency, "Be'el Shamayn (spoke) to me through seers and diviners, 'Do not fear, for I made you king and I shall stand by you.'" Similar encouragement comes to the Assyrian King Esarhaddon through several prophetesses, and to his successor Ashurbanipal through dreams sent by his god.[4]

In the course of Egypt's long and checkered history there were periods when social and religious conditions resembled those complained of by the Hebrew prophets. In one such time, shortly before the opening of one of the greatest periods of Egyptian history under the Twelfth Dynasty, an "Eloquent Peasant" addressed his complaint to Rensi, the High Steward: "O Chief Steward, my lord, greatest of the great! . . . Desire to live long, as it is said: Doing justice is the (very) breath of the nose. . . . If thou veilest thy face against violence, who then will punish meanness? . . . Do not plunder of his property a poor man; . . . he who takes it away is one who stops up his nose. . . . Do justice for the sake of the Lord of Justice. . . . Justice lasts unto eternity; it goes down into the necropolis with him who does it. . . . he is

---

[3] Cf. W. von Soden, "Verkündigen des Gotteswillens . . . ," *Welt des Orients* I, 1950, pp. 397-403; C. Westermann, "Die Mari-Briefe und die Prophetie in Israel," *Forschung am Alten Testament*, 1964, pp. 171–88; 2 Kg. 21:14–20; Is. 7:4.

[4] Cf. ANET, pp. 449–51.

remembered for goodness. That is a principle of the word of god" (i.e., of the divine order).

These words, of course, are a man's plea for justice for himself, unlike Amos' and Isaiah's denunciations, in the name of Yahweh, of the powerful who take advantage of the helpless. Yet it is significant because of its appeal to a transcendent source and principle of justice. Another Egyptian writer longs for death because "Hearts are rapacious; . . . there are no righteous; the land is left to those who do wrong." Again, a man named Ipuwer of the third millennium B.C. is bold enough to denounce to the Pharaoh himself the social chaos prevailing, and to call on the Pharaoh to be one of whom "men shall say, 'he is the herdsman of all men; evil is not in his heart. . . . Authority, Perception and Justice are with thee.' " Once again, there are similarities to the denunciations of an Amos or a Jeremiah addressed to the king, but with the fundamental difference that the speaker does not come as a messenger of God.[5] In still another work, the *Prophecy of Nefer-rohu,* we have an example of pre-dated prediction like 1 Kg. 13:2, where a king is named whose deeds are known to the audience but are represented as having been predicted long before.

The religious revolution of the Pharaoh Amen-hotep IV (Akh-en-Aton) produced—if not prophecy—psalms remarkably like, e.g., Ps. 104. But a priestly reaction followed, and Egyptian religion became archaistic and legalistic. In the later period when Jewish apocalyptic pseudo-prophecy emerged it too found a parallel in Egypt. The Ptolemaic *Demotic Chronicle,* like Daniel, is a book of "prophecies," nationalistic in tone and predicting dreadful catastrophies to be followed by a glorious salvation. Even the device of reckoning days as years appears in it.

But in spite of these parallels in form and, to some extent in substance, the measure of the distance of Hebrew from Egyptian prophecy is the measure of the superiority of Hebrew religion. (One

[5] ANET, pp. 406, 408–10, 443; Am. 7:7–9; Jer. 22:13–19.

reaches a similar conclusion when the Biblical stories of Creation, Paradise and the Deluge are compared with their Babylonian and Sumerian prototypes.) Amos does not call on the Israelites to do justice because justice is eternal: he speaks at the immediate command of a God whose will it is that men do justly now. The Hebrew prophets were like watchmen who pass an urgent message from hill to hill, not with parrot-like repetition, but with constantly renewed vitality. For the prophetic tradition was a living thing, which had become part of themselves through their own commission at Yahweh's hand. Their God was not tied to his past, nor were his nature and will to be deduced by theoretical reflection upon a settled doctrine. He was a God known by his mighty acts in national history and in the prophet's own experience, one who, in the actual situation of every moment, had made and continued to make his own characteristic demands upon his people. The prophets spoke with his immediate authority.

There is nothing comparable to this in Egypt or elsewhere, as there is nothing like the *succession* of prophets which Israel knew.

FIVE STAGES OF THE PROPHETIC SUCCESSION

We may classify under five heads the literature produced, directly or indirectly, by the prophetic impulse before it died out about the end of the Persian period, under the growing pressure of the normative Law. (The vital spark of prophecy was then passed on to apocalyptic on the one hand, and to psalmody and the "Wisdom" literature on the other.) It must be emphasized that this five-fold classification is a classification primarily of the *literature* through which we trace the story of prophecy, rather than a definition of stages in the developments behind the literature. But, roughly speaking, these five kinds of literary records are successive, and correspond to successive epochs of the prophetic movement.

(1) There is first of all *the traditional and partly legendary literature relating to the Founder, Moses,* preserved mainly in the

several documents of the Pentateuch. These documents incorporate a few fragments of the old national saga, of which they are prose versions influenced by prophetic teaching.[6] To these may be added the several versions in which the Decalogue of Moses was preserved at various sanctuaries;[7] versions whose common elements witness to their descent from a single original, and whose differences point to its antiquity. Though Moses is an authentic historic figure, his influence is felt rather than clearly seen in the literature relating to him and written centuries after his time.

(2) The second body of material is the *narratives* in Judges, Samuel and Kings *in which individuals called "prophets" appear as actors in the national drama*, but in no sense are the center of it (except for Samuel, whose prophetic office is correlated with his work as national leader). Nathan and Gad, Shemaiah, Ahijah and Jehu ben Hanani only flit across the stage. They are important as maintaining the continuity of the prophetic succession.

(3) Thirdly, we have the *biographical and legendary material* that gathered around the names of *the pre-literary prophets Elijah and Elisha*, and which was inserted in blocks of narrative into the history of the monarchies in 1 and 2 Kings. Here the *acts and incidental sayings* of the prophets are the chief interest of the narrator; there is no extended discourse, and the historical circumstances recede into the background.[8]

(4) The fourth body of Biblical material, and by far the most important for the understanding of Hebrew prophecy, is the *classical literature of the Golden Age* of prophecy, the eighth, seventh and early sixth centuries B.C. This consists chiefly of *collections of oracles written down after having been spoken*. There is certain additional narrative matter, descriptive of the prophet's acts, or of the circum-

[6] Poetic fragments of the old saga can be recognized, e.g., in Ex. 15:21; 17:16; Num. 10:35, 36; 21:14–18, 27–29.

[7] With Ex. 20:3–17; cf. Deut. 5:7–21; 27:15–26; Lev. 19:3–18 and Ex. 34:14–26.

[8] The "sons of the prophets," or prophetic guilds, appear in both the second and the third bodies of material.

stances of his preaching—and also of his spiritual experiences—but in the main these records of the great days of prophecy comprise the *substance of the prophets' oracular utterances.* The speakers are known; a large proportion of the oracles attributed to them can be regarded as authentic; the collections are dated in general terms, and particular oracles sometimes are dated exactly; the historical circumstances are reasonably clear.

This material comprises most of the Books of Amos, Hosea, Jeremiah, Zephaniah and Nahum; and a substantial part of the Books of Isaiah, Ezekiel, Obadiah, Micah and Habakkuk. The balance of the material in these books is to be classified either under heading (5) as anonymous written prophecy, or as oracular utterances from nameless prophets whose messages have been included with that of the well-known figures mentioned above. The brief revival of spoken prophecy, in the late sixth and early fifth centuries, which has left its record in Haggai, Zechariah 1–8 and Malachi may be called a Silver Age.

(5) Finally, there is the most extensive of the bodies of literature relating to the prophetic movement, *post-classical written prophecy, anonymous and of uncertain date.* The collections of oracles of the known prophets of the eighth and seventh centuries appear to have been put together by their immediate disciples, and these collections were treasured and enlarged by later members of the prophetic school or party. The process went on for centuries, with the result that these anonymous supplements now comprise more than half (some would say, considerably more than half), of the prophetic canon of Scripture. The material which has been added includes some new major contributions such as 2 Isaiah and the semi-apocalyptic chapters 24–27 of Isaiah, in addition to briefer editorial insertions and additions by unknown minor prophetic writers. The result is that only one-quarter to one-third of a book like "Isaiah" can be attributed to the prophet of that name, the whole having gathered gradually around brief original collections of his work. More than half of the "Book of the Twelve" Minor

Prophets is post-exilic[9] and of unknown authorship and uncertain date.

It will be evident that when we ask who were the prophets, and what was their teaching, the answer is beset with critical difficulties, and cannot be given by indiscriminate quotation from the prophetic canon. If we agree to trace the line of prophetic succession back to Moses, it covers a thousand years and has left, as we have seen, a series of literary records of various kinds and differing value. The best procedure would appear to be to concentrate attention upon the material under (4) above, the recorded spoken oracles of the classical period. We can come to grips with these prophets of the eighth and seventh centuries better than with any others, because their literary remains are fairly extensive and are usually comprehensible in the light of known historical and religious conditions. Moreover, with some significant exceptions such as the Servant Songs and 2 Isaiah, there is little elsewhere in our records to compare in importance and value with these prophetic masterpieces. Yet even these cannot be viewed in isolation from the great succession in which they stood.

TRADITIONS OF THE FOUNDER, MOSES

The religion of Israel is one of the religions of mankind which bears the personal impress of a founder. Few scholars today question the historicity of Moses, though they differ in their estimate of the importance of his contribution to the developed religion of Israel. The traditions of Israel's beginnings are not easy to disentangle, but it may be confidently affirmed that the story of Moses, the Exodus and the Sinai covenant is the necessary foundation of the *historically conditioned theology* of Israel.

Four strands of evidence lead back to this distant figure of heroic proportions whom the later law-makers looked to as the fountainhead of the Law, whom the priests regarded as the first priestly

---

[9] The word "post-exilic" is a convenient designation of the period after the destruction of Jerusalem in 587 B.C., though it must be recognized that only a part of the total population was deported to Babylonia at that time.

Levite, and to whom the prophets looked back as their antetype and ideal. The first strand is the testimony of the main historical tradition that Israel's worship of Yahweh as a God of distinctive character began at Sinai (Horeb), where a federation of tribes became "Yahweh's people" through a covenant mediated by Moses. The nation had been born out of Moses' personal religious experience, together with the soul-stirring common experiences in which this new God's power and will were made known to the people. The uniqueness of Yahweh was a cardinal tenet of Israelite faith. It was he and no other god whose summons and purpose were evidenced in historic events, the particular significance of which was interpreted by his spokesman Moses. At the head of the national tradition, and explaining it, was the figure of this man who had been a prophet like the prophets of the eighth century: a man who knew the presence and the moral will of God as an intense experience, who discerned his summons in current events and situations, and who declared that Yahweh demanded obedience and loyalty to the provisions of his covenant as the condition of his continued blessing and salvation. Hosea's word, "By a prophet Yahweh brought Israel up out of Egypt,"[10] belongs to this living tradition about Moses.

The second strand of evidence leading back to Moses is the character of the b^{e}rith, or covenant, which in historic times served as a kind of national constitution. In 1 Sam. 10:25 this is called "the manner[11] of the kingdom," and it is said to have been inscribed as a document and deposited in the sanctuary. When David was anointed king at the sanctuary of Hebron through the free choice of the elders of Israel, he "made a covenant with them in Yahweh's presence."[12] What this meant becomes clearer in the account of another coronation ceremony two hundred years later, that of the

[10] Hos. 12:13 (EVV).
[11] The word *mishpat* means a judicial decision, the execution of a decision (judgment), the principle exemplified by the decision (justice), or the customs and standards accepted as right. Here it means almost the "nature" of the kingdom.
[12] 2 Sam. 5:3.

child Jehoash, when the priest "made a covenant between Yahweh and the king and the people, and also between the king and the people."[13] This was first of all a renewal of allegiance to Yahweh, and the public acknowledgment of Yahweh's justice and mercy as the "custom and right" of the community to be upheld by the king. Further illustrations of the operation of this covenant of religion and social ethics as a kind of national constitution may be seen in the demands made upon Rehoboam at the Disruption, and in the covenant made in 621 B.C. by King Josiah and his people, as a result of which Jeremiah comments: "He judged the cause of the poor and needy; then it was well. Was not this to know me? saith Yahweh."[14] These covenants of the historic period are linked to the national tradition which had become a theological doctrine, viz., that at Sinai-Horeb Yahweh had entered into his special relation to the tribes, on terms summarized in a Decalogue and capable of expansion into successive codes of law.[15]

The existence of the several versions of the Decalogue—the "use" of Shechem or the "use" of Bethel[16]—is the third strand of evidence pointing back to Moses. The formulation of religious obligations so largely in terms of social ethics is a significant common feature of this covenant tradition and the teaching of the prophets.

In the fourth place we have clear indications in the words of the prophets themselves that they believed their message was not new, but was a recall to the essential religion of the formative period of Moses, "I am Yahweh your God (who brought you), from the land of Egypt . . . and there is no deliverer except me; I pastured you in the wilderness," says Hosea; and again, "By a prophet Yahweh brought Israel up from Egypt, and by a prophet he was

---

[13] 2 Kg. 11:17.
[14] Jer. 22:16.
[15] Such as the "Code of the Covenant," Ex. 20:23–23:33; the Deuteronomic Code, Deut. 12–26, the "Holiness" Code, Lev. 17–26, and the extensive statutory material of the Priest Code in Ex., Lev. and Num.
[16] Psalms 15 and 24:1–6, and Jer. 7:5–10 point to liturgical use of ethical formulae resembling the Decalogue.

preserved," but "they have transgressed my covenant, and sinned against my law."[17] "It was I who brought you up out of the land of Egypt, and led you through the wilderness for forty years," Yahweh says in Am. 2:10. And Jeremiah builds his argument on the same premise: "I spake not with your fathers nor commanded them, in the day when I brought them out of the land of Egypt, concerning burnt-offering or sacrifice; but this thing I commanded them: Hearken unto my voice."[18] The general prophetic teaching on the requirement of constantly renewed ethical obedience, and the relative unimportance of the cult, is here claimed as original in Israel's faith.

ACTORS ON THE STAGE OF HISTORY

There is not much that can be said about the second type of material, the incidental references to early and little known prophets in the histories of Judges, Samuel and Kings. These books in their present form are "religious" rather than "general" histories, so that the knowledge they give us of political events and social conditions is far from complete. They contain *selections* from various sources such as court annals, temple records, royal and prophetic biographies and popular tradition—edited with comments in order to teach the lesson that Yahweh had been constantly at work through persons and events of history. This was "prophetic" teaching, and these books were undoubtedly put together by disciples of the prophets.

It can readily be understood that these historians would not fail to draw attention to the work of their forerunners, the "prophetic makers-of-history,"[19] even though little was then known about them. Some dramatic action or striking utterance marked the impact upon the older national story of a spirit like that of the well-known prophets of a later day. Samuel, like Elijah, and Elisha, is accorded

---

[17] Hos. 13:4, 5 (following reading of Greek and Syriac in v. 5); 12:13 EVV.
[18] Jer. 7:22, 23.
[19] Cf. Chap. 3, pp. 53–54.

the role of king-maker in the records, and his famous dictum to
Saul recalls a similar word of Hosea.[20] Nathan's rebuke of David
for an outrage against one of his subjects recalls Elijah's similar
rebuke of Ahab and Jeremiah's scathing indictment of Jehoiakim.[21]
Ahijah commissions the leader of a revolt against the slave-labor
policy of Solomon, as Elisha commissions Jehu ben Nimshi to
extirpate the cult of Baal Melkarth in Israel and to usurp Ahab's
throne.[22] The prophet Jehu ben Hanani denounces Baasha in language resembling that used by Amos concerning Jeroboam II.[23]
Nathan, Gad and Micaiah, like Isaiah, were counsellors of royalty,
and the solitary courage of Micaiah in opposing the professional
prophets of victory was displayed again by Jeremiah.[24]

These prophets of an earlier day are remarkably like their successors in these particulars. They are remembered for having maintained the continuity of the succession, and appear among the
actors of Israel's dramatic history. But the references to them are
brief, and they left behind them no body of teaching.

THE ELIJAH AND ELISHA NARRATIVES

The story of Ahab's reign over northern Israel begins at 1 Kg.
16:29 in the bald annalistic fashion of the preceding chapters, following immediately upon a summary in six verses of the reign of
the great Omri. But almost at once Ahab's story expands into a full-
blooded narrative, which continues for six chapters until it, too,
concludes with the usual editorial formula at 1 Kg. 22:39, 40. Even
a cursory examination will explain this sudden blossoming-out of the
historian when he comes to the time of Ahab, who certainly was
not a greater man than Omri his father. The additional material
celebrates the deeds of Elijah and certain other prophets who

[20] 1 Sam. 10; 15:22, 23; cf. Hos. 6:6.
[21] 2 Sam. 11:2–12:15; 1 Kg. 21; Jer. 22:13–19.
[22] 1 Kg. 11:29–40; 2 Kg. 9:1–3.
[23] 1 Kg. 16:1–4; Am. 7:9.
[24] 1 Kg. 22:5–28; Jer. 26—28.

appeared in this reign and gave to it unusual significance in the eyes of the narrator. For the first time (if the story of Samuel, which is of a different sort, be excepted), we find a cycle of narratives in which a prophetic figure continues to hold the center of the stage, and which appear to have been gathered together in one of the sources utilized by the editor of the Book of Kings. Four of the chapters concern Elijah; the remaining two are concerned with the part played in the Syrian wars by Micaiah ben Imlah and two other prophets who remain anonymous.

Elijah is one of the most arresting personalities in the Old Testament story. His name was linked with that of Moses by later religious thinkers, and in Malachi we find the expectation that this prophet who, like Moses, had died mysteriously, would come again to herald the Judgment and the Messianic age: "Behold, I will send you Elijah the prophet before the great and terrible day of Yahweh come."[25]

Elijah's appearance in the pages of the Book of Kings is as sudden and unexplained as were his appearances to his contemporaries.[26] The editor introduces him at 1 Kg. 17:1 as the well-known figure he had become. His origin is as mysterious as Melchizedek's; we are told only that he was a "Tishbite" who lived in Gilead on the borders of the desert. It is not obvious why in later days Elijah was coupled with Moses rather than with Amos and Isaiah to whom he was centuries nearer in date, and for whose work his was the preparation. Perhaps the reason was that he was an elusive figure but one essential to the tradition, like Moses—an assured fact of history whose distant greatness made him a symbol. A sure instinct recognized Elijah as the leader at a critical turning point, and the same instinct traced back to Moses, at least in principle, all that was distinctive in the beginnings of Israelite religion. Elijah, like Luther, went back to the sources: as Luther to the New Testament, Elijah to Horeb the mount of God. His mighty voice recalled Israel to her

[25] Mal. 4:5, 6 (EVV); cf. Mt. 17:3, 10–13.
[26] 1 Kg. 18:7–12; 21:20.

primary loyalty to Moses' God. The cry was taken up by greater
men who followed Elijah, men of deeper insight and greater spiritual
power. But the fact remains that he was the forerunner, as in the
later eschatology he became the forerunner of the Messiah.

The circumstances of Elijah's ministry are fairly clear. Ahab (or,
more probably, his father Omri for him) had made a marriage
alliance with the royal family of Tyre. Since political alliances at
that time involved a mutual recognition of deities, and since Jezebel,
Ahab's Tyrian bride, was not one to take her privileges lightly, the
priority of Yahweh as Israel's peculiar God was threatened. Already
the Israelite cultus had come to share many features of Canaanite
worship. But now that the cult of the great storm-god Baal-Hadad,
who in one of his local forms had become the national god of Tyre,
was installed at Samaria under the propagandist patronage of the
queen, the distinctive relationship of Yahweh to Israel was in
danger. On this, Elijah joined issue.

1 Kings 17 opens with the prophet's sudden appearance—"like
a meteor," as Loehr puts it—and his announcement to the king that
a great drought is imminent. This is a direct challenge to Baal in
his own sphere, the giving of fertility through rain. "In this country,"
says Elijah, in effect, "it is Yahweh who gives and withholds rain."
We are reminded of the words of Hosea a century later: "[Israel]
did not know that it was I who gave her the grain and the new wine
and the oil, and multiplied for her silver and gold, which they used
for the Baal (image)."[27]

Having startled the king with this pronouncement, Elijah prudently
goes into hiding by the brook Cherith, where he is fed by ravens until
the brook dries up. Nothing is to be gained by attempting to ra-
tionalize this miracle and the others in the stories of Elijah and
Elisha. The narrator plainly intended his audience to understand
that they were the sort of men who *could* perform miracles, and for
whom miracles were performed by Yahweh. We must be prepared

[27] Hos. 2:8 (EVV).

to apply a certain "legendary discount" to the narratives. The question is not whether, in the abstract, miracles can happen, but whether a particular series of miracle-tales can be taken at its face value, when it includes a story of bears eating children because they were rude.[28]

The stories concerning Elijah are on a rather higher level than those that concern Elisha. The ravens that fed Elijah, the unfailing cruse of oil, the revival of the child, and finally the coming of fire and rain from heaven in answer to Elijah's prayer—all testified to the power of Yahweh to give what the people had been wont to ask from the Baal. It is even claimed that Yahweh's power extended into the territory of Jezebel's god, the Sidonian village of Zarephath. These preliminary incidents lead up to the main episode in chapter 18, where, in a familiar scene, Elijah faces the prophets of Baal and puts their power and Yahweh's to the test. We note the dervish frenzy of Baal's prophets, and the dramatic completeness of what follows, when the lone representative of Yahweh repairs his ancient and neglected altar. We should not ask where Elijah obtained such quantities of water to pour on the altar in a time of drought, for that is a dramatic necessity of the story.[29] The main thing is the triumph of the representative of Yahwism on the crucial issue of the bringing of rain.

It is possible to consider the following story of Elijah's flight to Horeb in more than one light. Micklem[30] makes the suggestion that this is a misplaced account of Elijah's call to prophesy, but this cannot arise out of chapter 19 as it now stands. Here Elijah is in flight from Jezebel, a natural sequel to the tremendous nervous strain of the single-handed contest at Mount Carmel. But whether it be a flight or not, the significance of the journey is its direction. The first halting place is Beersheba, sanctuary of the northern tribes from

---

[28] 2 Kg. 2:23, 24.
[29] That is, the story in its present form. A. Alt's source analysis indicates that the contest-story has been combined with a distinct drought-story.
[30] N. Micklem, *Prophecy and Eschatology*, 1926, p. 93.

patriarchal times. From Beersheba the prophet travels "forty days and forty nights" (an indefinite but considerable distance) to Horeb, Moses' "mount of God," known in Judaean tradition as Sinai. Here, we are told, he lodged in a cave, and Peake[31] suggests that this may refer to the traditional "cleft of the rock" where Moses was when Yahweh "passed by," as he now "passed by" Elijah.[32] A great wind, an earthquake and (volcanic?) fire provided the setting for a second Mosaic revelation. But they brought no message to Elijah. Only when the reverberations of the stupendous display of natural forces had subsided did the prophet recognize the voice of Yahweh in the awful hush that followed.

To interpret the "still, small voice" as the voice of conscience is to read into the passage what is not there. "The voice of thin stillness" is a silence that could be heard, as it is sometimes said that a darkness is so great that one can feel it. The point is that the awesome phenomena which had spoken to Moses did not bring to Elijah the message he expected. But Yahweh spoke to him in the stillness of mountain and desert, as Elijah's recent experiences flashed back into his mind.

This may be interpreted as a rebuke to the violence of the man who with his own hands had slain the devotees of Baal. The days when Yahwism was to be propagated by violence were over, and the mountain peaks of the eighth century prophets, in all their moral grandeur, were already above the horizon. Or, it may be a rebuke to any tendency, whether at Carmel or at Horeb, to identify Yahweh too closely with natural powers. He was not a storm-god, but a god of the moral will and of the historic covenant. Again, the voice which follows the stillness and inquires: "What doest thou *here*, Elijah?" suggests that the prophet was wrong in going back to Horeb, for Yahweh's presence was not localized there, nor was the cry "back to Moses" an adequate formula for this later day.

As we observe the sequel in the story of Naboth's vineyard

[31] *The People and the Book*, ed. A. S. Peake, 1925, p. 261.
[32] 1 Kg. 19:11; cf. 33:21–23.

(chapter 21), where Elijah resists the new royal despotism in the name of the morality of the covenant, we see the new emphasis on the ethical features of Mosaism which was to characterize the prophets of the next century. The return to Moses was not to mean the revival of primitive nature elements in the concept of deity, nor yet (as the Rechabites hoped) the recovery of conditions of life that had passed away. The stillness Elijah heard was the stillness where Amos was to hear Yahweh roaring as a lion for covenant-justice to roll down like waters. It was a voice that recalled Israel, not to the *locality* of Sinai, but to the religious fervor and moral austerity associated with the vital origins of her faith. The voice called her away from Canaanite associations in life and religious ritual, away from sacrifice even at the ancient Yahweh altar at Carmel. (So Hosea and Jeremiah were to deny that the sacrificial system had any Mosaic sanction at all.[33]) Like Moses, Elijah received a theophany at Horeb, and died under mysterious circumstances. Their basic resemblance is that each stood forward at a moment of supreme crisis in Israel's religious history, and became the symbol of a crucial decision.

Elisha was the servant and disciple of Elijah, and appears to have carried on as Elijah's successor through most of the second half of the ninth century B.C.[34] Some of the material that relates to him is of a religious and literary quality resembling that of the Elijah narratives (e.g., the story of Naaman, 2 Kg. 5), but in the remainder the miraculous and legendary elements are so marked as to suggest folk tales. Moreover, there are curious repetitions of material from the Elijah cycle: each fills a widow's failing cruse, each raises to life a mother's only son, each is made responsible for instigating the revolution of Jehu, and each at his death is called "the chariot of Israel and the horsemen thereof."[35] Elisha

[33] Hos. 6:6; 8:11–13; Jer. 7:22.
[34] The material relating to Elisha is found in 2 Kg. 2—9:3; 13:14–21, together with a brief insert in the Elijah cycle establishing his connection with Elijah, 1 Kg. 19:15–21.
[35] A phrase meaning, apparently, "Israel's sure defence": 2 Kg. 2:12; 13:14.

is undoubtedly an historical figure standing in the prophetic succession, but the fact that he was remembered chiefly as a wonderworker and head of the prophetic guilds[36] suggests that he made no distinctive contribution to the "increasing purpose" of prophecy, comparable to that of Elijah.

THE GOLDEN AGE OF PROPHECY[37]

So far as we know, the great days of Hebrew prophecy began with Amos. The qualification is necessary because, though Amos is the first to leave behind him any extensive record of his utterances, he may not have been the first to be worthy of such a literary memorial. But it was Amos or his disciples who initiated the practice of preserving in writing the substance of spoken oracles. It has been conjectured that this resulted from the ban placed on the prophet by the priest of the royal sanctuary at Bethel.[38] If so, this repressive act had the opposite of the desired effect. Another explanation[39] is that this echoed a change in Assyrian imperial policy, from dealing with Kings to dealing with peoples—hence the need for publication.

Amos' prophecies are dated under Uzziah of Judah and Jeroboam of Israel, the two monarchs whose long, contemporary reigns were a "Victorian Age" in Palestine. The point is emphasized that he spoke *during the two years before* a memorable earthquake[40] which brought to Israel the beginning of the doom he had predicted.[41] We learn from his apologia before the priest of Bethel that Amos was not a professional prophet but a layman, a simple herdsman who, among his flocks, was seized with the conviction that he must

---

[36] The legends of their master doubtless come to us from the "sons of the prophets."

[37] Only a very brief survey of classical prophecy is given here, as it provides the material for succeeding chapters.

[38] Am. 7:12–13; cf. Jer. 36:4–8.

[39] By my colleague John S. Holladay, Jr., in an unpublished paper.

[40] Am. 1:1; see Chap. 1, note 16. This earthquake was still spoken of centuries later; cf. Zech. 14:5.

[41] Am. 8:8; cf. 3:15; 4:11, 12; 6:9–11.

prophesy to—and against—Israel. As a Judaean, he was heir to the Puritan strain in the tradition of Yahwism. But, though the only narrative in the Book of Amos places him at Bethel, it is not to the northern kingdom only that he speaks: the inhabitants of Zion are castigated in the same breath with the men of Samaria. To the sturdy peasant's contempt for the refinements of civilization is added an awareness of the hollowness of the apparent prosperity of the cities, and a keen insight into its human cost and spiritual consequences. "They drink from bowls of wine," he says, "and anoint themselves with the best oils; but they are not pained by the crushing of Joseph."[42]

The oracle with which the Book of Amos opens has seven strophes or stanzas uniform in arrangement, working up to an unexpected climax enforced by the suspense of anticipation. One after another the surrounding nations are summoned to the judgment bar of Yahweh to answer for their atrocities in war. But Israel is called to account for the atrocities of peace which are no less terrible, and which are constant rather than occasional. The exploitation of the poor and the debauchery of worship are sins against the light which has been given her. Yahweh's punishment is suggested in a swift glimpse of a panic-stricken army.

Next, Amos argues from the causal connection of events in the natural world to the moral realm where Yahweh is supreme. "Does a lion roar in the forest without having taken prey? . . . if evil befall a city, is it not Yahweh who has done it?" The moral law is inexorable, and Yahweh has no favorites. His past favor is all the more reason for his punishment of Israel. "You only have I known of all the families of the earth: therefore I will punish you."[43] And further, the worship which lends its sanction to a luxurious and unjust society will be destroyed by the just God it professes to serve: because he is just, men may not drown the cries of the oppressed with the noise of hymns, nor buy off the

[42] Am. 6:6.
[43] Am. 3:2.

deity with increased offerings.[44] This certainty that justice is a primary demand of Yahweh leads Amos to declare the fallacy of popular beliefs; such as, that God's past favors would be continued irrespective of Israel's way of life; that he was pleased by sumptuous sacrifice; that on the Day when he would show his power, the discomfiture of their enemies would follow. But no—"I hate, I despise your feasts," and, "Woe unto you that desire the Day of Yahweh; . . . it will be darkness, not light."[45]

The historical doctrine of a chosen nation does not mean for Israel an election of unconditional privilege, for other nations too are under Yahweh's control: "Did I not bring up Israel out of the land of Egypt, *and* the Philistines from Caphtor, and the Syrians from Kir?" It is the *sinful* people, not the peoples who do not worship Yahweh, which will be destroyed. When once, as here, the categorical imperative of morality is recognized as universal, we are not far from monotheism.[46]

The prophet Hosea's ministry is dated in the reign of Jeroboam II of Israel and also in the reigns of four successive kings of Judah, the last of whom began to rule more than twenty years after Jeroboam's death. Apparently the stable dynasty of Judah was held to provide the only reliable chronology, for, of the six kings that followed Jeroboam at Samaria, four were assassinated and succeeded by usurpers. The political chaos was made worse by a feud between pro-Assyrian and pro-Egyptian political parties. The result was anarchy, with every man's hand against his fellow. The class struggle added its toll to the depredations of outlaws. Prophets and priests were as degraded as the people. The corruption which Amos had pictured had now reached an advanced stage, and society was disintegrating. "There is no truth, nor goodness, nor knowledge of God in the land."[47]

[44] Am. 5:21–23; 4:4, 5.
[45] Am. 5:18.
[46] It should be added that 9:8b–15, with its modification of the prophet's message and its clear reference in v. 11 to the fall of Jerusalem as already in the past, is a post-exilic appendix. See below, p. 88.
[47] Hos. 4:1.

One feature of the situation that is brought out by Hosea is the essential identity of popular Yahwism with Baal worship, the Canaanite form of the widespread fertility cult. The mysteries of life and death and generation have always gripped the mind of man, and it was believed that the needed fertility of fields and herds could be promoted by religious exercises based on the life-cycle of vegetation, animals and men. The fertility cult was at once a primitive natural science and a religion. According to its mythology, a male deity died annually when vegetation withered, was mourned and sought in the underworld by his goddess consort, and was brought back to earth by her with the resurrection of vegetation in the Spring; they were then remarried, to insure the generation of new life. It is not surprising that "sacred" prostitution was a feature of the cultus of this form of religion.

The recognition that Hosea's wife, on whose story much of the prophet's message turns, was probably one of these temple prostitutes, helps to solve the difficulties of chapters 1 and 3 where the story is recounted. Both in 1:2 and in 3:1 Gomer is described as an adulteress when Hosea married her, not, as the story has usually been interpreted, an unfaithful wife. It has been suggested by T. H. Robinson that the prolonged seclusion required of her in 3:3 was a period of deconsecration necessary to free her from her obligations and special status as a temple functionary.[48] Hosea's love for Gomer is a two-fold mystery in which he discerns the direction of a divine hand: why, in the first place, he should have felt this compelling, spiritual love for a woman who herself was satisfied with sensuality, and why he should love her still when she returned to adultery. In the light of his own experience the prophet reasons from the divine love which chose Israel at the beginning to a love which yearns over her still, though she has lapsed into the disloyalty and immorality of the Baal cult. As in that terrible travesty of the highest human relationship the glory and wonder of true love are unknown, so "my people are destroyed

[48] Cf. the provision for the temporary deconsecration of a priest, in Ezek. 44:19.

for lack of knowledge"[49] of the God they worship. Hosea speaks of judgment that cannot be averted by superficial professions of repentance; but he speaks more of love undefeated by evil. The final word remains with mercy.[50]

The ministry of Isaiah at Jerusalem was, in its earlier part, contemporary with the ministry of Hosea in the north. As a boy this man may have heard his fellow Judaean Amos preach at Bethel or Jerusalem. The looming threat of Assyrian power which is felt but not named by Amos, and which Hosea mentions specifically,[51] becomes for Isaiah a concrete fact, filling the background and providing the occasions for the crises of his life work. He watches while the northern kingdom is forced to pay tribute to Tiglath-pileser in 738 B.C., while her territory is partitioned and depopulated five years later and her independent political existence is ended in 721 with the capture of Samaria by Sargon. It was the appeal of the Judaean king, Ahaz, for help against Israel and Damascus which brought the Assyrian armies into the field in 734, and Isaiah denounced this appeal as evidence of a fundamental distrust of Yahweh as the nation's bulwark.[52] Ahaz, indeed, introduced an Assyrian altar into the Temple in deference to his new overlord.[53] Judah remained loyal to the Assyrians until 705, when Hezekiah was persuaded to join in the general revolt of subject peoples which followed on the death of Sargon. Again Isaiah opposed the royal policy with its dependence upon entangling political alliances rather than upon Yahweh's power to defend his people. When the royal policy failed and Sennacherib's armies stood at the gates of Jerusalem, the prophet's faith in Yahweh's purpose and ability to defend his city did not falter.[54]

[49] Hos. 4:6.
[50] Hos. 5:14, 15; 6:4–6; 10:12–15 and 2:14–23; 11:8, 9; 14:1–8.
[51] Am. 5:27; Hos. 5:13; 8:9; 9:3; 10:6.
[52] Is. 7:9; 8:5–8.
[53] 2 Kg. 16:10–13.
[54] 2 Kg. 19:6, 7; Is. 37:6, 7, 21–35.

"The preaching of Isaiah," says von Rad, "represents the theological high water mark of the whole Old Testament."[55] The exalted sovereignty and majestic "holiness" of Yahweh which overwhelmed Isaiah in the vision that made him a prophet,[56] provide the key to his teaching. "Holiness" is that which pertains to deity: the "awe-full otherness" of the divine, which has no necessary ethical content in itself. But "Yahweh of hosts is exalted *by justice,* and the holiness of the Holy God shows itself *in righteousness.*"[57] The uniqueness of Yahweh among the gods is in his character, and in his sovereignty over the history of his people and of other peoples with whom they have contact. In time of national danger, the way of safety is not reliance upon armaments and alliances, but quiet confidence in Yahweh and loyalty to the way of life he has enjoined.[58] Isaiah sees no likelihood that the people will hearken and avoid inevitable judgment; the hope of the future lies with the faithful few who will be the surviving "remnant" of the nation, and the center of its renewal when the storm has passed.[59]

Micah of Moresheth-Gath was a Judaean contemporary of Isaiah, with a somewhat briefer ministry. While Isaiah spoke from his vantage point in the capital city where he was in touch with public life and world affairs, Micah was the peasants' champion who laid the responsibility for their suffering at the door of the proud city in the hills. Cities, to Micah, were hot-beds of iniquity and centers of oppression; they were Canaanite in origin and were built with blood: "*Therefore,* on account of you, Zion shall be plowed like a field, and Jerusalem shall become heaps (of stones)."[60] The very metaphors are rural. The evil which bulks largest in Micah's eyes is the reduction of the peasants to serfdom, through the seizure of

---

[55] *O.T. Theol.,* ii, p. 147.
[56] Is. 6.
[57] Is. 5:16.
[58] Is. 7:3–9; 28:14–18; 30:12–18. Cf. von Rad, *O.T. Theol.,* ii, p. 160, "This is what Isaiah called faith—leaving room for God's sovereign action."
[59] Is. 10:20–22; 6:9–13; 7:3; 37:31–32.
[60] Mic. 3:12.

their land by the wealthy.[61] He uses the metaphor of cannibalism of those who batten on the bodies of the poor. And the priests, the prophets and the rulers are no better.[62]

Moresheth-Gath, where Micah lived, was in the fair and fertile hills southwest of Jerusalem. He pictures the invading army advancing on the city, and ravaging the countryside he loved so well.[63] For the peasants will suffer too when their oppressors are punished. To Micah, Jerusalem and Samaria are distant and alien in spirit, though near at hand. Yet his disagreement with Isaiah who declared that Yahweh would defend Jerusalem is apparent only: they agreed as to the conditions which made the judgment of Yahweh inevitable.

The long reign of Manasseh (696–641 B.C.) was an interval of silence in the Golden Age of prophecy. That king reverted to cult practices which the prophets of the eighth century had condemned, and persecuted their successors who had the courage to resist him.[64] Only after his death did prophecy blossom again in Jeremiah, Zephaniah, Nahum and Habakkuk, though it is possible that the words of a prophet of Manasseh's reign have been incorporated in the later Book of Ezekiel.[65]

Jeremiah lived through one of the most cataclysmic periods of his people's history. His ministry began about 626 B.C.,[66] the year when the last great king of Assyria died, and when the barbarian hordes burst into Palestine from the north. As a young teacher he witnessed, and probably had his part in the Deuteronomic Reform of King Josiah, with its far-reaching consequences both religious and political. He shared the excitement during the death struggle of Assyria, and he mourned the untimely death of Josiah at the hands

---

[61] Mic. 2:1–2; 3:1–3, 10.

[62] Mic. 3:5–7, 11.

[63] Mic. 1:10–16.

[64] 1 Kg. 21:16.

[65] Cf. Jas. Smith: *The Book of the Prophet Ezekiel,* 1931. In addition, a judgment on Manasseh is ascribed in 2 Kg. 21:10–15 to unnamed contemporary prophets.

[66] J. P. Hyatt, Interp. Bi., V, 1956, pp. 779, 798 takes 626 B.C. to be rather the year of Jeremiah's birth and dates his call in 609.

of Pharaoh Necho. With Necho's final overthrow at Carchemish Jeremiah recognized that world power had passed into the hands of Babylon. In the last momentous years of the Judean monarchy he was the outstanding religious leader of his people. Having endured the rigors of Nebuchadrezzar's two sieges and watched the coming of the doom he had predicted, the prophet survived into the "Indian summer" of Gedaliah's governorship, only to go into Egypt and oblivion when Gedaliah died tragically, and winter came.

The Book of Jeremiah has been transmitted to us in two editions, the Hebrew and the Greek, the latter of which is considerably shorter and has a different order of sections. In addition to a large number of prophetic oracles in their original poetic form, there are oracles condensed into prose, and also considerable extracts from a biography of the prophet, perhaps by Baruch, the companion-secretary of the prophet's later years.

When Jeremiah received the call to prophesy[67] he was still a lad. His shrinking from the task is characteristic, for he was by nature sensitive and retiring. But he recognizes the sovereign guidance of God in the converging and determining forces which have moulded his life. Now, when he catches sight of a blossoming almond tree men called "the Wakeful" (because it blossomed early), he exclaims its name aloud; and the conviction wells up within him that this is no chance encounter. It is a *sign*. Yahweh is awake to perform his word. Then the steam from a boiling pot that blows on him from the north is another sign, for from the north, even then, hordes of enemies were pouring on their mission of destruction.[68]

It has been argued that Jeremiah at first supported hopefully the Deuteronomic Reform, but that later he came to suspect the motives of the Jerusalem priests who stood to benefit by the exaltation of the central sanctuary. He saw how impotent is a law to

[67] Jer. 1:6; 16:2.
[68] In Jer. 4, 5 and 6 are found oracles depicting invaders formerly taken to be Scythian barbarians but now thought to refer to the Chaldaeans.

change men's hearts, and repudiated the sufficiency of sacrifice with a thoroughness which the priesthood could not approve.[69] At a festal gathering in the Temple courts he bluntly challenged the popular superstition that Yahweh would preserve his sanctuary inviolate: unless Judah repented, it would be destroyed like the earlier Shiloh.[70] Having challenged the hierarchy and the king,[71] Jeremiah was forced into hiding, where he committed his prophecies to writing in a further and vain attempt to influence the nation's course.[72] He was still in hiding when the city fell in 597, but then emerged to take up a position of leadership. Believing that Yahweh had given the city into the hands of the Babylonians, he counselled the exiles to accept their position, and strongly opposed the second revolt as a result of which the city was again taken and, this time, destroyed.[73] Rescued from the dungeon into which his "unpatriotic" conduct had brought him, Jeremiah was still under guard when the city was taken. He was not deported like so many of his countrymen, but remained as spiritual monitor of the shaken community, until taken forcibly to Egypt by those who fled there after the assassination of Gedaliah the governor.

Jeremiah was no weeping willow, but a storm-tossed oak grown from a tender sapling. His sensitive spirit was torn between love for his people and fidelity to the truth of God. Inner strength came to him as he wrestled with God on the heights of an intense personal religion, as we learn from his "Confessions,"[74] so that what he *was* became more important for the history of religion than what he *said*. Essential religion can never again be equated with an operative cult, but becomes the spiritual pilgrimage of man vividly aware of his divine environment. Sin becomes, in Jere-

---

[69] Jer. 8:8, 9; 7:21–23.
[70] Jer. 7:1–15; 26:1–6.
[71] Jer. 26:7–15; 22:13–19.
[72] Jer. 36.
[73] Jer. 29:1–20; 28; 21:1–10.
[74] The term that has been applied to such passages as 11:18–23; 12:1–6; 15:10–21; 17:9–18; 18:18–23; 20:7–12, describing his spiritual struggle with God.

miah, not transgression of certain taboos or commandments, but the stubborn wilfulness which makes free and humble fellowship with God impossible. Hence for him sacrifices are irrelevant, and the "old covenant" has failed. But Yahweh will make a covenant of a new kind; he will put his law in the *mind*, so that it becomes an integral part of personality, and man becomes capable of the obedience he owes.[75]

The prophet Ezekiel was a contemporary of Jeremiah, but one in whom the prophetic impulse took a different form. He was first and last a priest (1:3). He differed from the other prophets in defining Israel's supreme sin as her stubborn indulgence in idolatry that has rendered her ritually unclean, and as her disobedience to Yahweh's "statutes and ordinances" (e.g., chap. 16; 5:7; 36:17). As von Rad says, her failure was "a failure in the sphere of the holy."[76] In his vision of the restored Jerusalem of the future the most elaborate provisions are made to safeguard the ritual holiness of the priesthood (44:15–27). That is a far cry from Isaiah's vision of Yahweh's holiness as connoting ethical exaltation. Furthermore, the ideas and phraseology of the prose sections of the book have remarkable similarities to the priestly documents of the Pentateuch, especially to the Holiness Code of Lev. 17–26.

Yet, if the traditions embodied in the book are to be trusted, Ezekiel was also a poet of no mean order. The brilliant poetic imagery of the oracles against Tyre and Egypt (e.g., chaps. 27–28 and 31) is in such marked contrast to the prosaic sermons (e.g., chap. 20) that they seem to come from different hands.[77] A probable explanation is that both prose and poetry ultimately go back to the prophet but that the oracles preserved in prose were largely recast in later priestly circles.

Other distinctive features of Ezekiel's prophecy are his fondness

---

[75] Jer. 31:27–34.
[76] G. von Rad, *Old Testament Theology*, vol. ii, p. 224.
[77] The tradition in Josephus (Ant. X, 5, 9) that Ezekiel left behind *two* books may be an early recognition of this fact.

for symbolic actions, his elaborate allegories, and above all the strangeness of his psychic experiences of paralysis and levitation.[78] The descriptions of his visions are among the most elaborate in the Bible: in chap. 1 the glory of Yahweh on his heavenly throne; in chaps. 8–11 the departure of this glorious presence from the sinful city, and in 43:1–5 its return to the re-created holy community of the future.

Not surprisingly, scholars have come to widely differing conclusions about the amount of material in the book that can be traced back to Ezekiel himself; about the editorial process through which the book reached its present form; about the dating of its several elements; and about the tradition that places Ezekiel in Babylonia when his prophecies are chiefly directed to the "house of Israel" in Palestine.[79] It seems that Ezekiel prophesied in Jerusalem from 593 to 587 B.C. when he was deported to Babylonia with the second group of exiles. Since the doom he predicted had now fallen on the sinful city, his message to his people is changed from condemnation to hope and promise, as in the famous picture in 37:1–14 of the resuscitation of an army from the dry bones of an old battlefield. Each individual man is to be responsible for his own sin, but he can repent and live. By the power of Divine grace a new and holy Israel will be reborn.[80]

What must be said about the remaining prophets of the classical period can be set down more briefly. Zephaniah is the prophet of the *Dies Irae*. The affirmation of Amos that "the Day of Yahweh will be darkness and not light" is expanded by Zephaniah into a terrible picture of universal catastrophe, when all the earth will be devoured by the fire of Yahweh's jealous anger. The prophet appears to have caught the feeling of terror inspired by rumors of

[78] Ezek. 2:8–3:3; 4:1–17; 5:1–4; 12:1–7; 17:1–10, 22–24; 19:1–14; 23:1–21; 3:26; 4:4–8; 8:3; 11:1.
[79] On the history of Ezekiel criticism, see O. Eissfeldt, *The Old Testament, an Introduction*, 1965, pp. 365–82; H. H. Rowley, *Men of God*, 1963, pp. 169–210.
[80] Ezek. 18:19–24; 34:24–28.

impending invasions, but the overthrow he pictures is more than that; it is a divine judgment in universal cataclysm, a day when Yahweh himself will officiate at a cosmic sacrifice.[81] Only a remnant, "an afflicted and poor people, who take refuge in the name of Yahweh"[82] may hope to escape and live to see the beginnings of a new world order.

The prophecy of Nahum is a paean of exultation over the approaching destruction of Nineveh, cruel task-master of the world. At long last Isaiah's prediction will be fulfilled, that Yahweh would punish the arrogant boasting of the king of Assyria.[83] The moral sovereignty of Yahweh is now to be vindicated. With unsurpassed brilliance of imagery the prophet portrays Yahweh's overthrow and spoiling of his people's ancient foe.

The prophecy of Habakkuk seems to come from a time when Judah had endured an invasion by the Chaldaeans, and has traditionally been dated shortly before the fall of Jerusalem in 597 B.C. But the description in some particulars does not seem to fit the situation at that date, and the book has been related by some scholars to other situations, either earlier when Assyria was under Chaldaean attack, or as late as Alexander the Great.[84] The prophet questions the consistency of the divine moral government of the world, and especially the silence and inaction of God when evil triumphs. He receives the answer that every evil doer shall bring his own woe upon himself, whereas "the righteous shall live by his faithfulness."

POST-CLASSICAL ANONYMOUS WRITTEN PROPHECY

To call the prophets of the classical period "writing prophets" is to beg the question, for it is uncertain to what extent they were

[81] Zeph. 1:7–18.
[82] Zeph. 3:12; 2:3.
[83] Is. 10:12; Nah. 2:13–3:7.
[84] Cf. O. Eissfeldt, *The Old Testament, an Introduction*, 1965, pp. 417–20.

themselves responsible for the recording of their oracles. If the
silencing of Amos by the priest of Bethel initiated the process of
writing down prophetic messages, close friends and followers of
the prophet would be the ones to undertake the task. Jeremiah is the
only one of the speaking prophets who is said to have dictated to
a secretary, and in that case he had been prevented from speaking
and was trying to gain a hearing by an alternative method. In the
classical period it is the spoken word which is primary, and the
record is subsequent to it.

In the post-classical period a new stage has been reached. Instead
of being recorded speech, prophecy is deliberate literary composition,
almost entirely anonymous. Much of it is supplementary to, and
modelled on, the oracles of the classical prophets. The forceful
personality whose name was remembered for the part he played in
religious history and for his God-empowered speech, now gives
place to the minor preacher and poet, the imitator, the commenta-
tor and the scribe. Original utterance bearing with it its own
authority is succeeded by conscious imitation of "the words which
Yahweh cried by the former prophets when Jerusalem was inhabited
and in prosperity."[85] Literary forms, especially the form of prophetic
visions, become stereotyped, and the exegete and scribe begin to
take the prominent place they always have in the religion of a book.
At this time the older collections of prophetic oracles were re-edited,
and the supplementary work of the same hands can be traced in
different books of the prophetic canon with a fair measure of
assurance.[86] One obvious motive is to counter-balance the old prophecies of doom with the promise of a glorious future, now that the
doom had been fulfilled. Of this the epilogue to Amos (9:9–15)
is a conspicuous example.

Two exceptions must be made to the above generalization. The
first is that there is *some* recorded spoken prophecy, as, for example,

[85] Zech. 7:7.
[86] As by R. E. Wolfe, in "The Editing of the Book of the Twelve," ZAW 53
(1935), pp. 90–129.

in Obadiah and in Joel, not to mention the prophets of the "Silver Age" in the Restoration period, Haggai, Zechariah 1–8 and Malachi. It is difficult to draw the line, especially when it appears that the writer is incorporating older material. But the fact that the material from this later time is so largely anonymous indicates that those from whom it comes were not public figures whose words demanded preservation.

Again, by no means all of written prophecy can be said to be of minor importance, compared to the work of the great prophets of the eighth and seventh centuries. There is work of the first rank, though of a different kind, in the Persian period. The greatest heights of all are reached in those fragments from an unknown prophet incorporated in the latter part of the Book of Isaiah and known, since Duhm, as the "Servant Songs."[87] Around these has been woven that lyric, exultant promise of the new day known as 2 Isaiah, where the message is presented in a series of cantos, and in which monotheism reaches its most explicit Old Testament expression. This is turn has been edited and added to by a lesser man who pictures Israel's triumph in material terms. The last six chapters of Zechariah, Isaiah 24–27, and the second part of Joel show us written prophecy in its later stages, on the eve of making way for true apocalyptic such as is found in Daniel 7–12.[88] Of Ezekiel it has been said with some justification that this prophet "stands at the source of the apocalyptic tradition."[89]

---

[87] Is. 42:1–4; 49:1–6; 50:4–9; 52:13–53:12.
[88] On the distinction of apocalyptic from prophecy, see above, Chap. 1, pp. 4–6.
[89] *The Jerusalem Bible*, 1966, p. 1131. Cf. Ezek. 1:4—2:2; 47:1–12.

5

THE PROPHETIC WORD

The prophets were men of the Word of Yahweh. They were possessed by it as their predecessors had been spirit-possessed. The difference was that they were not speaking with tongues, but with the understanding. Their prophetic experience of divine presence and power had a content as of intelligible speech. They had an irresistible compulsion to speak what they had heard when the "hand" or power of Yahweh was on them. The Word and the commission to utter it were parts of the same fundamental and characteristic experience. "Yahweh said to me, Go, prophesy. . . . Now therefore hear the word of Yahweh"; "Go, and tell this people . . ."; "To whomsoever I shall send thee thou shalt go, and whatsoever I command thee thou shalt speak. . . . Then Yahweh put forth his hand and touched my mouth; and Yahweh said to me, Behold, I have put *my* words in *thy* mouth."[1] Ezekiel in vision was made to eat a scroll on which were inscribed the words he was to speak.[2]

It is clear from these and other passages that prophecy—as already emphasized—is not to be equated with divination of the

[1] Am. 7:15–16; Is. 6:9; Jer. 1:7, 9.
[2] Ezek. 2:8–3:3.

future. It is equally clear that the prophets were something other than ethicists, preachers or theologians. Theirs was a positive and urgent message that was neither derived from tradition (though the tradition was part of it), nor produced by reflection upon an existing body of religious belief. They spoke at an immediate divine demand. They spoke in Yahweh's name, as spokesmen and interpreters of his mind and will. Having stood in the heavenly council,[3] they were as ambassadors plenipotentiary sent upon a mission by their Lord: "I heard the voice of Yahweh, saying, Whom shall I send, and who will go for us? Then I said, Here am I. Send me." And as personal envoys of the divine ruler they were endowed with adequate authority: "See, I have this day set thee over the nations and over the kingdoms, to uproot and to tear down, to destroy and to overthrow, to build and to plant."[4]

THE PROPHETIC ENDOWMENT

Although inspiration by the spirit of God is claimed by Ezekiel and later prophets,[5] Mowinckel has shown convincingly that the prophets of the classical age reject the thought of spirit possession as explaining their powers, and attribute these rather to the compulsion of Yahweh's word.[6] In so doing they distinguish themselves from the ecstatic prophets of the times of Samuel and Elisha, and from their spirit-crazed contemporaries in whom the old tradition persisted.[7] A man who behaved abnormally was popularly believed to be under the influence of a spirit which had come upon him from without. This was the explanation given of Joseph's wisdom, of Bezalel's artistic skill, of Gideon's courage, of Samson's

---

[3] 1 Kg. 22:19–23; Jer. 23:18; Am. 3:7.
[4] Is. 6:8; Jer. 1:10. "The 'Word' may be regarded as a potent 'Extension' of Yahweh's Personality": A. R. Johnson, *The One and the Many in the Israelite Conception of God*, 2nd ed., 1961, p. 17.
[5] Ezek. 11:5; Is. 48:16; 61:1; Jl. 2:28 (Heb. 3:1).
[6] S. Mowinckel, JBL, LIII, 1934, pp. 199–227.
[7] Cf. 2 Kg. 9:11, "this mad fellow"; Jer. 29:26, "every madman who prophesies"; Hos. 9:7, "the prophet is a fool, the man of the spirit is mad."

strength, of Saul's prophetic frenzy and his later melancholia, of the treachery of the Shechemites, of the sudden disappearances of Elijah and of the lying of Ahab's court prophets.[8] In most instances the spirit is said to be the spirit of God or of Yahweh. But in 1 Kings 22:19–23 the "lying spirit" put in the mouth of the false prophets is described as a member of the heavenly host distinct from Yahweh, yet under his control.

It is noteworthy that Micaiah in this same context does not attribute his own knowledge of Yahweh's purpose to a "true" spirit, but to his own apprehension by prophetic insight of what had taken place in the heavenly court and of what was about to happen on the field of battle. This grasp of the moral and spiritual realities of a given situation, coupled with the certainty that he must proclaim them in unmistakable terms, marked off a prophet like Micaiah or Amos from his ecstatic predecessors and contemporaries. His utterances had substantial comprehensible content which was lacking in their uncontrolled and incoherent spirit-speech. Where the ecstatics were possessed by sheer, undifferentiated spirit-power, the great prophets were possessed by the mind and holy will of Yahweh. They were his voices, speaking in the first person on his behalf, whether or not their oracles as they have come down to us are prefaced by the messenger's introductory formula, "Thus saith the Lord." What they proclaimed was a Word from Yahweh—definite, relevant, urgent.

Significantly, the type of a true prophet, according to Deut. 18:15–18, is Moses, with whom God spoke "mouth to mouth, plainly, and not in riddles."[9] The divine self-disclosure was not in the mysterious, garbled cries of *glossolalia*, but as it were in a direct contact of mind with mind assuming the form of intelligible speech, "as a man speaks to his friend."[10] The audition was, of

[8] Gen. 41:38; Ex. 31:2–3; Jg. 6:34; 15:14; 1 Sam. 19:23–24; 16:14; Jg. 9:23; 2 Kg. 2:16; 1 Kg. 22:23.
[9] Num. 12:7–8.
[10] Ex. 33:11.

course, an inner religious experience of the prophet which is subject to psychological examination. The point is that what he perceived to be a divine manifestation had articulate meaning. It was a *Word*. Sometimes, owing to the vividness with which this presented itself to the prophet's consciousness, it is called a *Vision* or "revelation."[11]

We may still regard this consciousness of possession of and by the Word of Yahweh as the mark of an ecstatic state of mind. But it is a very different kind of ecstasy from the dervish frenzy of the lower levels of prophecy, "a more refined and spiritual exaltation, which is better known by other names."[12] "The idea of hearing," says Lindblom,[13] is only a means of describing the inspiration by which the high ideas emerged in the soul of the prophet." There was a light in the prophet's mind that kindled his awareness and illumined his understanding. "Thus spake Yahweh to me with impelling power" (literally, "with strength of the hand"), says Isaiah. "The Lord Yahweh showed me," says Amos. "Then Yahweh put forth his hand and touched my mouth; and Yahweh said unto me, See, I have put my words in thy mouth," says Jeremiah. And again, "My heart within me is broken, all my bones lose their strength . . . because of Yahweh, and because of his holy words." But the result is that the prophet becomes "full of power, and of justice and of strength to declare unto Jacob his transgression."[14] His prophetic consciousness is of great intensity: Elijah was "very zealous for Yahweh."[15]

Such intensity and exaltation of spirit, resulting from a recognized divine impulsion, is then a *new* kind of prophetic ecstasy, related to

---

[11] Is. 1:1; Jer. 14:14; Hab. 2:2–3. Cf. J. Lindblom, *Prophecy in Ancient Israel*, p. 108.

[12] As Rowley describes it, while at the same time affirming that "there was a large element of abnormality in the higher prophets"; H. H. Rowley, *The Servant of the Lord*, 2nd ed. 1965, p. 123.

[13] Lindblom, *op. cit.*, p. 121.

[14] Mic. 3:8.

[15] 1 Kg. 19:14. Lindblom calls this an "ecstasy of concentration" in contrast to a mystical "ecstasy of absorption."

the concentration and absorption of the mystic, the artist and the genius, but different because of its action element. As Rufus Jones says of mystical experience, "when the powers of the mind are fused and unified, overbrimmed and revitalized by intense mystical concentration and unification, the whole interior self becomes an immensely heightened organ of spiritual apprehension in correspondence with the real world to which it belongs."[16] "It is quite clear," says Mowinckel, "that the prophets speak and act in a state of mental high tension . . . (in which) the ideas, thoughts, etc., which in one way or another have been created in a person will rise above the threshold of consciousness, and in a flash attain sudden clarity."[17] There is nothing here of the outpourings of the subconscious mind released by religious frenzy, as there is nothing of a merely passive mysticism of feeling. The mystical experience of the prophets (if it may be called that) was a mysticism of faith, of understanding and of action. They were supremely alive to the moral realities of the actual human and social situation; they were not aloof from it, as the mystic tends to be. They remained acutely conscious that they themselves were part of the scene, while at the same time knowing that they were spokesmen to it of the mind of God. "With the breaking up of the daughter of my people, I am broken," says Jeremiah.[18]

The new type of prophetic ecstasy expressed itself in a new kind of ecstatic speech, clearly intelligible, direct and radical, and charged with strong emotional force. Clarity of perception and moral earnestness were combined with imaginative, artistic mastery of language. The concreteness and vividness of the Hebrew tongue provided ready materials for an utterance of direct and urgent appeal. The dignity and importance of the message raised the forms of speech to an artistic level previously unknown. Sometimes the prophet felt that he was repeating the actual words of Yahweh, as in Jer. 3:11, 12; sometimes that Yahweh was actually using his

[16] Rufus Jones, *Pathways to the Reality of God*, 1931, p. 41.
[17] Mowinkel, *op. cit.*, p. 214.
[18] Jer. 8:21.

mouth and his tongue with which to speak, as in Jer. 2:9 and Is. 6:7. In any case he must speak as befits an ambassador.

THE CALL AND COMMISSION OF A PROPHET

The assurance of having a divine call and commission was a primary element in the prophetic consciousness. Westermann makes the point that the call never had a human witness, hence the prophetic office could not be institutionalized.[19] Amos, the herdsman protested that he prophesied not of his own choice, but at an irresistible divine command which had uprooted him bodily from his accustomed way of life. Isaiah, the aristocrat, heard the voice of the divine sovereign calling for a messenger, and knew that the call was meant for him. Hosea, the lover, perceived in the imperiousness of a love which tortured his mind and broke his heart, a summons to speak of a divine love that no evil could quench. Micah, the peasant, was possessed by his message and the power to deliver it. Jeremiah, the shy and sheltered youth found himself thrust into the forefront of great events and clothed with an authority that terrified even himself.[20]

Coupled with his sense of this overwhelming compulsion by the divine will and the divine choice was the prophet's recognition that he had been set apart from other men and consecrated to a task from which there was to be no release. To be sanctified was to be set apart for Yahweh's use, like an offering in the temple. "Before thou camest forth out of the womb I sanctified thee"; Yahweh declares to Jeremiah, "I had appointed thee a prophet to the nations."[21] Isaiah, who knew himself as a man of unclean lips, dwelling in the midst of a people of unclean lips, was cleansed and set apart from the people who would *not* turn again and be healed. Hosea set himself apart by the choice he made before his neighbors. Amos abruptly left home and occupation.

The call appears to have come to each prophet in a time of

---

[19] C. Westermann, *Forschung am A.T.*, 1964, p. 175.
[20] Am. 7:14, 15; Is. 6:1, 8; Hos. 3:1; Mic. 3:8; Jer. 1:1–10.
[21] Jer. 1:5.

intellectual and emotional tension. "The year that King Uzziah died" marked the end of an epoch. The social strains following Jeroboam's wars and a series of natural calamities appear in the pages of Amos as affecting all but the very wealthy. Hosea spoke out of a welter of vice and confusion, bordering on anarchy. Micah cried out that the cities were draining the life-blood of the countryside, and a foreign invasion must shortly come to complete the destruction. Jeremiah and Zephaniah began to prophesy when the world empire of the Assyrians was tottering under the onslaught of barbarian hordes, which were soon to appear on the northern horizon of Palestine. Nahum shouted that Nineveh was about to fall with world-shaking crash.

In such times of general excitement it is readily understandable that men of unusual spiritual endowment should have critical religious experiences. Where the story of a prophet's call is recorded at all fully, as with Isaiah and Jeremiah, this experience appears to have been marked by a degree of ecstatic rapture not subsequently repeated, and certainly not characteristic of the prophet's later day-to-day communion with Yahweh. The significant thing is that this original experience introduces the prophet into a new, standing relationship to his God.[22] The subsequent oracles which from time to time he delivers are not necessarily dependent upon a repetition of this original experience, but are derived from his standing knowledge of Yahweh's nature and will and awareness of Yahweh's continued presence. These have become integrated with the primary ecstasy in a total personal experience on a new level, as in genuine "conversion."

Related to the prophet's continuous special relationship to God, is his acknowledged responsibility as an intercessor. "The prophet, like the priest, had a dual role. It was his responsibility (a) to call with (or upon) the 'Name' of Yahweh, and (b) to speak in his 'Name.'"[23] His commission lays upon him a direct measure of responsibility for the spiritual condition and fate of his people. Though set apart for his task and often forced to stand alone, the

[22] Cf. Jer. 1:9; 23:28.
[23] A. R. Johnson, *The Cultic Prophet in Ancient Israel*, 2nd ed., 1962, p. 56.

prophet in his approach to God, speaks for the people to whom he belongs, and who cannot or will not acknowledge their spiritual necessity. In his own person he feels the weight of the very divine judgments which find utterance through his lips. Amos interceded for the people, saying: "O Lord Yahweh, forgive, I beseech thee: how can Jacob survive?" The power of intercession was recognized as part of the endowment of a true prophet: "If they be prophets, and if the word of Yahweh be with them, let them now make intercession to Yahweh of hosts." Both Jeremiah and Isaiah received royal appeals to pray for the nation in times of extremity.[24] Examples of the language of such prophetic intercession are found in Jer. 14:7–9, 19–22.

Prayer was made also for Yahweh to give a word or oracle when a special situation seemed to demand one and it had not come unasked: "Behold, they say unto me, Where is the word of Yahweh? Let it come now!" cried Jeremiah.[25] The giving of oracles in response to a special request is recorded, e.g., in 2 Kg. 19:14–34; 20:1–6; Jer. 37:3–10; 42:1–22. In the last case, ten days elapsed before the answer came.

The predominance of references to Jeremiah in this connection is due partly to the fact that the records of his ministry are more extensive and intimate than is the case with any other prophet, and partly to the fact that intercession was particularly congenial to one of Jeremiah's sensitive and understanding spirit. For the endowment of a prophet did not obliterate the human and personal factor. The tender-heartedness and gentle nature of Jeremiah and Hosea stand in contrast to the austere and virile puritanism of Micah and Amos, and to the assured dignity of the aristocrat Isaiah. Even when they speak what is essentially the same message, as when they condemn social injustice, their manner of doing so is individually characteristic.[26] That is only to say that the divine Word found expression through human minds and in natural speech.

[24] Am. 7:2, 5; Jer. 27:18; 18:20; 37:3; Is. 37:1–4.
[25] Jer. 17:15.
[26] Cf. Jer. 5:1–9; Hos. 6:4—7:7; Mic. 3:9–12; Am. 8:4—10; Is. 5:8–16.

THE POWER OF THE WORD

Even the words of everyday speech, according to the Hebrew way of thinking, were something more than sounds conveying ideas. "Talk" was not "cheap." Words were felt to be charged with the vital force of the speaker's person, and, once uttered, continued its effective expression even in the speaker's absence, or after his death. A death-bed curse or blessing was especially powerful; the words of the dying Isaac, Jacob and Moses[27] are represented as determining factors in the subsequent history of the Israelite tribes. A man's name represented him in a more than formal way; as Pedersen puts it: "To know the name of a man is the same as to know his essence."[28] David sent his followers to greet Nabal with David's name, expecting a particular reaction.[29] To mention the name of God was all the more significant; it was to invoke his presence, which was not to be done lightly or in a defiling context, as we are reminded by the fourth Commandment.[30]

Thus the word uttered through the prophet had the power of Yahweh in it, and manifested his presence in a given situation.[31] "Yahweh has sent a word against Jacob, and it will light upon Israel." "I have hewn them by the prophets, I have slain them by the words of my mouth." "My word . . . shall accomplish that which I please." It was entirely in keeping with this conception that the centurion should say to Jesus: "Speak only a word, and my servant will be healed."[32]

The inherent potency of the prophetic word has particular significance when it refers to future events. These were not merely foreseen, but *willed*. The court prophets of Ahab announced in

---

[27] Gen. 27:27–40; 49:1 ff.; Deut. 33:1 ff.
[28] J. Pedersen, *Israel*, I–II, 1926, p. 245.
[29] 1 Sam. 25:5.
[30] Cf. also Am. 6:10; Ezek. 43:8.
[31] Cf. J. Lindblom, *op. cit.*, p. 114: "Precisely because it was a divine word from Yahweh's own mouth the prophetic word was a word with effective power. . . . By his word Yahweh made the heavens and the earth."
[32] Mt. 8:8.

advance a victory at Ramoth-Gilead in order to insure that victory. When the words of Yahweh were put in the mouth of Jeremiah, he was thereby "set over nations and kingdoms," as a force affecting the future course of their histories. In the names of their children Isaiah and Hosea articulated the divine word, to influence that future when the purpose of God must find realization.

Sometimes a prophet would pronounce his message through a striking symbolic act. Ahijah of Shiloh tore his new cloak into twelve pieces, giving ten of them to Jeroboam with the words: "Thus says Yahweh, God of Israel: See, I am tearing the kingdom from the hand of Solomon and I will give you ten tribes." The dying Elisha commanded King Joash to shoot arrows on his behalf in the direction of Damascus, as "Yahweh's arrow of victory over Syria." The court prophet Zedekiah "made for himself horns of iron, and proclaimed: 'Thus says Yahweh, With these you shall push the Syrians until they are destroyed.'" Even the great Isaiah went about Jerusalem for three years "naked and barefoot" (like a captive slave), to show the doom of the Egyptians and Ethiopians on whom Judah was relying for help.[33]

The consciousness of the prophet that he had within him a word expressing the divine *will* shows itself in the sense of compulsion under which he labored. His mission was not of his own choosing. "The Lord Yahweh hath spoken; who can but prophesy?" cries Amos. And again, "I was no prophet . . . but Yahweh said unto me, Go, prophesy." Human prudence would keep silent, but the divine word must find utterance.[34] Isaiah felt himself sent out with a hopeless and impossible task, and the stories of Elijah and of Jonah illustrate how some prophets would fain have escaped from the relentless will which drove them on. From the beginning Jeremiah protested in vain against the charge that was laid upon him; in an excess of agony he cursed the day he had been born to labor and sorrow and shame. He contended with God,

[33] 1 Kg. 11:29–31; 2 Kg. 13:14–19; 1 Kg. 22:11; Is. 20:2–6.
[34] Am. 3:8; 7:14, 15; 5:13.

the master of his destiny, and acknowledged the defeat of his own
will as Yahweh's victory: "Thou art stronger than I, and hast
prevailed."[35]

Before such conviction the anathemas of priests, the denunciations of professional prophets, and the strong hand of the civil
authorities were of no avail. Even that most wounding of all blows,
the defection of intimate friends, struck Jeremiah to the heart, but
did not slay his faith: "I have heard the defaming of many; 'Let us
denounce him,' say all my familiar friends. But Yahweh is with me
like a dreaded champion."[36]

THE AUTHENTICATION OF THE WORD

Since the phenomenon of "false prophecy" was well known to
the classical prophets,[37] the question arises: how were they themselves so sure that their message came from God, and was not
merely the projection of their own views and desires? For their
voices were trumpet notes of no uncertain sound. Only occasionally
is there any suggestion that a pronouncement is provisional, as when
Amos admits as a possibility that Yahweh will be gracious to the
remnant of Joseph, and when Jeremiah finds confirmation of his
presentiment in a subsequent experience. "Then I knew," says the
latter, "that this was the word of Yahweh."[38] Before that, Jeremiah
himself had not been sure.

If that was so, how much more difficult it must have been for the
prophets' audience when two of them of apparently equal standing
like Jeremiah and Hananiah contradicted one another.[39] As Skinner
says, "in externals there was nothing to distinguish the one kind of
prophet from the other. Both spoke in the name of Yahweh; both
spoke with the accent of personal conviction; and both could appeal
to ecstatic experiences as the seal of the genuineness of their oracles.

[35] Jer. 20:7.
[36] Jer. 20:10.
[37] Cf. Is. 9:15; 28:7; Jer. 5:31; 14:14; 29:8; Hos. 9:7; Mic. 3:5, 11.
[38] Am. 5:15; Jer. 32:8.
[39] Jer. 28.

Yet they could not both be true interpreters of the one thing which it was important to know—the actual purpose of Yahweh."[40] The criterion offered in Deut. 18:22—fulfillment of a prediction—was useless at the moment when the prediction was uttered. There can be no doubt, however, that the destruction of Jerusalem and the exile of Judaeans to Babylon showed that the pre-exilic prophets of divine judgment had been right, and this resulted in the preservation of many of their oracles as true words from Yahweh.

Nevertheless there were certain criteria more immediately available to the prophets' hearers—even if conclusions drawn from them were not infallible. The first test was clear and specific: a prophet who proposed apostasy to the worship of other gods[41] could have no claim to speak for Yahweh. A second test was the moral character of the prophet, especially when it was painfully obvious that this was bad. If, as Isaiah says, they were drunken and confused while discharging their sacred office; if, as Jeremiah says, they were known liars and adulterers, stealing from one another the oracles they announced as revelations, or were in the business of prophesying only to make a living and, to quote Micah, "declared war against him who put nothing into their mouths,"[42] such men's words would not carry conviction. Even simple people would not be fooled indefinitely.

The third criterion required a more subtle intelligence. Was the prophet sincere? As Rowley says, "insincerity is not always transparent, and such a charge may be more easily believed than proved."[43] There were at least grounds for suspicion when a man prophesied what king or people wanted him to say, as when the court prophets of Ahab cried, "Attack Ramoth-Gilead and be victorious!", and Jeremiah's colleagues promised, "Peace! Peace!", when (Jeremiah adds grimly) "there is no [prospect of] peace."[44] What

---

[40] J. Skinner, *Prophecy and Religion*, 1926, p. 188.
[41] Deut. 13:1–5.
[42] Is. 28:7; Jer. 23:14, 30; Mic. 3:11.
[43] H. H. Rowley, *The Servant of the Lord*, 2nd ed. 1965, p. 115.
[44] 1 Kg. 22:12; Jer. 6:14, cf. p. 54, note 55.

the hearers could be sure of was the sincerity of a Micaiah who braved the wrath of the king to affirm: "As Yahweh lives, what Yahweh says to me, that will I speak!"[45] Furthermore, when the true prophet had no word from Yahweh he remained silent, while the false prophets were all too ready to "retail visions of their own."[46]

The true prophet had his own criteria. In the first place, these were psychological. "Who could mistake straw for wheat?" cries Jeremiah. "Is not my word like fire, says the Lord, and like a hammer which breaks the rock in pieces?"[47] The quality of his religious experience was obviously different from that of the false prophets. The clarity and decision of his message and the irresistible impulse to speak it carried the conviction that the word had come to Jeremiah from beyond himself. His sudden insight into the moral and spiritual realities of a situation was like the solution of a problem or the unveiling of a mystery. "The Lord Yahweh will do nothing without disclosing his (confidential) plan to his servants the prophets."[48] This was the fitting and inevitable answer, the inescapable corollary. It was an experience that could bear no other interpretation than that of a divine revelation. What caused the prophet an inner agony he could hardly bear and could not avoid could hardly be attributed to self-projection. Even the stern Amos shrank from the judgment he was called upon to pronounce. Isaiah cried: "Lord, how long?" and Jeremiah could not restrain himself when he heard the alarm of war, and felt that his own soul was the battleground of the wrath of God.[49]

Indeed, not only was the impulse to speak independent of the prophet's own volition; sometimes it was contrary to it, as when Jeremiah said "Amen" to Hananiah's prediction of a quick release of the exiles, but then went on to declare that the true word of

[45] 1 Kg. 22:14.
[46] Cf. Jer. 28:10-12; 42:7; Hab. 2:1; Jer. 23:16 (*Jerusalem Bible* translation).
[47] Jer. 23:28-29.
[48] Am. 3:7; Cf. Jer. 23:22. The Hebrew word *sôd* means both "counsel" and "council."
[49] Am. 7:2, 5; Is. 6:11; Jer. 4:19, 20.

Yahweh was to the opposite effect.[50] The word of doom was as disagreeable to speak as it was unwelcome to hear. The very fact that these men felt compelled to declare, in the face of a dearly held *religious* expectation, that the Day of Yahweh would mean darkness and not light, was to them an authentication of that message.[51] The further fact that Jeremiah and Habakkuk went so far as to question the righteousness of Yahweh's actions[52] shows how vividly they were conscious of a will other than their own.

The true prophet's assurance was further corroborated by the power of utterance that accompanied his exalted mood. The tradition concerning Moses was that he was not eloquent but slow of speech, so that Yahweh had to promise to help him speak and to tell him what to say. Similarly Yahweh says to Jeremiah, who also had protested that he did not know how to speak: "Whatsoever I command thee thou shalt speak; ... behold, I am making you this day a fortified city."[53] The prophetic oracle often rises to great heights as poetry or rhetoric. Sometimes it suggests the stateliness of a royal proclamation, at others the gravity of a judicial deliverance, or the differing notes of authority of the commander, the teacher, or the master of assemblies. The gift of such language is to the prophets a gift indeed, the gift by Yahweh of a vessel to contain his word. They *see* a word which other men do not see, but they *speak* words which other men can hear, and in a manner that commands attention even though it may not produce obedience.

It was not a light matter to sustain such a ministry, always difficult, often perplexing and disappointing, and sometimes dangerous. But the prophets were conscious of an enabling power within them which was itself an assurance that their commission was genuine. "I am full of power," says Micah, "to declare unto Jacob his transgression," much as Jeremiah feels himself brimming with *Yahweh's*

[50] Jer. 28:5–14; Cf. 17:16.
[51] Am. 5:18; 8:9, 10; Zeph. 1:14–16; Jl. 2:11.
[52] Jer. 12:1–4; Hab. 1:4, 13, 14.
[53] Ex. 4:10–12; Jer. 1:7, 18.

anger.[54] The latter, most gentle and sensitive of all the spokesmen of Yahweh, became like a fortified wall against which the furious assaults of men were broken. It was Yahweh, he well knew, who was his only strength, his stronghold and his refuge in time of trouble.[55] The enabling power of religion, then as now, was the best evidence of its reality.

The second of the prophet's criteria was rational. This was the test of consistency with the terms of his original commission in the radical experience of his call; of consistency, further, with Yahweh's will as made known in the past history of Israel, and through earlier prophecy. The dooms and "Woes" of Amos are echoes of the fearsome roar and withering blast with which Yahweh had spoken to him at the first; they also point to the intensification of past afflictions and disasters which had failed to turn Israel from her evil way.[56] As Hosea's wife was defiled so Israel was defiled, and her love was "like a morning cloud, and like the dew that goes early away." But Yahweh was constant; when Israel was a child he loved him, and called his son out of Egypt.[57] The calls of Isaiah and Jeremiah were determinative of their subsequent teaching, and are the key to it.[58]

The third criterion for the prophet was the moral worth and immediate relevance of his message. Amid moral confusion, he was able to distinguish good from evil, and to define it as justice, humanity, faithfulness and truth.[59] "My people are ruined for lack of knowledge," cries Hosea; "Yahweh has a quarrel with the inhabitants of the land, because there is no truth, no love and no knowledge of God in the land."[60] It is this true knowledge of God and understanding of his ways which the prophets would declare

[54] Mic. 3:8; Jer. 6:11.
[55] Jer. 16:19.
[56] Cf. Am. 1:2; 2:6–8, 13–16; 4:6–12; 5:16–18.
[57] Hos. 3:1; 6:4; 11:1.
[58] Is. 1:2, 26; 30:9–17; Jer. 7:2–15, 21–28.
[59] Is. 5:20; 1:16, 17, 26; Am. 5:14, 15; Hos. 4:1, 2, 6; 6:6.
[60] Hos. 4:6, 1.

through their censures and exhortations. They give testimony, impart knowledge, explain their message "precept upon precept, rule after rule, a little here, a little there" (as mockers described the tireless reiteration of the prophetic theme). Such a clear and constant word was self-authenticating; it fitted the situation as a key fits the lock. "Yahweh has sent a word against Jacob, and it shall light upon Israel, and all the people shall recognize (it)." So with the prophet himself: "Yahweh caused me to know, and I understood it."[61]

The urgent and immediate importance of the word for men in the situation in which they stood helped to produce in these spokesmen of Yahweh the certainty that it came to them from him. It disclosed the real facts, the underlying moral and spiritual conditions; it explained the situation and would determine its outcome (failing, i.e., radical alteration in those conditions through genuine repentance). Of course, the divine possibilities of such a change of heart were a part of the total encompassing spiritual situation. It is Yahweh's will, says Hosea, to betroth Israel to him in righteousness and in justice, in love and mercy and faithfulness. This was "to *know* Yahweh"[62] as Hosea and Jeremiah knew him, as the ultimate fact in the heights and in the depths of human experience.

The demand for a sign from heaven to authenticate the prophetic declarations of Jesus is familiar from the Gospels.[63] This was an old expectation, as is evident from Deut. 31:1: "If a prophet arises among you . . . and he gives you a sign or a wonder . . ." God himself, according to the tradition, had given a sign to Moses to confirm the reality of his call. Jeremiah found assurance in two experiences closely associated with the time of his commissioning, those of the almond branch and the boiling cooking-pot.[64] The

[61] Is. 9:8, 9; Jer. 11:18.
[62] Hos. 2:19, 20 (EVV).
[63] Mt. 12:38; Jn. 2:18.
[64] Ex. 4:1-9; Jer. 1:11-16.

wonders that preceded and accompanied the Exodus were thought of as awe-inspiring manifestations of the power of the God who had undertaken to deliver Israel.

Only exceptionally are such signs represented as miraculous. The shadow which went back ten steps on the sundial of Ahaz is the only example from the period of classical prophecy that shares this feature with the story of Gideon's fleece and the fire which consumed his offering.[65] Normally a prophetic sign was a present token of a future still to be realized according to the prophet's word. Isaiah gave to his sons names embodying themes of his teaching, and then set aside and sealed a scroll of which the names would remind the hearers when the time of fulfillment came. An approaching harvest would witness to king Hezekiah a more distant but sure deliverance. The capture of a Pharaoh by his enemies would signal the approaching doom of the Jews who had sought refuge in his domain.[66] In each instance the prophet faces the future in full confidence that Yahweh's word through him will be fulfilled.

In the last analysis, the word was authenticated by its own inherent worth and weight rather than by signs, and by the personal power of the men who spoke it. It was novel, unconventional, even startling. It came as a new, disturbing and creative element into a situation, and faced men with the necessity of a moral decision. The speakers were men of that passionate conviction which divides men into two camps, making disciples of some and enemies of others. They risked their reputations and their lives with utterances which searched the moral foundation of settled conditions, and of hoary taboos and practices. Their words threatened the prerogatives of those who held power, ecclesiastical, political and economic. They were a felt force within the community, recognized as a power making for righteousness and challenging the accepted standards and method of society. With all their personal differences, there was in all the prophets a characteristic persistent common quality and a

[65] Is. 38:7–8; Jos. 10:12–14.
[66] Is. 7:3; 8:1–4, 16–18.

creative vitality, which accorded with their claim to speak the word of God.

THE FORMS OF THE WORD

The Word of Yahweh has come down to us in the words of the prophets, which were spoken before they were written down.[67] Initially these were preserved only in the memories of the prophets themselves or of their disciples—as when Baruch entered on a scroll the oracles which Jeremiah had pronounced from the day of his call to the fourth year of king Jehoiakim.[68] The forms in which the records of prophecy eventually were enshrined in a written scripture are various. Some of these records are in prose and some in rhetorical poetry.

The prose forms are of at least five kinds: (a) *Autobiographical narratives* in the course of which the prophet quotes or summarizes certain of his oracles (e.g., Is. 6:1–13; Jer. 18:1–11); (b) *Biographical narratives*, again containing oracles (e.g., Is. 7:1–17; Jer. 26:1–24; Am. 7:10–17); (c) *Historical narratives* in which a prophet and his oracles are mentioned, but not as the sole interest of the narrator (e.g., 1 Kg. 22:1–23; Is. 36:1—37:38); (d) *Prose summaries or variants* of oracles originally in poetic form (e.g., Is. 37:33–35, cf. vv. 28–29, especially v. 34a and 29d; Jer. 22:11–12, cf. v. 10); (e) *Longer addresses or sermons* ascribed to a prophet but in which apparently his thought has been recast and expanded by later traditionists[69] (e.g., Ezek. chaps. 16 and 18).

The most characteristic form of prophetic record is the oracular poem embodying Yahweh's word spoken by a prophet as his messenger. It is relatively brief, ranging usually from two to eight or ten verses, directed to a particular audience and situation, and structured so as to be complete in itself. Most frequently it is introduced with

[67] The reference, of course, is to the classical prophets of the eighth to early sixth centuries B.C. and not to later prophecy like 2 Is. See above, pp. 64–65.

[68] Jer. 36:1–4.

[69] As in the long sermonic discourses of the Fourth Gospel, contrasting with the forms of Jesus' teaching in the Synoptic Gospels.

the messenger's preface "Thus says Yahweh!" with which we may compare the Rabshakeh's address to Hezekiah, "Thus says the great king, the King of Assyria!"[70] Other designations of the prophetic oracle sometimes found are *ne'um Yahweh* which means something like "whisper" or "inward revelation" of Yahweh,[71] and a term *massa'* which in other contexts is to be translated "burden." The latter comes from a common verb meaning "to lift"; what is lifted here is the *hand*, in the gesture accompanying a solemn oath or curse.[72] Thus the term is used chiefly as the title of doom oracles on Israel's enemies, and once of a sworn judgment on an Israelite king.[73]

The predominant content of the pre-exilic prophets' oracles is the pronouncement of divine *judgment*, usually accompanied by an *accusation* which sets out the reasons for the impending doom of the accused. The judgment may be pronounced upon the nation's enemies, on Israel (or Judah) herself, or occasionally on an individual or a royal dynasty.[74] Oracles against foreign peoples, by name or more ambiguously, are found grouped together in the books of the major prophets, in Is. 13–23, Jer. 46–51 and Ezek. 25–32. Amos 1–2 begins with a series of such oracles culminating in a parallel accusation and judgment upon Israel. Obadiah and Nahum pronounce the dooms respectively of Edom and Assyria. It may well be, as the oracle-complex in Am. 1–2 suggests, that the pronouncement of doom on the nation's enemies was expected of prophets whether at court or in the temple worship, and that those who eventually were seen to be the *true* prophets were those who saw that the ethical demands of Yahweh and his consequent judgment rested primarily on Israel herself.

---

[70] Is. 36:4. Cf. the preface of Hezekiah's message to Isaiah in 37:3.
[71] This may introduce an oracle as in Num. 24:3, 15; conclude it as in Is. 3:15; or occur in the course of it at points requiring solemn emphasis, as in Jer. 2:9, 12.
[72] Cf. Ex. 6:8; Ps. 106:26; Ezek. 20:5–6; Rev. 10:5–6. For the pronouncement of judgment with an oath, cf. Is. 5:9; 14:24.
[73] Is. 13:1; 17:1; Nah. 1:1; Hab. 1:1; etc., and 2 Kgs. 9:25.
[74] For instances of the last-named, cf. Is. 22:15–19; 1 Kg. 14:7–11; 21:17–24.

The basic form of the judgment oracle is well illustrated in Mic. 3:9–12:

> *Summons to the accused*—"Hear this, you heads of the house of Jacob!"
> *The indictment*—"who abhor justice and pervert all equity . . ."
> *The connecting link with divine judgment*—"Therefore, because of you . . ."
> *The sentence of the judge*—"Zion shall be plowed as a field . . ."

There are many variants of this basic structure. The summons to hear the indictment may be addressed not to the accused, but to "heaven and earth," "mountains and hills," "Assyria and Egypt," to act as the judge's assessors or "a special type of 'jury.' "[75] The indictment sometimes appears to stand by itself[76] as a prophetic denunciation of wrongdoing, but the consequent judgment is implied or appears nearby in the literary context as presently arranged. Westermann has demonstrated in an exhaustive study that the announcement of divine judgment is the basic Word, to which the various forms of denunciation or reproach are related directly or by implication.[77] The phraseology is largely derived from the forms of accusation and judicial sentence in the law courts.

The pattern of a lawsuit in which the nation is accused and condemned to suffer punishment[78] is only one of several forms in which the prophets proclaimed Yahweh's imminent judgment. In Is. 5:8–12, 18–23; Am. 5:18–20; Hab. 2:6–19 and other passages, "Woes" are pronounced upon evil-doers. It would be more accurate to say that the cry of lamentation, *"hôy,* Alas for . . . ," is uttered

---

[75] As suggested by G. Ernest Wright in *Israel's Prophetic Heritage,* ed. B. W. Anderson and W. Harrelson, 1962, p. 47. Cf. Is. 1:2; Mic. 6:2; Am. 3:9.
[76] Is. 29:15–16; 1:10–17; 3:13–15; Jer. 3:1–5; 8:4–7.
[77] C. Westermann, *Grundformen prophetischer Rede,* 1960; Eng. tr. *Basic Forms of Prophetic Speech,* 1967.
[78] On this see G. Ernest Wright, "The Lawsuit of God," *Israel's Prophetic Heritage,* chap. III.

concerning those who deserve to die, for the setting-in-life is now not the lawcourt but the funeral.[79] Again, as for example in Is. 1:10–17; Am. 3:2–8, the prophet reasons with and admonishes his audience like an authoritative teacher. In Is. 5:1–7 he makes use of a parable to evoke self-condemnation, and in Is. 28:23–29 of a parable of a quite different type to clarify a theological issue.

The counterpart of the *Threat* or *Judgment-oracle* is the *Promise* or *Salvation-oracle*. Beyond doubt the majority of those now included in the books bearing the names of pre-exilic prophets are anonymous additions from a time when the doom they had foreseen had fallen on the Hebrew kingdoms. A characteristic opening is "in that day . . . ," as in the appendix to the Book of Amos, 9:11–15, where the reference to the catastrophe of 587 B.C. as in the past is unmistakable. Similar introductions are "At that time," "In the later time," "In the later days." An example is the famous prediction, found in both Is. 2:2–4 and Mic. 4:1–4, that the nations will "beat their swords into plowshares" when Zion has become a pilgrimage center for all mankind.

In spite of the predominance of Judgment-oracles in the classical prophets' words, the Salvation-oracle is certainly present in one or other of at least four forms. The first is the assurance of the imminent overthrow of the nation's enemies, a type of prophecy which the nationalist court prophets proclaimed with less discrimination. Isaiah assured King Ahaz that the threat posed by the Syro-Ephraimite invasion would be averted, and again that "the arrogant boasting of the king of Assyria" would be punished, and Jerusalem delivered from his threat.[80] In the second form the promise of deliverance is presented as an alternative to judgment, conditional on the nation's response: "If you are willing, and obey, you shall eat the good things of the land; but if you refuse and resist, the sword shall consume you."[81] In Hosea we find a third type of Salvation-oracle,

---

[79] Cf. Jer. 22:18–19.
[80] Is. 7:3–9; 10:12–19; 37:21–29.
[81] Is. 1:19–20 (Confraternity translation). Cf. Jer. 21:8–9; 22:2–5.

where the loving mercy of Yahweh overtakes and overflows, as it were, his disciplinary judgments.[82] Finally, there are the oracles of promise where Jeremiah, standing with his people under the darkness of Yahweh's present judgments, yet looks to a day of restoration visible to the eyes of faith: "When seventy years have elapsed for Babylon I will visit you and I will fulfill my Promise to you and bring you back to this place."[83]

It is impossible to say how far the prophets themselves were responsible for the building up of groups of related oracles into larger compositions such as are found in chaps. 1 and 2 of the Book of Amos, and in Is. 9:7 (EVV 9:8)—10:4 and the related 5:15–30. Part of the effect is produced here by the linking of single oracle-units in a larger composition, and there is no reason why this may not have been due to the prophet's own plan. Certainly the vast majority of the individual oracles show the marks of careful preparation for public proclamation in an impressive form.

This is illustrated by the distinction from these "public" oracles of what may be called "private" oracles, where the prophet tells what Yahweh said to *him*, commanding him to speak. Sometimes, as might be expected, these appear in the autobiographical narratives and incorporate the "Word" that is to be published, as in Is. 6:9–13 and Jer. 2:1–3. Sometimes they are given simply as an introduction to the "public oracle," as in Is. 30:8–14.

A particular type of "private" oracle worthy of special notice is the short enigmatic phrase which seems to be the form in which the Word spoken was first crystallized in the speaker's consciousness. Am. 8:13 and Jer. 1:11–12 provide familiar examples. In each case a *single word* emerges, charged with a double meaning through assonance: *qayis*, "fruit"—*qēs*, "end!" These are oracles in embryo, and become the texts for what then is publicly proclaimed. In Is. 8:1, 3–4 a private embryonic oracle of four words is expanded into an intelligible message. The names of Isaiah's and of Hosea's chil-

[82] Hos. 2:16–25 (EVV 14–23); 11:8–9; 14:5–8 (EVV 4–7).
[83] Jer. 29:10; cf. 31:2–6, 20; 31:31–34.

dren[84] embody the gist of prophetic Words. The scornful name given by Jeremiah to his opponent Pashhur, "Terror on all sides," is a summary of the denunciation which follows (Jer. 20:3–4). This primary "embryonic" form of an oracle may be preserved in the text of a published oracle, as in the play on words—ṣᵉdāqā, ṣᵉʿāqā— which forms the emphatic climax of Is. 5:1–7, or the similar play on forms of the verb '-m-n in Is. 7:9b. Containing as these do the quintessence of developed oracles for publication, it seems that they preserve the first articulations of the Word in Isaiah's mind.

THE SUBSTANCE OF THE WORD

The common element in the various oracle types is that each is the expression or formulation of Yahweh's personal and moral *will*. He is present over against his people as a living reality, not at all like the religious objects in the static pattern of ritual and myth, which was dominant in contemporary religions and influential in official Yahwism. The prophetic oracles constantly inject into the religious situation the clamant moral demands of an active and interested deity. They contribute to ethical vitality by calling for response and decision, and by relating the present to the future in terms of the historic purpose of Yahweh and his moral government of the world. As Eissfeldt puts it, the content of the prophetic utterance is a communication of the will of Yahweh to a present which cannot be separated from the future; the future is not determined by chance but by the same will which makes these moral demands in the present, so that the prophet's announcement of the future is a righteous act of Yahweh's present will.[85]

The communication of the divine will is at the same time a disclosure of the divine nature. Yahweh is holy, terrible, true and just. He is zealous for his name and for his covenant, and jealous, because he is not merely one among many gods but a different kind of god. He is mighty not only as possessing mysterious super-human

---

[84] Cf. Is. 7:3; 10:21–22; 8:3; Hos. 1:4, 6, 9.
[85] Cf. Eissfeldt, *The Old Testament, an Introduction*, p. 79.

power, but as the author of historic judgments and deliverances which are recognizable as divine acts rather than as chance happenings. He is free in decision and in act, but he is not capricious. In judgment and in mercy he is consistently true to himself, and to the meaning of his covenant with Israel.

To speak the word of such a God was, for his representative, to declare the inexorable facts in any given situation. The prophet reveals the moral and spiritual reality behind appearances, *what is*, as against what seems, what is felt on the level of the senses, or what is desired or feared. He interprets the present experience of his auditors in the light of wider experience, that of his own call and communion with Yahweh and that of his people's religious history. The divine nature, purpose and activity give meaning to the past, urgent importance to the present and ultimate significance to the future. In these circumstances the prophetic oracle is at the same time a revelation and a categorical imperative, an accusation and a present judgment, a word of doom and a word of promise.

6

THE THEOLOGY OF THE PROPHETS

The prophets were not theologians; rather, they were conscious instruments of an immediate divine commission and demand. Their God was primarily a subject of experience rather than an object of thought. For this reason it may be questioned whether one should speak of the prophetic theology. But two considerations may be advanced in justification for doing so. The first is that a similar objection might be made to the discussion of New Testament Theology, for the New Testament writings are not primarily formal theological documents, and it is impossible to compile from them a completely consistent and at the same time all-inclusive system of doctrine. But the attempt to relate the significant religious ideas of the New Testament in a coherent statement is not invalidated because the writers differ in viewpoint and emphasis, and show evidence of developing thought and experience.[1]

A second consideration is this: a theology is implicit in any serious religious utterance. If the prophets provide no thought-out system of doctrine, this is largely because they receive their message in flashes of insights; they are not teachers so much as messengers sent on an errand. Their oracles, however, are not just miscellaneous and

[1] Cf. the opening pages of J. Moffatt: *The Theology of the Gospels*, 1919.

unrelated fragments. Springing, as they do, from intense personal experience of the tension between the living reality of Yahweh and the world of man's everyday life, these oracles express in terms of the moment the prophets' central convictions as to the nature and relationship of God and man. This is the stuff of theology. Furthermore, these convictions are often in such marked contrast to the religious outlook of the prophets' contemporaries that the implicit theology has a distinctness that invites formulation.

To say this, of course, is not to overlook the fact that the theological concepts and emphases of the different prophets show considerable variation. Isaiah's theological interests and insights are not the same as those of Amos. Jeremiah does not seem to speak the same theological language as Ezekiel. "The symmetrical patterns into which we try to fit (Hebrew religion) are shattered time and again by historical crises, changes of cultural environment, and the work of great, creative personalities."[2] What is common to the canonical prophets is a new attitude to tradition, a new appreciation of Yahweh's active participation in the current affairs of Israel, and a new turning toward the future. As Lindblom says, "The ideas of the prophets concerning God, the election of Israel, the divine revelation, and the moral demands of Yahweh were not new; they were old ideas, but applied by the prophets in a new way."[3]

HERITAGE AND FULFILMENT

For all Israelites, belief in Yahweh as the God with whom as a people they stood in a peculiar and unique relationship was fundamental. God was a presupposition of thought rather than an object of thought.[4] This relationship had been established at a definite time in the historic past. Then and subsequently Yahweh's words and deeds had given direction and meaning to Israel's life and his-

---

[2] G. W. Anderson in *The Old Testament and Modern Study*, ed. H. H. Rowley, 1951, p. 309.
[3] J. Lindblom, *Prophecy in Ancient Israel*, 1962, p. 314.
[4] Cf. C. Westermann, *A Thousand Years and a Day*, 1962, p. 242.

tory. There is consequently no argument needed for the existence of
Yahweh, nor as to his personal concern for the people of his
covenant. His attributes of might and justice, faithfulness, mercy
and truth were vivid in the common tradition. The prophets continued to appeal to this heritage, even when they recognized that
some things had entered the tradition that were not native to it and
indeed were incompatible with it. Israel *knew about* Yahweh well
enough. She formally acknowledged his initiative in her historic past
and professed to serve him now in the cultus of her various sanctuaries, in particular at Jerusalem. But she did not know him as a
child knows his father, or a wife her husband, in an intimate relationship where she responded freely and naturally to his purpose
for her life.[5] She did not know him in the present as she *knew of*
him in her past. Yahweh had become a figure of tradition rather
than a fact of life, a theological postulate rather than a present
reality.

Thus what we find in the classical prophets is not so much new
teaching as a new realization of the nature and presence of the God
with whom men have to do. The divine personal qualities are
restated in dynamic terms. Yahweh is still the God of the fathers,
the Holy One of Israel, whose name was revealed through Moses.
He is a God of transcendent glory and of awful power in natural
phenomena and in events; of inscrutable and determinate purpose,
all-seeing, wise and just; true and faithful, and eager to be gracious;
watchful and active in revealing his concern. But his demand for
obedience and loyalty is more peremptory than had been assumed.
He will be terrible in his response to the obstruction of his will by
Israel as well as by Israel's enemies. Although his presence continues
to be connected in a special way with Zion and even with Sinai, he
is not a localized or territorial deity, but a God whose power, concern
and even self-revelation range far beyond Canaan's borders.[6] He is not
a god, but God.

[5] Cf. Is. 1:2–3; Hos. 4:1; 11:1–3; 2:1–13 (EVV).
[6] Am. 1:3—2:3; 9:7; Is. 6:3; Jer. 27:1–15; Mal. 1:11.

GOD THE LORD

It was long customary to say that ethical monotheism first found expression in Israelite religion through the eighth century prophets. But this, if anything, is the consequence rather than the burden of their message. The doctrine first becomes explicit in the sixth century introduction to Deuteronomy and the contemporary 2 Isaiah.[6A] Indeed, it can be argued that the religion of the patriarchs and of Moses was in effect a monotheism even if not theoretically defined as such. The incomparable nature of Yahweh, his personal and unique relationship with Israel, and the prophets' own immediate experience of God as a personal confrontation, made inevitable a doctrine of ethical monotheism when later they became organizing principles of religious thought. But that was not yet.

Meanwhile the greatness and gravity of the life-enveloping, life-directing and decision-demanding reality of God burned like a fire in the souls of these men. It was at once a light in darkness and a flame which threatened to consume them. The word "god" gained new content, because so overwhelming an experience put the formal worship of the cultus, like the worship of other gods, into an altogether different category. Yahweh indeed was recognized in the cultus as Israel's special deity because of the tradition of the Exodus, the covenant, and (later) because of his special relationship with the Davidic dynasty and with Jerusalem. But in like manner Chemosh was the special deity of the Moabites.[7] Elijah's challenge, "If Yahweh be God, follow him; but if Baal, then follow him"[8]—called for more than a choice between rival claims to allegiance. It meant a decision as to the meaning of the idea of "god," for Yahweh was not just the better of two deities of the same sort. The content of the concept of deity was defined by what Yahweh has shown himself to be, and in that context Baal was not a god at all.

[6A] Cf. Dt. 4:35, 39; Is. 43:10–11; 45:5, etc.
[7] Cf. the language of the Moabite Stone, ANET, pp. 320–21; and 1 Kg. 11:5–8.
[8] 1 Kg. 18:21.

The prophets proclaimed Yahweh as the Incomparable One, not just a national god superior to, but not essentially different from, the gods of the nations. They "emphasized the spiritual, personal and moral aspects of the nature of God . . . (They) always had to fight on two fronts; against naturalism and against nationalism."[9]

The unique and all-embracing fact of God possessed the prophets in their experience of the call to undertake their life work. From that they derived their urgent sense of mission. The divine fact was to them a personal presence with a name, one who confronted with his summons his chosen instrument. The prophet was awed by a majesty, and aware of irresistible might. Yet he was not terrified by weirdness or crushed by power. It was a personal will that called for his own surrender and obedience. Justice, truth and mercy were then no abstract concepts but constituents of Yahweh's character and of his dominant purpose, claiming the loyalty of the prophet as a king claims the services of his ambassador.[10] He knew Yahweh as a personal will demanding the obedience of Israel as it demanded his own, the determining factor in the nation's historical situation even as it burned like a fire in the prophet's mind. It was that same will which settled the course of history, not by predetermining events but by exhibiting before men a way of life that must be chosen or rejected. Yahweh was eager to pour blessings upon a people who would be responsive to his purpose; he was also ready to resist with inevitable destruction their refusal and stubborn pride.

It is with this passionate and righteous will that the final reckoning must be made, as men order their lives and frame their plans. For they cannot soothe that will with sacrifices, nor subject it to their control by magical means, by the mechanism of the cult or by political power.[11] It is the will to righteousness and mercy without which man cannot live.[12]

[9] Th. C. Vriezen, An Outline of Old Testament Theology, 1958, p. 32.
[10] Am. 7:15; Is. 6; Jer. 1:4 ff.
[11] Am. 5:21–24; Is. 1:11–15; Jer. 7:21 ff.; Is. 2:6–21.
[12] Hos. 14:3; Is. 1:9; Jer. 16:5 ff.

The second distinctive element in the prophetic consciousness of God is the intensity of feeling associated with the realization of the divine presence. The "love" of God is not an idea that takes its tone from his kindly provision in Nature for human need, nor from his gracious personal Providence—though both of these are included in it. The Divine love is terrible in its depth and poignancy. Only in the height and depth of human experience can its meaning be glimpsed, as in the agony of a husband's unrequited devotion, in a father's yearning over his infant son, and over that same son when grown to man's estate and become wayward.[13] The anger of Yahweh at sin is not the cold anger of a judge upholding law, but the passionate anger of a master whose goodness has been flouted, of a guardian whose helpless wards have been maltreated. Hence the formal worship which takes no account of Yahweh's real nature and which does not stir the depths of life, is rejected by God, not with indifferent disdain, but with the loathing of one whose being is outraged. There is no sorrow like unto his sorrow, for indignation and pity contend together in the heart of God. The execution of his judgments means the death of hope. Feeling so intense may for the moment even deflect the operation of Yahweh's will, so that he changes his mind at the prophet's intercession with respect to a particular judgment.[14] But in the end his righteous will prevails at whatever cost to himself, for it is himself.

The third important element in the prophetic apprehension of God is closely related to the first two. Yahweh is such a being that he is an active and interested party to what happens among men. Though he is the Lord of nature, it is as the Lord of history and of common experience that his essential nature can be most definitely distinguished, and most clearly grasped. He is not a static cosmic framework of beauty, truth and goodness, nor an impersonal force making for righteousness through the mechanical enforcement of the moral law. First and foremost Yahweh is one characterized by dy-

---

[13] Is. 1:2, 3; Hos. 2:2 ff. (EVV); 11:1–4, 8, 9.
[14] Am. 7:1 ff.; Hos. 11:8, 9.

namic personal qualities, a participant in life. He is known by and
in his acts. He is a "Doer," rather than a static "Being." "The
appropriate expression for history in the prophetic books is, therefore, 'the work of Yahweh.' "[15] He is righteousness in action. Yet his
righteousness cannot be realized except in human behavior and
relationships, through the conscious choice of men. Hence it is that
he reveals himself most really not in holy words, mystic ecstasy or
material phenomena, but in the moral groundwork of experience. A
man discerns God's presence in the ethical choices and decisions
which he must make, and in virtue of which he is a morally conscious and responsible person. "Men . . . have become persons because God has addressed them, and they have had to make a decision in his presence. This was something new in Israel."[16] And
since conscious experience is for the individual what history is for
the nation, the sphere of moral decisions, Yahweh becomes known
in personal experience and in history as he cannot be known definitively in any other way. Here he is unique, alone in his exaltation,
universal in his manifestation.[17]

Hence, the supreme importance to the prophets of the call which
came to them as individuals, and of the tradition of the covenant
people's history to which they constantly allude.[18] In the relationship
of man to God, the character and behavior of both parties is the
fundamental fact. No expert priestly knowledge can bridge the gap
at another point; no cultus can bring people and God together in
impersonal terms; no amoral offering can serve as a substitute which
makes the bridging of the gap unnecessary. Yahweh is one who wills,
feels, knows, speaks and acts in the here and now. It is with him
alone, and with him as he really is, that man has to do. "Am I a
God near at hand—and not a God afar off? Can any hide in secret

[15] Am. 3:7; Is. 5:12, 19; 28:21; Zeph. 1:12; 3:5; H. W. Wolff, in *O.T. Herme-*
neutics, 1963, p. 338.
[16] von Rad, *O.T. Theol.,* ii, p. 76.
[17] Am. 5:4–7, 14, 15; 9:7, 8; Hos. 7:11–13; Is. 5:16; 10:12 ff.
[18] Is. 6; Jer. 1:4 ff.; Am. 2:9, 10; 3:1, 2; Hos. 6:7; 8:1; 12:9, 13 (EVV); Is.
28:14 ff.; Mic. 6:1–5; Jer. 2:6, 7; 11:3–5.

places so that I cannot see him? Do not I fill heaven and earth? It is the oracle of Yahweh."[19]

God is near, but he also is far—immeasurably exalted, inexpressibly different. He is the king who does not die.[20] The fact of his intercourse with men after the fashion of a man and the language of human experience used to describe this are probably necessary for human apprehension of deity. But "I am God, and not man; the Holy One in the midst of thee."[21] The word "holy" marks the gulf between man and God, between the weak and the powerful, between the familiar and the mysterious, between the transitory and the eternal. "In biblical language 'holy' is best understood as meaning 'divine,' or 'wholly other.' "[22] But *Yahweh's* "holiness" has the distinctiveness of his own character. It is the glory and moral majesty of *his* person, whose righteous will has been made known, and whose power embraces all life for the accomplishment of his purposes. "Yahweh of hosts is exalted *in justice,* and God the Holy One shows his divinity *by righteousness.*"[23] This divine fact dwarfs all other facts with which men are concerned. It is a tremendous, awful glory which only total moral blindness can hide from men, and from which, when they see it, there can be no escape. The land is filled with the glory of this presence; the ends of the earth tremble at Yahweh's rebuke. He is the God of all flesh, for he is the Maker and Lord of all.[24]

Before this living Lord of life, this "Other" who is sovereign, the pride of man must be abased, the hollowness of his pretensions be revealed, his material satisfactions be dissolved like smoke, his empires collapse in ruins. For Yahweh himself is the only strength and vitality of his people, the reality of social justice which maintains the fabric of society, the core of personal life, its spiritual

[19] Jer. 23:23, 24.
[20] Is. 6:1.
[21] Hos. 11:9.
[22] H. Ringgren, *Israelite Religion*, 1966, p. 74.
[23] Is. 3:16.
[24] Is. 2:10 ff.; 6:3; Am. 1:2; Mic. 1:2 ff.; Jer. 27:5.

principle, its moral framework.[25] He alone is great, is wise, is holy. His sovereign divinity he shares with no other gods, even if they be acknowledged as inferior. "She did not know that it was I who gave her the grain and the new wine and the oil, and the silver which I multiplied for her, and the gold, which they used for the Baal."[26] Yahweh is alone because he is unique, and he is *one* because he comprehends life in its total setting. Wonders and disasters both are his doing, for he is in control. Only he can claim man's obedience, which means to conform to his reality. Yahweh is *Lord*.

MAN AND HIS WORLD

The thought of the prophets is centered on God to such a degree that what they have to say of the nature of man is largely by way of contrast. As Yahweh is "God and not man," so man is "flesh and not spirit."[27] The distinction between the divine and the human is both metaphysical and ethical. As part of the natural world man is "flesh." The life of the flesh is the life of ordinary experience and physical satisfactions; it is inherently weak, and subject to corruption and death.[28] "Spirit," on the other hand, is not a constituent part of man's nature; it is a mysterious onset of power that may intrude into human experience from the divine side.[29] At this point the prophets spoke the language of their age. Their own great contribution was to show that God was to be distinguished from man, not only as supernatural Spirit, but as the ethically exalted One. Isaiah's experience in the temple was undoubtedly what Otto has called a "numinous" experience, but it culminated in an awareness of absolute qualitative difference, a gap which only God could bridge, and that in moral terms.

The Hebrews thought of man as an animated body rather than as an incarnate soul. His life is a breath-soul, and when the breath

[25] Is. 1:26; 17:10; 28:5, 6; Hos. 13:4, 9; Zeph. 3:5; Jer. 38:16.
[26] Hos. 2:8 (EVV).
[27] Hos. 11:9; Is. 31:3.
[28] Cf. Pedersen, *Israel I-II*, pp. 176–79.
[29] See above, pp. 91–92.

leaves the body the real man is no more. For in the grave—or Sheol
—to which he is gathered with his fathers, his shade persists as
little more than the echo and memory of a man whose real im-
mortality is in his posterity.[30] Life itself is Yahweh's gift, and it is
Yahweh's intention that man, in rendering him obedience, should
find satisfaction in this life and "eat the good of the land."[31] Man's
conscious life is compact of feeling, will and understanding; he
has "reins and heart,"[32] i.e., emotions and conscious volition. He
can devise and carry out his purposes, though always subject to
the unpredictability of the future and the possible intervention of
God.[33] There is no abstract distinction between thinking and doing.
Both are expressions of the intent of man's heart, and by his ways
and deeds he shows what he is in himself.[34] The highest human
power is the capacity to distinguish good from evil, and to know,
trust and obey God.[35] This capacity can be atrophied by misuse or
disuse, so that a man becomes ethically moribund and sceptical,
blind and deaf and dull of mind, until the truth and reality of God
can find no longer any opening for entrance into his experience.[36]

The traditional feeling of family and tribal solidarity persisted
too in the prophets' thought, though it was through intense individual experiences like those of Hosea and Jeremiah that an understanding of the integrity, freedom and responsibility of the individual
was to emerge alongside of social consciousness. Man is what he
is within a complex of social relationships. He is son, brother,
husband, father, neighbor; but the importance of the group remains
primary. The nation in its internal structure is ideally a family. In
relation to other nations and to its God it is a "people," or cor-

---

[30] Cf. H. Wheeler Robinson: *The Religious Ideas of the Old Testament*, 1913,
pp. 91 ff.
[31] Is. 1:19.
[32] Jer. 11:20.
[33] Is. 10:7, 12.
[34] Cf. Pedersen: *op. cit.*, pp. 128–133.
[35] Am. 3:10; 5:4, 14; Is. 5:20; Hos. 4:1; Jer. 9:23, 24 (EVV).
[36] Is. 6:10; Zeph. 1:12.

porate unit, with a corporate personality of its own.[37] It was not
simply a poetic metaphor for Isaiah to speak of the "daughter Zion,"
nor did the prophets attack an abstraction when they arraigned the
nation for its sins. The nation *as such* had received the revelation of
Yahweh, and had entered into covenant with him; the nation *as such*
had adopted a way of life which expressed its central life-direction
as clearly as did the "habit pattern" of an individual. Isaiah felt
himself unclean as a member of an unclean people; for her doom
Micah lamented as for his own. Jeremiah heard and joined in the
weeping of the tribal mother Rachel for the children who were
united in her continuing life.[38]

The moral condition of man as the prophets knew him was seen
in the "goal of life," defined by the pattern and methods of the
society in which he lived. That goal, as they saw it, was the continuance by all means of the life of the flesh, the increase of its
satisfactions, and the avoidance or postponement of its end in the
death of the individual and the dissolution of society. Man reveled
in the material and sensual satisfactions of life; he desired its ful-
ness measured in age, in honor, in prosperity and in progeny. He
sought by ritual means to increase the fertility of his family, his
lands and his herds, and to secure divine aid to prosper his enterprises. He sought further to make his own life secure by appro-
priating as large a share as possible of nature's bounty and of the
wealth produced by the community. By his strength, his cunning
and his acquisitiveness man exalted himself in the world, became
vain of his self-sufficiency and measured life only by his desires.
He did not acknowledge Yahweh as the giver of all good gifts,
nor was he grieved with Yahweh's grief for the hurt of his fellow
men.[39]

What was true of the individual was true of the nation. The
picture of Israelite society so clearly painted in the prophetic books

[37] Cf. Pedersen: *op. cit.*, pp. 54–57.
[38] Is. 1:8; 21 ff.; 6:5; Mic. 1:8 ff.; Jer. 31:15 ff.
[39] Am. 5:1; 6:1–6; 8:4 ff.; Hos. 2:5 (EVV); 7:3–7; Is. 2:6 ff.; 10:13, 14.

is that of a people devoted to this self-directed pagan way of life because in reality its goal was a pagan goal. The nation had set its heart on the wealth and buildings of its cities, its military power and alliances, the luxury of its court circle and the elaborateness of its sanctuaries. King and princes, judges and military officers, priests and official prophets, together formed the human framework of the social structure—its mainstays, as bread and water are the mainstays of life.[40] The community did not see that it shared the instability of leaders who were concerned with privilege rather than responsibility; since the foundations of society had been undermined by the corruption of justice and the neglect of truth and mercy, this human framework must collapse like a structure of wax before a fire.[41] The social institutions that were considered necessary to national existence and self-respect were not in fact what made a people out of a mass of men. Only when these were taken away would they learn that family feeling for the neighbor and an ethic of solidarity rooted in religion, are indispensable to a people.

The basic attitude of man was thus optimistic confidence in himself and in the way of life he had devised to secure his satisfactions. He felt himself autonomous. He was sure that the exercise of social power after the fashion of other nations, together with divine favor insured by many and costly sacrifices, were adequate to attain his ends. He refused to face the facts of human suffering and social degeneracy, or to believe that calamities which came were warnings of a final doom. He gave to the world of his own scheming the trust that was due alone to Yahweh, the Maker of heaven and earth and men. For in his heart of hearts he believed that he, and not Yahweh, was in control. The other gods whom he acknowledged as real divinities, even if subsidiary to Yahweh, were fit symbols of his self-sufficiency. For them, too, his hands

[40] Is. 3:1–7; 31:1; Mic. 3:1; Am. 6:1.
[41] Am. 5:11; Hos. 3:4; Mic. 3:9–12; Is. 5:13, 14.

had made, like the cities where their proud shrines were built. "For as many as are your cities, are your gods, O Judah!"[42]

REVELATION AND COMMAND

The prophets recognized that man's confidence in his way of life is necessary to his vitality, and that loss of confidence must bring collapse and dissolution. Man's self-commitment, therefore, must be to something secure and permanent.[43] The prophets consequently were not content to denounce particular sins against Yahweh's covenant; they pled also for recognition of the inherent instability of a man-centered society and for the transfer of confidence to a new center in the personal revelation and command of Yahweh. The religion to which Yahweh was only a name or a tradition was ineffective. It was poles apart from the prophets' own overwhelming apprehension of God as a present and active participant in life. Though they were not able to bring their audiences (except for small groups of disciples) to share that apprehension, they did continually appeal to acknowledged facts of the national religious tradition, to the moral obligations of the covenant, and to the meaning for a sinful people of the calamities which had already come.[44]

The possibility of revelation is not argued for; it is taken for granted. The messengers of Yahweh were on common ground with their hearers when they spoke of him as a God who had revealed himself supremely to Israel on certain great occasions in the past, and who from time to time still made known his will through priestly oracle and prophetic word. The question at issue was whether particular prophets on particular occasions had an authentic word, or spoke only "a vision of their own heart, and not out of the mouth of Yahweh." If the prophet Hananiah had a genuine revela-

---

[42] Jer. 2:28.
[43] Is. 3:1–8; 7:4a, 9b; 30:12, 15.
[44] Is. 30:1 ff.; 12–15; Am. 2:9–12; 4:6–12; Jer. 7:21–28; Hos. 11:1–2.

tion, Jeremiah was self-deceived, and on occasion Jeremiah wondered if Yahweh himself had not deceived him.[45] But, for the most part, he was sure that those who denied that doom was coming were false prophets. For he himself would fain echo their denial but could not, because of a will confronting him which was stronger than his desire. The power that compelled a prophet to speak as he had no wish to do, that filled him with complete assurance as he pointed to the sin that was destroying his people, that clarified his spiritual perception so that he discerned the unfolding of a consistent moral purpose, and gave him a sense of mission which neither indifference nor opposition could destroy—was a power like an inward fire, as real as his own existence.[46] His message came out spontaneously as from a crucible where his life was fused with the life of his people, by the white heat of the holy will of God. A flash of insight on occasion disclosed in otherwise trivial happenings a meaning coincident with Yahweh's known purpose, so that these became "signs."[47] Yahweh's purpose was evident in the connection, visible to the moral consciousness, between the community's sins and its experienced calamities.[48] Its presence was felt in the compulsion to speak even against the prophet's own desire, and its content known from the "prophetic" tradition of Yahweh's ethical characteristics.

Revelation was thus both a present experience and an objective element in the historical tradition. It had its place also in the cult.[49] The name of Moses is, indeed, mentioned only by Jeremiah (unless Mic. 6:4 be original) among the pre-exilic prophets. But there are fairly numerous allusions to the period of the Exodus, the Wanderings and the Conquest, as the time when Israel was constituted the people of Yahweh in a distinctive relationship of

[45] Jer. 23:16; 28; 20:7.
[46] Jer. 28:6 ff.; Mic. 3:8; Am. 7:10 ff.; Jer. 20:9.
[47] Is. 7:14; Jer. 1:11–14.
[48] Am. 4:6.
[49] Mic. 3:11; Hos. 8:12; Jer. 2:8; 18:18.

mutual obligation.[50] Israel claimed to know her God and to possess peculiar privileges because of that knowledge, gained by past revelation and experience. What Hosea emphasizes is that she does not know him as a present reality and a vital factor in her belief and behavior. Meaning does not cling to words which have lost their relevance: Isaiah's promise that Yahweh would defend Jerusalem has become a fetish, a deceitful word, when quoted in the altered circumstances of Jeremiah's time a century later. Furthermore, reliance upon such a promise of Yahweh becomes meaningless if at the same time his primary ethical requirements are being disregarded: "Will ye steal, murder, and commit adultery, and swear falsely, and burn incense to the Baal and go after other gods that you do not know—and then come and stand before me in this house which is called by my name, and say: 'we are safe'?"[51]

The reference here to the Decalogue of Ex. 20 and Deut. 5 is clear. Whatever one may hold as to the antiquity of any of the several *forms* of the Decalogue,[52] some such summary of the primary requirements of Yahweh's worship appears to have been part of the temple ritual from early times, probably in the form of a threshold liturgy.[53] In any case, the service of Yahweh had certain definite ethical associations which were believed to derive from ancient revelation.

In addition to this there was the recollection of a succession of national leaders and prophetic witnesses who had maintained the continuity of the religio-national tradition down to the present.[54] The representatives of this succession in Jeremiah's day were the cultic and court prophets. These formed an accepted element in society, and their claim to be heard presupposes such a recognition of their forerunners as is found in Jer. 26:17 ff. That Yahweh had

---

[50] Am. 2:9, 10; 3:1; 5:25; Hos. 9:10; 11:1; 12:13 (EVV); Jer. 2:2, 3; 7:21–26; 11:7, 8, 10; 34:13.
[51] Hos. 8:2; 4:6; Jer. 26:16–19; 7:9, 10.
[52] Ex. 20:3–17; Deut. 5:7–21; 27:15–26; Lev. 19:3–18; Ex. 34:14–26.
[53] Cf. Jer. 7:2, 9, 10 with Psalms 15 and 24.
[54] Am. 2:11, 12; Hos. 6:5; 12:10 (EVV); Is. 30:9, 10; Jer. 7:25; 26:5.

revealed himself at the beginning, and repeatedly since, was generally accepted as a fact. Yet it was not only through the prophetic word that revelation was believed to have come. The priests declared the will of Yahweh by use of the sacred lot, and in *toroth* ("rulings, teachings"), given in response to particular inquiries. "The Wise" formulated their religious reflections upon experience. The pragmatic test, applicable even to prophetic teaching, enabled emergent truth to be accepted as revelation, since Yahweh himself illumined man's mind, and was the source of all truth.[55]

There is this distinction, however, between revelation through the prophets and that through the priests and Wisdom teachers. In the former case the initiative lay with Yahweh, and the essence of the revelation was a summons and a commandment.[56] We are speaking here of the prophets whose words have become canonical because they were validated in experience and by history. The same criterion distinguishes these from the "false prophets," who did *not* summon men to obedience but sought to express with mantic power the human desire for victory and well-being, and so to insure that these would follow.[57] In the most famous of prophetic affirmations, Micah states the essential requirements of Yahwism to be just and merciful action toward men and humble obedience to God. Trust in Yahweh is demanded, and faith is necessary to the hearing and acceptance of the demand itself. Moreover, conformity to the right way requires repentance of the evil way of pride and self-gratification. Religion becomes responsiveness within a divine-human relationship, personal in its terms.[58] This points on to a high level of revelation not yet reached, when Yahweh's will is to be written in men's minds like a law upon tablets. *Then* obedience to him will be a spontaneous response to

---

[55] Mal. 2:4–7; Is. 28:5–8.
[56] E.g., Am. 5:14, 15.
[57] Clear examples of this are 2 Kg. 22:10, 11; Jer. 28:10, 11. A similar use of prophetic symbolism to embody a Word of Yahweh is made by Jeremiah in the same passage, and by Isaiah in 20:2–4.
[58] Mic. 6:8.

the divine reality whose nature is immediately and clearly known, so that there will no longer be need for external teaching *about* Yahweh and his commands.[59]

A second significant difference between revelation through the prophetic word and that through priests and the Wise is this. The latter was an enlargement of the body of religious knowledge in a relatively static, continuing situation; the former was a momentous message which called for decision, and gave special meaning and importance to the time and situation in which it was uttered. To the priests and the Wise, God was the Ancient and Unchanging; to the prophets he manifested his personal will in a special way at a particular moment. The former may be said to be media of traditional religious knowledge, the latter of a specific and unique self-disclosure in the light of which life's total setting must be understood. "Yahweh, who is the theme of Hebrew prophecy, is primarily the Lord of history. He is the Lord of Nature, too, but . . . the interest in Yahweh's creative activity is subordinated to the interest in His redemptive work. God is not described in metaphysical terms, as He is in Himself. The prophets bear witness to Him as the great Intruder in human affairs."[60]

ELECTION AND COVENANT

As Eichrodt points out,[61] the doctrine that Israel was a people chosen of God must be understood as an expression of the historically conditioned relation of Yahweh to his community. That relationship is deliberately distinguished from any natural or physical bond, which, being permanent, would give no special significance to time. Belief in a divine act of choice at a particular moment in history, on the other hand, gives to time special significance as the context of divine action and human moral response. It also gives to history a beginning and a direction. Revelation is thus par-

---

[59] As in Jer. 31:33, 34.
[60] N. W. Porteous, in *Record and Revelation*, ed. H. W. Robinson, 1938, p. 238.
[61] W. Eichrodt, *Theology of the Old Testament*, i, 1961, pp. 41–42.

ticularized and made concrete without in any way limiting its universality and permanent validity. Israel's assertion of her election affirms the fact of a revelation within the actual history of a continuing community. The personal manifestation of God to living men necessarily takes place at a point in space and time. This lends significance to places (Sinai, Zion, the hillsides of Tekoa), and to occasions. But that importance is conditioned by continuing response to the revelation, received there and then. Apart from a present moral response, the times and places of revelation remembered in tradition have no longer any real meaning. Nor have the Israelites any special status simply as children of their fathers. "God is able of these stones to raise up children unto Abraham."

The Old Testament doctrine of election and covenant is, then, an historical statement of fact, even though it be a fact that must be accepted by faith, and is otherwise meaningless. It declares that to Israel there has come a real historical experience of divine deliverance, associated with a personal manifestation of God and a summons to obey him. This is a philosophy of history (or rather, a *theology* of history) which finds its constituent elements in the experiences of the Israelite clans at the time of the Exodus, as these experiences came to be interpreted by prophetic insight. It cannot be proved to have originated with Moses, for the Pentateuch does not provide us with primary historical documents. Yet there seems to be no other sufficient cause to explain it prior to the eighth century. The writings of the prophets are evidence that they did not give the doctrine birth. They tell of a line of witnesses like themselves who had continued a tradition originating in the creative period of the Exodus, the Wanderings and the entrance to Yahweh's land.[62]

In this connection they speak of Yahweh as the Maker and Saviour of the nation. At Sinai Israel became Yahweh's people, and he became their God. Through the definitive experiences of that period the tribes were constituted a people, a "whole family,"

[62] Am. 2:11–12; Jer. 7:25.

whose unity arose from a new and special relationship to this deity
with his distinctive character. Having its origin at a particular time
and place, this was a relationship established by the historic act
of Yahweh. The terms of the covenant were laid down by its
sovereign, and specified an ethical norm of community life corresponding to his strongly marked personal characteristics. The
primary obligations of Israel were those of loyalty and obedience.
These were to be expressed in the exclusive worship of this unique
God of the nation, the heeding of his messengers, and the faithful
embodiment of his ethical standards in social life.

That this was the covenant doctrine of the prophets is evident
from their repeated denunciations of syncretisic worship and social
corruption, as departures from an ethico-religious obligation theoretically acknowledged. These are seen as grotesque and unnatural
perversions of the relationship with Yahweh. The proud self-sufficiency of those who held power and of national policy itself, was
rebellion, not obedience; they marked the choice of the world's
way rather than of the way of the covenant. There did not exist
that genuine intimate knowledge of Yahweh which was essential.
The covenant was his gift and required a real sharing of life.
It could not be thought of simply as a formal contract, conferring
on Israel a special status and a claim upon her God. It must
be a constant and conscious condition of the people's life if it
was to remain in force. Even the cumulative experience of history,
in which punishment and restoration testified to Yahweh's patience
as well as to his righteousness, gave no assurance that he would
go on indefinitely tolerating breaches of his covenant. There came
a point when the relationship was no longer real. The traditional
and cultic links alone could not keep it in being, for it connoted
a vital and not merely a formal relationship.

Thus there was nothing necessary or final about Israel's election,
should she fail to serve the divine purpose. It should not be made
a theological dogma. The unique deity, Yahweh, had in his sovereign freedom selected Israel to be the medium for his self-dis-

closure. She had been privileged and preserved in decisive moments in order to be the instrument of his purpose. But that purpose was not irrevocably committed to the historic survival of *this* nation. "Are you not like the people of the Ethiopians to me, O people of Israel?—Did I not bring up Israel out of the land of Egypt, *and* the Philistines from Caphtor, *and* the Syrians from Kir?"[63] Israel's election could be annulled by her own act. Yahweh will show his nature and purpose, as well by the rejection of his people now as by her original selection to be a people peculiarly his own. The *unrighteous* nation without distinction would be destroyed: it would destroy itself. For the conceit of unconditioned privilege had become nationalist pride, sustained by a superficial recollection of Yahweh's earlier deliverances that ignored their ethical purpose.

The fact of Israel's repeated defection from the covenant in the past without her having been abandoned by her God, is attributed by the prophets to his mercy, his patience and his persistence. It is his nature to be long-suffering. Yahweh's purpose to disclose his goodness and to finish creating a faithful people is not easily defeated. But his integrity cannot be outraged forever. Israel's persistence in her evil ways has brought her to a condition where she is no longer capable of response. She is on the brink of the doom which final faithlessness has made inevitable.

Yet the doom of the nation is not the doom of the covenant. In two notable ways the prophets affirm their certainty that Yahweh's purpose to create a people for himself and like himself will triumph in the end. Isaiah's teaching about the "Remnant" and Jeremiah's proclamation of the New Covenant are eschatological doctrines.[64] That genuine and spontaneous recognition of Yahweh in the common life which was to have been the essence of the old covenant, and of which the empirical nation had shown itself incapable, must in the end be realized, because Yahweh is God.

[63] Am. 9:7.
[64] Is. 1:27; 6:13; 7:3; 8:15.

Isaiah saw its beginnings in the small circle of his disciples. Jeremiah, apparently as a result of his disappointing experience of Josiah's reform, learned with Paul that what the Law could not do God could *and therefore would* do. The New Covenant was the fulfilment of the Mosaic covenant as the prophets discerned its central meaning:—a real, experiential knowledge of God which has become the creative power and norm of human life.

SIN AND JUDGMENT

"What gave rise to pre-exilic prophecy in its typical form? It was horror at the apostasy of Israel. The prophets saw that their people had lost their way and gone astray, away from their God and His will. The greater part of their teaching consists of pictures of the sinfulness of the people."[65] Hence one of the major contributions of the great prophets is their redefinition of sin, and the sense of dreadful reality with which they invest it. The nature of sin is defined by the nature of the Deity sinned against. Its seriousness is measured by his real importance in the thinking and in the lives of his professed worshippers. Sin belongs in that area of experience which is the meeting-place of man with God. If the nature of God be conceived as such that he will be satisfied with offerings and cultic honors meticulously performed, then failure here disrupts the normal relationship, and is sin. This is the stage and kind of religion represented in David's word to Saul: "If it be Yahweh that has stirred you up against me, let him smell an offering."[66] It is a stage from which the religions of the ancient East—apart from Israel—never really emerged.

But if religion is essentially a relationship between a God who speaks and acts, and a community whose part it is to hear and obey in trust and loyalty, then sin is any act or attitude or failure

[65] J. Lindblom, *op. cit.*, p. 320.
[66] 1 Sam. 26:19. On the other hand, "an act might be universally recognized as a vice or a crime; it did not follow that it was a sin." W. O. E. Oesterley and T. H. Robinson, *Hebrew Religion*, 1930, p. 166.

of man which disrupts that relationship. It *may* be a transgression with respect to cultic obligations, if thereby disloyalty to the Deity is given deliberate expression; note that "Thou shalt have no other god images in my sanctuary" is probably the meaning of the First Commandment. But worship at the sanctuary is to the prophets only one strand—and that not the most important—in the connection between Yahweh and his people. To rely exclusively upon it is to misconceive the nature of Yahweh and the consequent personal, historical quality of the connection. Thus the very cult service itself may become a sin, if it fails to express the genuine loyalty to Yahweh alone which is the fundamental requirement. This means loyalty to his characteristic covenant with its sacred social obligations, trust in him and obedience to the word of his messengers. Sin is disloyalty, unfaithfulness, mistrust, self-sufficient pride, disobedience. Its root is an ultimate scepticism about the reality of Yahweh's presence and power, or a total misconception of his nature which makes impossible any effective fellowship and partnership with him.

It is noteworthy that in the long catalogue of sins attributed to their people, the pre-exilic prophets seldom if ever describe sins against holy places, holy persons and holy things as sins against the God from whom their sacredness is derived. Instead, religious observances are judged by the moral standards applied in every other area of the people's life, for the moral standards are inherent in the religious standards. The one sin peculiarly directed against Yahweh is idolatry, the overt idolatry of polytheism and its image-worship, and the covert idolatry that used Yahweh's name in worship whose form and quality made it really the worship of Baal. For the rest, the sins against which the prophets inveigh are sins against men. These are sins also against God, for men are within his covenant.

The particular sins mentioned constitute a woeful list characteristic of unregenerate human societies generally: treachery, exploitation, oppression, cruelty, angry strife, greed of money, luxury and power; dishonesty, venal justice, lying, violence, murder. Their underlying principle is repeatedly defined as disobedience, rebellion, estrangement from God, love of evil. The resultant spiritual condition is corruption, perversion, instability, callousness, degeneracy. Sin is a concrete way of life. The terms used are suggestive: *ra'* and *resha'* denote a state of habitual wickedness; *'awon*—guilt, inherent evil; *pesha'*—deliberate transgression of a known commandment or moral standard; *ḥaṭṭ'ath*—defection from good. All are used of this general spiritual condition of guilt and estrangement from God, as expressed in a state of mind and a habit of life. "The *ḥaṭṭ'ath* of Judah . . . is engraved upon the tablet of their heart"; "I am full of power . . . to declare unto Jacob his *pesha'* and to Israel his *ḥaṭṭ'ath*."[67] The evil purpose and its concrete consequences belong together.[68]

Sin was thus sharply and profoundly distinguished from cultic faults. Ritual uncleanness might result from acts of commission or omission; it might be the consequence of inadvertence or of certain natural happenings which brought a person into the area of taboo. Ritual means were provided to remove the condition and stigma which precluded access to ritually "holy" things. Though sin, to the prophets, was viewed from a radically ethical standpoint, there was this analogy to ritual fault, that it was a condition of man over against the "holiness" of Yahweh. For *his* "holiness" had become for them something more than the mysterious and dangerous power of Divinity. It had taken on the quality of Yahweh's ethical personality. Sin is more, then, than the sum of wrong acts. It is a state of moral uncleanness resulting from such acts and giving rise to them.

Nothing man can do will automatically change this condition, though his repentant turning to God may pave the way for the divine forgiveness. But God must act, in punishment or in restoration. Apart from this no priest can absolve the sinner, nor can

[67] Jer. 17:1; Mic. 3:8.
[68] Cf. Mic. 2:1, 2.

elaborate community cultic acts of penitence—fasting, sacrifice
and prayer—compensate Yahweh for the community's disobedience,
or change the community's standing in his sight. Still less can
wealth, power or military alliances provide an alternative security
against the disabling corruption of sin. Certainly a feigned repentance and reliance on a formal dogma of election from which all
reality has evaporated are useless to deal with sin's dreadful reality.[69]

The full horror of that reality is symbolized in prophetic language
by the revulsion of nature itself against man's uncleanness. "How
long shall the land mourn? . . . For the wickedness of them that
dwell therein the beasts are consumed"; "Be astonished, O heavens,
at this, and be horribly afraid."[70] The unnatural perversity of
Israel puts her lower in the moral scale than the dumb beasts:
"The ox knows its owner, and the ass its master's manger, but
Israel knows not, my people does not understand."[71] Pagan nations
whose gods could not be compared with Yahweh had not acted
as Israel had done. "Has a nation changed its gods, which yet are
no gods? But my people have changed their glory for that which
is profitless."[72] The most elementary moral distinctions have become blurred. Men call good, evil, and evil, good. The perversion
of justice is as fantastic and unnatural as if men were to set out
to plough the sea with an ox.[73] It is sheer horror to the prophet
to realize that the people "love to have it so." They are so sunk
in spiritual torpor that they have lost the capacity for spiritual
response and moral responsibility. They are decrepit with age,
incurably ill, wandering, lost. With the rotting away of the social
bond of confidence in one another, in life and in God, the nation
is distintegrating.[74]

Why? Because, in a world where Yahweh rules, they have brought

[69] Is. 1:10–15; Am. 4:4, 5; 5:21–24; Hos. 5:13; 6:1–4; Jer. 3:10.
[70] Jer. 12:4; 2:12, 13.
[71] Is. 1:3.
[72] Jer. 2:11.
[73] Is. 5:20; Am. 6:12.
[74] Jer. 5:30, 31; Hos. 7:9; Is. 1:5; 3:8, 12; Jer. 8:22; 10:20.

punishment inevitably upon themselves. *They* have done it, but it is also *his* act, the effect of his unrecognized presence. "Behold, I will melt them and test them, for how else should I do?" "I will be like a moth unto Ephraim."[75] A doom must come which will be not only just but fitting. "You said: we will ride upon the swift; therefore they that pursue you shall be swift"; "You have carried (in procession) the shrine of your images; therefore will I cause you to go (in procession) into captivity"; "Instead of perfume, there shall be a rotten smell; and instead of a girdle, a rope; instead of dressed hair, baldness; instead of a robe, a wrapping of sackcloth; and instead of beauty, shame"; "They sowed the wind, and they shall reap the whirlwind."[76]

Only the seriousness of sin in Yahweh's eyes can explain the awful force of his reaction against it. His anger is hurt and indignant wrath. "I will meet them as a bear bereaved of her whelps." Yahweh will judge and recompense. Israelites need expect no special pity; their God will be deaf not only to their own prayers, but to the intercession of the prophets.[77] The sheer terror of the day of judgment is pictured in unforgettable language. "Men will go into caves of the rock and into holes of the earth, from before the terror of Yahweh and his glorious majesty"; "The bravest of warriors shall flee away naked in that day"; "That day is a day of wrath, a day of trouble and distress, a day of waste and desolation, a day of darkness and gloom, a day of cloud and thick darkness, a day of the trumpet and alarm . . . for he will make an end, a terrible end."[78]

There can be no escape but by an uncovenanted mercy from this destiny which Israel has carved out for herself. The people of Yahweh have been arraigned before the nations, and heaven and earth called to witness that her judgment is just. Yahweh sends his

[75] Jer. 9:7; Hos. 5:12.
[76] Is. 30:16; Am. 5:26, 27; Is. 3:24; Hos. 8:7.
[77] Hos. 13:8; Is. 1:15; Jer. 7:16.
[78] Is. 2:19; Am. 2:16; Zeph. 1:15–18.

witnesses to her, but there is little hope that she will repent before the blow falls. She is too hardened already, and the message can but confirm her people in their stubborn way, and set in high relief their persistent rejection of Yahweh's will. Desolation, exile and near extinction must come to purge away the dross. Before God's world can come to be, man's world must come to an end.[79]

SALVATION AND ESCHATOLOGY

"The Day of Yahweh," says Amos, "shall be darkness and not light." Other prophets such as Isaiah and Joel picture the awfulness of that Day in unforgettable terms.[80] But clearly Amos and the others are overturning a popular expectation that on the day when Yahweh exhibits his power by intervening on behalf of his people, the crisis of their history will be resolved in victory. As von Rad has shown, we have here an echo of the tradition of the "holy war."[81] This expectation seems to have been reinforced by the cultic celebration of *the Day*, the New Year's festival, when Yahweh's victory at Creation over the primeval forces of chaos was celebrated.[82]

There seems little doubt that on this two-fold foundation the cult prophets fostered an expectation that Israel's future was to be *shalom*—victory, well-being—or, in Amos' term, "light." Jeremiah observed sadly that they prophesied "*Shalom!, Shalom!*" when in fact *shalom* did not lie ahead. His own conflict with the priests and prophets of the Jerusalem temple was precisely on this issue, and also his confrontation with his colleague Hananiah.[83] Oracles proclaiming disaster to Israel's enemies unaccompanied by any criticism of Israel herself, as in Obadiah, Nahum, and Ps. 60:6-8 (EVV), may with probability be attributed to these spokemen of a religious

[79] Am. 3:9; Is. 1:2; 6:9, 10; 1:21–26.
[80] Am. 5:18; Is. 2:10–19; Jl. 2:1–11; cf. Is. 13:6–8; Ezek. 30:1; Zeph. 1:7–18.
[81] G. von Rad, *Old Testament Theology*, ii, 1965, p. 123.
[82] S. Mowinckel, *He that Cometh*, 1955, p. 132.
[83] Jer. 6:14; 26:1–15; 28:1–16.

nationalism. Indeed, in Amos 1–2 a series of such oracles is introduced to show with remorseless logic that Yahweh's judgment must
fall on the *sinful* nation, whether alien or not.

There is not sufficient evidence to show whether, in the popular
expectation, the "Day" of Yahweh's saving intervention was near.
The prophets certainly declared its imminence, as they revised its
meaning. They were sure that Yahweh must soon show his power
over his people because the moral and religious situation demanded
it, and unheeded afflictions gave warning of a final catastrophe.
Yahweh was about to show himself in his unmistakable character, by action in events determinative of the future. Israel would
be brought face to face with the awful reality of his righteousness,
and then her sinful condition, not her formal covenant status,
would decide the outcome. At the very least, she would be chastised,
and her dross purged away as in a refiner's fire.[84] But the coming
of Yahweh meant a new outpouring of his mercy as well as of his
righteous judgments. He would sift out the good as well as the
evil. "On that day Yahweh of hosts will become a glorious crown
and a beautiful diadem to the remnant of his people; a spirit of
justice to him that gives judgment, and of valor to those who turn
back the tide of battle at the city-gate."[85]

Isaiah here touches on his well-known doctrine of "the Remnant,"[86] a spiritual kernel of Yahweh's people which has survival
value in his sight. Its basic quality is faithfulness, and the patient
waiting for Yahweh that shows unshakable trust. On these conditions alone may men join the company of those whom disaster
cannot overwhelm. In Hosea and Jeremiah the thought of Yahweh's
mercy is much to the fore. But Hosea speaks sadly of Yahweh's
inevitable withdrawal until Israel repents, and Jeremiah of inescapable chastisement. "The people that escapes from the sword shall

[84] Am. 5:18, 20; 2:16; 3:14; 8:9; Is. 2:11–19; Hos. 5:9; Mic. 2:4; Zeph. 1:7–18;
Jer. 30:7.
[85] Is. 28:5–6.
[86] Cf. Is. 7:3; 10:20–21; 8:16–18; 30:15.

find grace in the wilderness," because "with everlasting love I have loved you." Yahweh's healing mercy will be present even in his judgment. When the nation's pride is broken his anger will vanish and his love will be like refreshing dew on the sun-baked earth.[87]

This hope and promise, however, does not contemplate simply a restoration of a state of blessedness after the purging judgment. The prophets look to a new beginning for Israel, and to a new relationship with Yahweh; not a renewal of the old covenant but a *new covenant*. This becomes most explicit in words of Jeremiah which echoed down the centuries to the time of the writers of that collection of Christian writings which became known as "the New Covenant (Testament)": "See, the days are coming, says Yahweh, when I will make a new covenant . . . , not like the old covenant which I made with their fathers . . . my covenant which they broke. . . . But this is the covenant which I will make with the house of Israel . . . : I will put my law within them, and I will write it upon their hearts; and I will be their God, and they shall be my people. And no longer shall each teach his neighbor and his brother, saying, 'Know Yahweh!', for they shall all know me . . . and I will forgive their iniquity and remember their sin no more."[88]

As von Rad puts it, the prophets share "the conviction that Israel's previous history with Yahweh has come to an end, and that he will start something new with her . . . the hitherto existing saving ordinances have lost their worth. . . . The prophets' message had its centre and its bewildering dynamic effect in the fact that it smashed in pieces Israel's existence with God up to the present, and rang up the curtain of history for a new action on his part with her."[89]

[87] Hos. 2:14–23; 5:5–7; 14:4–7; Jer. 3:12–13; 31:2–6.
[88] Jer. 31:31–34. Cf. Heb. 8:6–13; 10:16–17; 12:24; Gal. 4:22–31.
[89] G. von Rad, *Old Testament Theology*, i, 1962, p. 128.

7

THE PROPHETS AND HISTORY

The religion of Israel was historically oriented to a degree that was unique among contemporary religions. The documents of her distinctive beliefs as we have them in the Old Testament are gathered around a national story set in chronological time. The beginnings of Israel as a chosen people of God are traced to a specific event—her deliverance from Egypt under the prophetic leadership of Moses and her constitution through covenant as a society related to Yahweh in a unique way. Her beginnings could be traced still further back—still in broadly chronological continuity—to the call of Abraham and even to the Creation. This backward look of tradition, however, was by no means all. There was also a looking toward the future, to a Day when Yahweh would again intervene to deliver his people from all their tribulations.

The prophets made a major contribution to this historical consciousness of Israelite faith. They too remember the significant past of tradition. In the nature of the case they speak much of the future. But in a new way they stress historical events of the *present* moment, the *immediate* past and the *near* future. History for them is not simply a continuity from the beginnings to a hoped-for consummation. It is what Yahweh is doing *now*, within the experience of the present generation. They talk of Israel's life as it is, under the pressure of earthquakes, droughts, threats of invasion, corruption among rulers and ruled—and the failures of inherited religious institutions. History for them was not just the sacred tradition, though it included this. It was the arena where living men must be aware of *God as alive and at work*, if they were to know God at all.

Yet the Old Testament has no word for "history," or at least no single term as wide-ranging as the English word has become, denoting both the sequence of events and their record. Terms equivalent to more restricted meanings of the word do occur, such as that aptly translated "chronicles," and those meaning "memory" or "memorial."[1] The "chronicles" of a king's reign recorded events selected for their intrinsic importance, and doubtless also for their value in enhancing the ruler's reputation or otherwise serving the purpose of the chronicler. Memorial records of individuals or of how Israel came into being as a people, stories of persons, events and occasions from the past which were significant for later times embody the recollection of memorable experiences in a continuum of social tradition which is the essence of history. Yet Israel had apparently had no idea of "history" as an abstract concept, in spite of her undeniable feeling for historical experience as an aspect of reality.

The Old Testament is certainly characterized by the historical quality of its thought, as distinguished from mythological, mystical or metaphysical understandings of the reality with which men have to do. Hebrew faith and its literature are centered on a particular history of God's dealings with men, and on an interpretation of that history which becomes a way to the understanding of all history. "The self-manifestation of Yahweh in the history of Israel and of the world is for Israel the starting-point of all faith and all theology."[2] God had shown his presence and power in events of human history as normally experienced, rather than in miraculous intervention from

---

[1] *dibrē hayyāmīm*, 1 Kg. 14:19; *zēker*, Ex. 17:14; *zikkārōn*, Mal. 3:16.
[2] R. Rendtorff in *Offenbarung als Geschichte*, ed. W. Pannenberg, 1961, p. 41. Cf. G. von Rad, *O.T. Theology*, vol. ii, 1965, p. 418: "For Israel, history consisted only of Jahweh's self-revelation by word and action."

a supernatural realm. Man's temporal experience is not an illusion, for in it he meets the final fact of a God known by his activities in experienced events, which are recognized and interpreted by prophetic insight. The "acts" of Yahweh are shown to be such by the Word of Yahweh through his messengers.

The prophets of the eighth and seventh centuries made a special contribution to this religious understanding of experience and to the philosophy—or rather, the *theology*—of history derived from it. In doing so they developed a distinctive feature of the religious tradition which goes back to the creative historian of the "J" document in the Pentateuch, and probably to the prophetic genius of Moses. The new thing in the prophets was their awareness of the currents of world history which flowed around the Israel of their own day, and which were being used by Yahweh in his further dealings with his people. Israel's history with God was no water-tight compartment enclosing her special covenant story. She must come to terms with the fact that the Yahweh who had brought Israel from Egypt also had brought the Philistines from Caphtor and the Syrians from Kir.[3] The meaning of Israel's history lay not alone in her distinctive tradition but also in her experience of, and response to, Yahweh's present judgments and mercies in the wider world, where, too, he was Lord.

THE INTERPRETATION OF HISTORY

"History," says Tillich, "is the totality of remembered events, which are determined by free human activity and are important for the life of human groups."[4] This definition brilliantly combines the subjective and objective meanings of the word. History is the current of events, but *remembered* events, whether in the living memory, in tradition or in some form of record. These events are selected for record or preserved in memory because they are felt to have an importance beyond the moment of their happening, and such valuation opens the way to different interpretations of events as men's

[3] Am. 9:7.
[4] In *The Kingdom of God and History*, ed. J. H. Oldham, 1938, p. 108.

interests and standards of value differ. Again, history has to do with events "determined by free human activity," i.e., with what happens in, and as a result of, man's decisions and actions under given conditions. Yet "Nature, too," Tillich acknowledges, "has a share in the making of human history, . . . but nature itself has no history because it has no freedom."[5] It is in man's autonomy of decision and response —even within limits—that there lies the new and unique, unpredictable and unrepeatable element which distinguishes human history.[6]

Thus we may define history as the record and interpretation of significant human experience. Only in a restricted sense can we speak of the life-*history* of an individual; it is with events remembered for their importance "for the life of human groups," as Tillich says, with which we are primarily concerned. The on-going life of a self-conscious community has its own memory which powerfully affects its character and actions, much as in the case of the individual. Indeed, a community's living tradition, together with its political organization and social ethic, contributes even more largely to its self-consciousness than do race, language and dominant religion. A group without significant, formative memories is sub-historical, and even an historically self-conscious community has many members in whom this consciousness is dim. Further, "the pure fact is not as such historical. It only becomes historical when it can be brought into relation with a social tradition,"[7] i.e., with the common memory which relates a living past to a living present.

Thus the historian's task is wider than the establishment, as exactly as possible, of the facts of what has happened, and the conditions under which it happened. He must look for meanings, causes and consequences, so that the event becomes significant in a stream of events which ultimately reaches the point where the historian stands. Inevitably, he will have his *own* "way of envisaging and correlating

---

[5] *Op cit.*, p. 108. But cf. C. Oman, *On the Writing of History*, 1906, p. 2: "One cannot eradicate physical phenomena in the world from the sphere of historical enquiry."
[6] "History is not shaped by physical events simply, but by events compounded with ideas."—C. R. North, *The O.T. Interpretation of History*, 1946, p. xii.
[7] Christopher Dawson in *The Kingdom of God and History*, p. 200.

a certain series of events," so that "history is not a purely objective thing."[8] "History involves two distinct operations," says Professor Shotwell, "one of which, investigation, is in the field of science, while the other, the literary presentation, is in the field of art."[9] The former has come into its own only since the eighteenth century, but the latter, which is as old as the historical consciousness, has not been and cannot be displaced; for the historian must interpret the events and conditions he is describing in the light, not only of other historical facts, but of *all facts* so far as he knows them, and of all truth, so far as he understands it.[10] If his understanding is very limited, or if he deliberately adapts his story to serve some special interest or support some thesis, the picture will be to that degree distorted. But even the most impartial writer cannot pass an entirely objective judgment upon his subject matter, which largely comprises the words and actions of other men.

There is a division among historians as to whether the emphasis should be on the scientific or on the artistic, interpretive part of their task. "History is a science, no less and no more," declares Bury roundly; "claiming for history," as Wood comments in quoting him, "the same standards of impartiality or disinterestedness, the same endeavour after accuracy of measurement, as are characteristic of physics."[11] Oman declares that history "is the investigation of evidence . . . about series of events concerning which we are able to make some conclusion. (It) is not a tale of logical processes or necessary evolutions, but a series of interesting happenings."[12] But, asks

[8] As Oman, who has no use for philosophies of history, admits in *op. cit.*, pp. 7, 8; cf. p. 213: "It is the bias of interpretation which makes what we may really call 'history,' which is a way of looking at facts rather than a recapitulation of them."

[9] *Enc. Brit.*, 13th ed., 1926, p. 527.

[10] "There are no bare facts for the historian. The observer's inevitable interpretation of the event may become, in turn, a new 'fact' of history." H. W. Robinson, *The O.T., Its Making and Meaning*, 1937, p. 76.

[11] J. B. Bury, as quoted by H. G. Wood in *Christianity and the Nature of History*, 1934, p. 12.

[12] Oman: *op. cit.*, pp. 7, 9.

Weiser, "how do 'happenings' become 'history'?" He answers, "when a more-than-individual linkage of spirit becomes visible, by which separate events gain meaning and relation: 'history' is happenings that have become meaningful."[13]

When men find meanings and values in history, they do so in relation to some philosophical or religious viewpoint. This they believe provides them with a moral standard and a frame of reference outside history, and with a clue to its understanding as a whole. The interpretive element is more than the personal approach of the writer; it is a coherent scheme of things into which the facts of history appear to fit, and which they illustrate. Certain events, conditions and persons are seen to be *momentous*, because they are important or even decisive in a stream of historical experiences which, *as a whole*, has direction and meaning. Past events are not a miscellaneous succession, heterogeneous and irrelevant, but find order, unity and immediate relevance in a scheme of things which embraces human experience past and present. Meaningful history is part of the present environment of life.

The distinctively religious interpretation of history sees man's social (as well as his individual) life as the arena of the moral judgments of God, and the course of history, with all its relativity and ambiguities, as ultimately conforming to the Will of God. It recognizes man's freedom, and the conflict of one man's will with the wills of other men, with circumstances, and with the active purpose of God. It recognizes, too, an inexplicable element of tragedy in man's experience, an element which marks also God's own relationship to his world. It is aware of the presence and activity of God in persons and events, and in the continuing stream of a community's life. Finally, it finds the meaning of human life, past, present and future, in its relationship to One who makes himself known under the conditions of time but who is not bound by those conditions, and in whose hands are the issues of life.

[13] A. Weiser, *Glaube und Geschichte im A.T.*, 1931, p. 20.

NATURE RELIGION AND HISTORICAL RELIGION

The groundwork of the religious interpretation of history is laid in the Old Testament, and its deepest insights are to be found in the words of the prophets. Indeed, the central religion of the Bible is inseparably bound up with certain historical events of which, among other things, it is the interpretation. "What distinguishes the prophetic view of history is that it is coherent, morally conditioned and purposive. . . . Israel was the pioneer of history-writing, and became so by virtue of its religion."[14] The reality of God in temporal experience, and the recognition of his characteristic activity in what happens and what has happened with decisive consequences in the past, mark it as an historical religion.

Within the Israelite people itself a mortal struggle developed between the proponents of a form of nature religion not essentially different from that of neighboring peoples, and the representatives of the distinctively Israelite historical tradition. The forms of worship and religious practices were in many respects, especially in earlier times, those of nature religion, and to the end this left upon them its indelible mark. Clear-cut historical religion challenged nature religion most strongly in the phenomenon of prophecy, and eventually modified the cult-forms and transformed the meaning given them.[15] Prophecy further demonstrated its religious independence of any particular cult-forms and actual shrines. For this reason the religion of Israel did not perish when its sanctuary was destroyed, but lived to pass on its torch to the super-national religious communities of Judaism and Christianity.

The nature religion made its most direct impact upon Israel in the religion of the Canaanites among whom the Israelites settled after their conquest of the land. From incidental allusions to it in the Old Testament, as well as from its influence upon the popular religion of Israel, it seems clear that Canaanite religion conformed to a general

[14] Lindblom, *Prophecy in Ancient Israel*, pp. 324–26.
[15] Cf. A. C. Welch, *Prophet and Priest in Old Israel*, 1936, Chap. III.

pattern of beliefs and practices found at the time in Mesopotamia, Egypt and Syria. This religion sought to understand man's natural environment as a manifestation of divine powers, and to influence, if not to control, that environment in man's interests. Two supreme principles or powers were believed to reside in the natural-divine environment—that of sexual fertility derived by observation from animal life, and that of death and resurrection derived from the cyclic process of vegetation. Man sought through myth and ritual "in an imitative participation in the archetypical,"[16] to relate himself effectively to these divine forces of nature in order to secure the constant renewal of the life of his family, and the life of animals and vegetation on which his sustenance depended. Other aspects of nature, too, impressed him as the work of divine powers, to be related in some way to the life forces: the regular rhythm of day and night and of the seasons, and the heavenly bodies which appeared to govern it, together with the occasional catastrophes of storm and drought, fire and flood, famine and pestilence.

There is no space here to discuss the many and various forms assumed by this nature religion, in official national cults and in popular religious practice. It will suffice to mention certain elements which mark its fundamental difference from the historical religion which appeared in Israel. In the first place, its gods and goddesses were personified natural forces who had come into being, according to the different mythologies, from the ground-stuff of nature. They were not the ultimate reality, and there had been a time when there were no gods. Though the creation of the known physical world was the work at a later stage of a god or gods, this creation was not thought of as the beginning of a forward movement of human history, but as the initiation of the recurrent cycles of the natural world.[17] For "nature-religion finds the divine . . . in those aspects of [the world] which are recurrent, and may be regarded as exemplifications of unchanging laws, and not in the particular and non-recurrent

---

[16] W. Pannenberg, in *O.T. Hermeneutics*, p. 320. Cf. *idem.*, pp. 315–16.
[17] Cf. Weiser: *op. cit.*, pp. 23 ff.

events which make up history. . . . The Hebrew prophets . . . repudiated all such worship. The ground for this is clear. Nature is in itself
non-moral as it is non-personal. History is the sphere in which character counts and moral issues are involved. It is, therefore, the proper
sphere for the revelation of a God who is personal and cares for
righteousness."[18]

There could thus be no question of a personal and moral relationship between the nature gods and their worshippers, or of any
meaning in events beyond their indication that the gods were for
the moment pleased, indifferent or angry. This religion required the
performance of certain "religious" acts and the observance of certain
taboos; the only sin was failure to fulfil the cultic requirements. For
the whole apparatus of the cult was essentially a kind of sympathetic
magic, which, *if correctly performed*, would harness the divine forces
for the satisfaction of human desires. This left no place for the qualitative measurement of life, or for rational and moral continuity
between the experiences of succeeding generations. The community
undoubtedly remembered past events, but it had no history, no past
alive with meaning. For it lived always in the revolving circle of the
present.

On the other hand, as James Barr puts it, "in Hebrew thought the
sequence of historical events, or of some historical events, is a purposive movement toward a goal; it is certainly not cyclic in the sense
of something recurrent, but is non-recurrent, non-reversible and
unique." Barr makes the point, however, that it is not strictly correct
to call this a linear view of time, as is often done, in sharp contrast
to a cyclical view. The Hebrews too were sensitive to the rhythms of
"seedtime and harvest, cold and heat, summer and winter, day and
night," and of "festival times, and days and years."[19] We might say
that for them time was a meandering stream, ever turning back
upon itself and yet moving on irreversibly to its goal. Even that is
not the whole story, for von Rad is undoubtedly right when he

[18] C. H. Dodd, in *The Kingdom of God and History*, p. 21.
[19] J. Barr, *Biblical Words for Time*, 1962, pp. 139–42; Gen. 8:22; 1:14.

remarks that Israel's "experience of what we call time and ours are different." What *we* call past, present and future were inter-penetrating. The future was so vividly present to the prophets that they could speak of it as something which Yahweh *has done*: e.g., "therefore my people have gone into captivity" (Is. 5:13). The past was past, but it was not over and done with. It could be relived, as is evident in the (to us) strange sequence of pronouns in the ritual for presenting first-fruits in Deut. 26:5–11: "My father (!) was a wandering Aramean who went down into Egypt and sojourned there few in number (!), and there *he* became a nation, great mighty and populous. And the Egyptians treated *us* harshly. . . . Then *we* cried to Yahweh the God of our fathers . . . and Yahweh brought *us* out of Egypt . . . and gave *us* this land. . . . And *now* I bring the first of the fruit of the ground which thou, O Yahweh, hast given *me*."[20]

The power of Yahweh was seen in nature, but he was not identified with natural forces, for he was before them. There was in Israel no theogony, or tale of Yahweh's origin. Creation provided the setting primarily for human history and for Yahweh's revelation of his will in that history,[21] and only in a secondary way the setting for the ceaseless round of growth and decay, of life and death and resurrection. Even the cult legends (as Weiser remarks)[22] are in their character not mythological but historical, and connect the holy places and ceremonies to a living tradition of the religious community. Into man's experience of the changeless natural rhythm had come something that was not part of it, something *new* under the sun. At the Red Sea and at Sinai, Yahweh had shown himself in a novel and different way as a novel and different god, relating himself to the world of experience through unique events with no dependence upon the cycle of nature.

These events, and those that succeeded them, gave to Israel the historical consciousness and perspective which set her free (if she

[20] Cf. G. von Rad, *Old Testament Theology*, vol. ii, 1965, pp. 99, 104.
[21] Cf. J. Hempel, *Gott und Mensch in A.T.*, 1926, p. 65.
[22] Weiser: *op. cit.*, pp. 35 ff.

would accept her freedom) from enslavement to the perpetual round of existence. They did so, in the first place, by creating a people on a basis other than race or territory, the basis of a religion essentially new because of the distinctive content given it by Moses. The people had an historical origin at a point in time which was not at the beginning of all things, and a subsequent history organically related to this origin. Time as event and as duration could thus be measured qualitatively; it became something more than perpetual succession. The meaning of religion was seen in the light of particular events recognized as acts of God. A significant past had determinative effect in the present and for the future.

In the second place, this historical quality distinguished the higher Israelite conception of God and of the community's relationships with him. "The presuppositions of the historical lie in its concept of God."[23] Yahweh was a deity not bound to physical nature, nor confined to self-manifestation through natural phenomena and priests who interpreted these as omens. He was the free, living, active God participating in events to make them historic. He made known his nature and will through prophets who stood in the midst of history and disclosed its significance. As Ps. 103:7 puts it: "He made known his ways to Moses, his acts to the people of Israel." Barr comments: "If God had not talked with Moses and identified himself, and told Moses what he intended to do, then the children of Israel would not have tried to leave Egypt and there would have been no divine act of deliverance."[24] The terms of the divine part in the making of history are *personal*—will, purpose, concern, justice, mercy—rather than simply the supernatural power and mystery that hedge divinity. The will and purpose with which Yahweh confronted his people at the supreme moment of the Exodus remained characteristic of him in his subsequent dealings with them, and in his insistent moral demands upon the nation of his special choice.

The relationship of such a god to his people was therefore not

[23] W. Pannenberg, in *Old Testament Hermeneutics*, p. 316.
[24] J. Barr, *Old and New in Interpretation*, 1966, p. 77.

formal, mechanical, magical, but intelligent, ethical and personal. The framework of association was not the cult but the "covenant," a living structure of personal relationships which traced its inception to an historic occasion when the tribes had become "Israel," the people of Yahweh. Within the terms of the covenant the cult had its place as a form expressing the relationship of worshippers to their god. But what mattered was the reality which it purported to express. This was the obedient response of his worshippers to Yahweh's will in their daily social behavior, and their confident trust in his power to save his people from calamity and to achieve through them his historic purpose.

THE LIVING TRADITION OF ISRAEL

"You only have I known of all the families of the earth: therefore I will visit upon you all your iniquities."[25] Amos and his hearers drew radically different conclusions from premises which they held in common, viz., the tradition of Yahweh's unique relationship to Israel and to her history. This tradition is of great importance as the background, not only of the prophets' appeals to past mercies and warnings, but of their own advance in the understanding of the historical quality of religious experience.

The elements of the tradition are familiar from the compendious religious history which, introduced by Genesis, follows from Exodus to the end of 2 Kings an ostensibly continuous narrative. This narrative in its present form is composed of different types of material from various periods—including the large sections of legal matter in the Pentateuch—and it came to its present form after the time of the great prophets, and to a considerable extent under their influence. The significant thing is that there stands in the forefront of the religious documents of Israel, as the *rationale* of her cult, her ethic and her social organization, this document which is both history and doctrine. The beliefs and customs of the religious society are ordered

[25] Am. 3:2.

and unified on an historical principle, and related to momentous occasions and unique individual experiences in the past of a continuing community.

It is further significant that this doctrinal history in its final form follows the lines of the much earlier versions of the national story known as J and E, large portions of which it incorporates. There is some reason to suppose that the prose narratives of J and E are in turn dependent upon cycles of national ballads with similar purpose and content.[26] The fragments of this ballad literature which remain have a noteworthy connection with important episodes of the national-religious epic; e.g., the Red Sea deliverance, Ex. 15:21; journeys and battles before and during the conquest of Canaan, Ex. 17:16; Num. 10:35, 36; 21:14, 15, 27–30; Jos. 10:12b, 13; Jg. 5.

The prophetic writings themselves bear witness to the contemporary existence of a well-formed and generally recognized religious-historical tradition. Amos refers three times to Israel as the people which Yahweh "brought up out of the land of Egypt"; once to her selection by Yahweh to receive his self-revelation; twice to the forty years in the wilderness, and again to the conquest and occupation of Canaan.[27] Hosea, too, speaks of Israel's religious origins in the period of her Exodus from Egypt, under the leadership of "a prophet"; the period when her "Maker" brought her into being as a people. There are references to "the covenant" and the giving of "the law," to the wilderness sojourn and even to one specific incident at Baal-peor narrated in Num. 25:1–3. From the period after the Conquest Hosea makes special mention of the establishment of the monarchy and the revolution of Jehu.[28]

Isaiah makes no reference to the Exodus tradition; his supreme concern is with the activity of Yahweh in the history of his own time. The book of Micah, in a single passage of somewhat doubtful

[26] Cf. Eissfeldt, *The O.T., an Introduction*, pp. 132–34.
[27] Am. 2:9, 10; 3:1, 2; 5:25; 9:7.
[28] Hos. 2:15; 8:13; 12:9, 13 (EVV); 11:1; 13:4, 5; 12:13; 8:14, 12; 9:3, 10; 8:4; 13:10; 1:4, 5.

authenticity, speaks not only of the deliverance from Egyptian bondage but names Moses, Aaron and Miriam, and goes on to mention the episode of Balak and Balaam.[29] Zephaniah, like Isaiah, does not touch on the tradition. Jeremiah, on the other hand, alludes to the Exodus, to Moses and the giving of the law, to the Covenant, to the wilderness wanderings and the occupation of Canaan, and—in the later period—to Samuel and to the destruction of Shiloh in the Philistine wars.[30]

The prophets, then, were speaking to a people who had a living tradition of historical events and persons through which their distinctive religion had been mediated, and of which it was an interpretation. This remains true in spite of the fact that in practice many of the people had fallen into the ways of nature religion, holding the two in an uneasy association without recognizing their incompatibility. With urgent insistence the prophets reminded them that the first commandment of the religious tradition in virtue of which they were "Israel," was an exclusive loyalty to their peculiar god. Their history was not to be turned into a mythology that had no connection with present experience except to explain its permanent conditions. There must be a living continuity in the character of religion, between the distinctive dynamic elements of the tradition and the present service of Yahweh.

The high points in the national religious tradition, such as the deliverance at the Red Sea and the covenant-making under Moses, embodied and exhibited for all time the central faith of Israel. As von Rad says, "The historical acts by which Jahweh founded the community were absolute. They did not share the fate of all other events, which inevitably slip back into the past. They were actual for each subsequent generation."[31] We should add that they were made actual through constant use in worship as a point of reference, so that, although historical in origin, they served as a powerful symbolic

[29] Mic. 6:4, 5.
[30] Jer. 7:22; 11:7; 31:32; 34:13; 15:1; 2:2 ff.; 7:12; 26:6.
[31] G. von Rad, O.T. *Theology*, vol. ii, p. 104.

myth in the sense of "a lived experience of the significant past reality."[32] So Yahweh became to Israel a God whose righteousness and mercy were known to be displayed in past and present social and personal experience. He had created this people before they had any connection with a land of their own; this almost unique independence goes far to explain how the Jewish people have survived in their Dispersion. They were the people of a covenant, which was a life-relationship with a living God. He was known to them as a personal will at work in the on-going experiences of a living community with its own peculiar origins, self-awareness and expected destiny. Yahweh was known as a Doer of "mighty acts," who told his prophets what he had done, was doing and was about to do.

The primary requirement of the service of such a God was the free response of men to his self-revelation and his commands. He delivered his people that they might serve him; he brought disaster upon them as a result of their neglect and defiance of his will. The consummation of his purpose in history must be seen not only in the light of his justice, his mercy and his proven power, but of the unconditioned freedom with which he chose, and might reject, his people.

This is the inner history of Israel as the prophets read it, the true history, of which they themselves were makers as well as spokesmen.

HISTORY THE SPHERE OF YAHWEH'S ACTION

The prophets and their fellow Israelites were agreed that the great events enshrined in their tradition had been saving, revealing actions of Yahweh. But, in the general view, such events belonged to the past, or to a coming "Day" of final victory and salvation. Men did not discern signs of Yahweh's activity in the present; they grew sceptical of moral values and cynical because nothing seemed to happen to mark his presence in the expected way. "They say in their heart, Yahweh will do neither good nor harm"; "They say, Let him hurry up, let him hasten his work, that we may see it."[33]

[32] R. A. F. MacKenzie, *Faith and History in the Old Testament*, 1963, p. 73.
[33] Zeph. 11:2; Is. 5:19.

To the prophets, on the other hand, the God of the classical tradition was visibly present and active in the present, and his moral demands were immediate. Yahweh would reveal himself in mighty acts of judgment, as truly as in mighty acts of salvation long ago. To the "scoffers" Isaiah retorted: "Yahweh will arise . . . that he may do his work, his strange work, and bring to pass his act, his strange act."[34] If Israel did not discern him it was because they were obsessed with other things: "The harp and the lute, and wine are their feasts; but they regard not the work of Yahweh, neither have they considered the operation of his hands."[35] Yahweh had smitten them with famine and drought, with pestilence and war, but they had not made the obvious deduction. "Does a lion roar in the forest," cried Amos, "when he has no prey? . . . Does disaster fall on a city, and Yahweh has not done it?"[36]

Man's life experience, then, is not wholly determined by its natural environment and circumstances. These are only the setting for God's word and man's response, the choices and actions which mark him off as a man. In the interplay, the struggle and the uniting of wills something happens. It is in this area that Yahweh's will is present as the finally determining factor. Not only is he the author of man's "spirit," his life force; but he himself participates as a personal will of constant righteousness, above and independent of natural processes, injecting himself into critical situations with historic consequences.[37]

Hence, Yahweh's will is the force of history, his purpose provides its continuity and his character its ultimate explanation. Amos summoned Israel to consider the atrocities of the neighboring peoples—and then her own—that she might realize why things happened as they did, and happened to her. "The preaching of the prophets which precedes the coming event," says Zimmerli, "takes away from it the

[34] Is. 28:21. Cf. the translation in the *Jerusalem Bible*, 1966—"his extraordinary deed, . . . his mysterious work."
[35] Is. 5:12.
[36] Am. 4:6–11; 3:4, 6.
[37] Is. 37:7, 33–35.

anonymity of a meaningless stroke of fate."[38] Yahweh must act according to his nature. Isaiah asks almost despairingly: "Why will you be stricken again, that you continue to revolt?"—revolting against a will whose demands are known and whose effective power is visible in a desolate countryside and cities burned with fire.[39] Yahweh is the creator of a world which is more than the physical setting of life—of the world of man's thoughts and actions, the world of his social intercourse and of his people's history. By Yahweh's support that world can be "established"; by his veto all human plans and effort are brought to nought. "It shall not stand, neither shall it come to pass." Man's freedom is limited by the over-ruling purpose which can use an enemy's destructive fury as its unwitting servant, and then "punish the fruit of the stout heart of the king of Assyria, and the glory of his high looks."[40] Destiny is not fixed by the stars; it is not with fate, but with a consistent, personal will, a righteous all-encompassing purpose, that man has to do.

This purpose is sovereign, but it does not come upon man with the crushing weight of an avalanche, meaningless, inexorable and pitiless. It is not sheer power, but is like the strength of maturity in dealing with youth, or of man in training his domestic animals to obedience. What Yahweh does is morally conditioned: "If you are willing and obedient, you shall eat the good of the land; but if you refuse and rebel, you shall be devoured by the sword."[41] For the moral law expressed in the ethical conditions of Yahweh's worship is the solvent and the ferment of social history. The words of Yahweh in the prophet's mouth are real forces at work among the nations "to pluck up and to break down and to destroy and to overthrow—*and* to build and to plant."[42]

The peoples of the earth strove to make themselves secure by eco-

---

[38] W. Zimmerli, in *O.T. Hermeneutics*, p. 102.
[39] Am. 1, 2; Is. 1:5–7.
[40] Is. 7:7, 9; 10:5–19.
[41] Is. 1:2, 3, 19, 20.
[42] Jer. 1:10.

nomic domination, by armaments and alliances, in the struggle for self-perpetuation which became a struggle for power. But the area of social history was precisely the area where Yahweh's power was most evident, where his guidance and support were indispensable. So it was "Woe to the rebellious children, saith Yahweh, that take counsel, but not of me. . . . Woe to them that go down to Egypt for help, and rely on horses, and trust in chariots because they are many . . . but they look not to the holy one of Israel. Now the Egyptians are men, and not God; and their horses flesh and not spirit: and when Yahweh shall stretch out his hand both he that helps shall stumble, and he that is helped shall fall."[43] Thus when Jeremiah learns of the battle of Carchemish where Egypt and the Neo-Babylonian power were locked in a contest for world supremacy, he declares that it is no ordinary day; "for that day is a day of the Lord Yahweh of hosts, a day of vengeance, that he may avenge himself upon his adversaries."[44] And Isaiah predicts that the Assyrian wars will be a winnowing process, in which Israel will learn by the action of God in history wherein lies the sole security for the nation's life: "And it shall come to pass in that day that the remnant of Israel . . . shall no more lean for support upon him that smote them [Assyria], but shall lean upon Yahweh, the holy one of Israel, in truth."[45]

History, then, is to the prophets the area of Yahweh's free purposive action. The meaning of social experience, past and present, is to be found in the truth about God, about his nature, his purpose and his part in what happens in the world. Good and ill are not predetermined; nor do they fall out by chance. Moral distinctions are real. Their consequences are evident and ultimately inevitable because Yahweh is who he is, and his power is what it is. With evil and with evil-doers he has a perpetual controversy, and heaven and

[43] Is. 30:1; 31:1, 3.
[44] Jer. 46:2–10.
[45] Is. 10:20.

earth are called to witness that his accusations are just.[46] Israel, like other nations, must face the reality of Yahweh's justice; his choice of her means peculiar responsibility, not unmoral privilege: "See, I will set a plumb-line in the midst of my people Israel. . . . Are you not like the people of Ethiopia to me? . . . See, the eyes of the Lord Yahweh are upon the sinful people [whichever it is], and I will destroy it from off the face of the earth." Israel still looks to Yahweh's past actions in history as the basis of her present religion and life. She will learn that that basis itself is under his scrutiny; that his present action, not his action in the past, will determine national fortunes in accordance with his truth.[47]

THE INTERPRETATION OF SIGNIFICANT MOMENTS

The historian attempts to find some rational or moral principle of order in remembered social experience. He finds clues to such a principle in particular occasions and events, in personal and social decisions which have a significance beyond themselves because they affect the future, and perhaps "change the course of history." In these moments the elemental forces which determine history's course disclose themselves, and enable men to reflect upon their total experience in the light of that disclosure. The past gains meaning in itself, and meaning also for man's understanding of the present situation in which he must live, decide and act.

The Israelite tradition was pivoted upon certain events of the Exodus, the Covenant-making at Sinai and the Conquest, which were decisive in their effect, but which also were extraordinary in themselves. They were "signs" and "wonders." The plagues of Egypt, the crossing of the "Reed" Sea and the phenomena at Sinai can be explained as natural events arrayed in the hues of legend. They became legendary, firstly because they were awe-inspiring, and sec-

---

[46] Hos. 4:1 ff.; Is. 1:2 ff.
[47] Am. 7:7, 8; 9:7, 8; cf. Am. 1, 2, and Is. 29:14.

ondly because they belonged to a unique series of happenings with profound religious consequences. As a result of them an actual historical people with a distinctive religion came into being. The meaning of its history became visible. This *meaning* gave unity and order to the tradition which was now so largely the mould of Israel's self-consciousness as a people.

With respect to the main events of the tradition the prophets and their hearers would be in general agreement. But the former were alive, as the latter were not, to the fact that the self-disclosure of Yahweh through unusual and disturbing (but non-miraculous) events had not ceased long ago. Earthquake and drought in the natural environment, famine and pestilence and war in the community's recent life, were acts of Yahweh. Like his deeds of old, they expressed his character and purpose. His reality was making itself felt in the world of historical experience, where, unlike the nature gods, he disclosed his distinctive presence and power. "Yet the people have not turned to him who smote them . . . they say in pride and arrogance, the bricks have fallen, but we will rebuild with hewn stone."[48] They had come to associate Yahweh too exclusively with the events of the tradition, and especially with its extraordinary elements, often heightened in legend to the miraculous.

To the prophets, on the other hand, Yahweh's ancient deeds were of a piece with his activity in the present. His participation in the affairs of his people belonged not only to the original, creative epoch, and to a future "Day" of his return in power. It was constant, and the course of his struggle with and for his people had been continuous up to and including the present. As the past had been charged with meaning for that time and for the time to come, so current history was to be seen as current revelation.[49] Israel's was a living rather than a static tradition. Past and present were not merely successive. They

---

[48] Is. 9:13, 10; cf. Am. 4:6–11. Note the contrast between the recurrent festivals of the cult and Yahweh's new deed, Is. 29:1 ff.
[49] Cf. Is. 6:1; 14:28, where a turning point in social history becomes an occasion of revelation.

were to be measured in qualitative terms, in the light of the known character of Yahweh, the living God.

This purpose and power of Yahweh, evident in current events and conditions, had become supremely real and luminous to these prophetic spokesmen in their "call." That intense personal experience was an event among other events; it, too, was a "fact of history." As Weiser points out,[50] it was not a blessed, mystic experience of union with the *being* of God; it was rather a convulsive moment when the prophet felt himself plunged into God's activity. Here and now was his dynamic presence, unquestionably real and active, and able "to make things happen," in what would happen. It was a presence in which the prophet was awed by the majesty of Yahweh's holy will, made vividly aware of human weakness and folly, and convinced of Yahweh's purpose to "make history" now as he had done long before.

The "call" was a supreme moment in experience in which the truth about all of life became evident. In the light of it the prophet surveyed the current scene, and was able to bear his witness. He was not a puppet, but a conscious instrument. Though similar "ecstatic" moments sometimes recurred, it is clear that these were occasional, and that the prophet's ministry was governed rather by the memory of Yahweh's summons, and by the fact that he stood in the line of succession of Yahweh's messengers.

What was given him as new was the "word" of Yahweh, and this— not his own teaching—was to be the effective power at work in his world and in his time. It set the processes of history in motion, as when Jeremiah at Yahweh's word laid stones to be the foundation upon which the throne of a future conqueror would be erected.[51] The "word" was the concrete expression of Yahweh's personal will. And the moment when the word came to the prophet was uniquely significant in his life as part of the life of his people. It displayed the meaning, and loosed the power of Yahweh's action. It brought together the two aspects of Israel's history: the tradition of Yahweh's

[50] Weiser: *op. cit.*, p. 81.
[51] Jer. 1:9, 10; 43:8 ff.; see chap. 5.

decisive, constitutive acts which had created this people in a particular epoch of the past and the consciousness of Yahweh as a living
God, always "present in the present," his will meeting the wills of
men and the collective will of the community. He was "a God at
hand, and not a God far off" (Jer. 23:23), a God who met men most
directly, not in the sanctuary, but in the actual, concrete experience
of life in which their history was being made. His "Day" would be a
revealing, transforming, catastrophic moment of divine self-disclosure
on the plane of history.

THE RELIGIOUS IMPORTANCE OF THE PRESENT

The prophets thus placed unusual emphasis on the religious importance of the present in which they and their auditors lived, in
contrast to unwarranted reliance upon tradition and an equally unwarranted optimism as to the future. In some way the past and the
future were part of that present. The resulting difficulties in trans-
lating the Hebrew tenses are well known, and they indicate a different way of apprehending time and its passing. There is, indeed,
recognition of time as *duration*, long or short;[52] of time as marked by
repetition of events,[53] and by the succession of cause and effect.[54]
Phrases like "the former time" and "the latter time"[55] clearly differ-
entiate past and future from the present. But, as is shown by the
verb forms, thought is concentrated upon the action or event itself,
as begun, continuing or completed. Time contains the total experience. Past and future are extensions of the present, and (so to speak)
are *present in* the present.

This is particularly important for understanding prophetic thought.
One familiar example is the so-called "prophetic perfect," the use of
the perfect tense, as of a completed act, to express the prophet's

---

[52] Is. 6:11; Jer. 29:28; Is. 10:25.
[53] Jer. 7:25.
[54] Am. 3:3 ff.
[55] Is. 9:1 (EVV), cf. *The Old Testament, an American Translation*: "days gone
by," and "time to come."

certainty of what Yahweh is about to do. Another example is the way in which the prophets speak as if their hearers had committed the sins of their ancestors: "Your fathers . . . went far from me . . . and I brought *you* into a land of plenty . . . therefore will I still accuse *you* . . . and your children's children"; "because your fathers forsook me . . . and *you* have done evil more than your fathers . . . therefore will I cast *you* forth."[56] The psychic solidarity of the whole includes all the generations, just as it includes the three or four generations living at one time. There is thus peculiar force in the address of Isaiah to his Judaean contemporaries: "You rulers of Sodom . . . you people of Gomorrah." As the youth lives in the man, so the nation's past and future are embraced in its present consciousness: "I am Yahweh thy God from the land of Egypt; I will again cause thee to live in tents."[57]

Because of their overpowering certainty of Yahweh's intercourse with themselves, his present activity in current social history seemed obvious to the prophets. Immediately after Jeremiah's call and commission, he discerned "signs" of what Yahweh was about to do.[58] They were able to identify the God of their ecstatic experience with the God of Israelite tradition, and, indeed, we may say that the experience was inevitably conditioned by their own possession of the tradition. But it was the *essence* of the tradition which concerned them, viz., the nature of Yahweh as a God of ethical will, showing himself in historic events and through individual prophets and leaders, and setting moral obedience as the primary condition of his service. The religious quality of these men is demonstrated by this insight; before they became prophets they were of the stuff from which prophets could be made.

To such minds, the past of their people and especially its great occasions of divine action were real and vivid. The evident meaning of the tradition was like a flood-light on the present situation. More-

[56] Jer. 2:5, 7, 9; 16:11–13.
[57] Hos. 12:9 (EVV); cf. Is. 5:1 ff.; 1:10.
[58] Jer. 1:4–16.

over, the future lay in that present, waiting to be revealed. In a world where Yahweh's moral demands were being enforced by the power of his consistent will, the consent or the indifference and rebellion of men brought inevitable results. It is characteristic of the prophetic oracle of doom that its effective conclusion is introduced by "therefore." "You have not returned to me, saith Yahweh. Therefore thus will I do unto thee, O Israel."[59]

The reality of history thus lay in the events in which God participated for his own purposes, not in the temporary successes of man's self-centered will-to-power. "You rejoice in what is nothing, saying, have we not by our own strength captured Karnaim? For I am raising against you a nation, saith Yahweh." An "end" was at hand, though their absorption in immediate profit-seeking beclouded men's minds to the developments which marked Yahweh's presence.[60] The premature rejoicings of the "tumultuous city" failed to take account of the realities of the situation; it was, in fact, a day of ruin. Not outward appearances but moral realities are the determining factors; they are the great and constant fact, because Yahweh too is at work in all that happens. He gives men "signs" of what he is doing, if they have the faith to accept them; "signs" that will be fulfilled as the present unfolds to reveal that which lies hidden in its depths.[61]

The present moment is the focal point of consciousness where a man can apprehend the reality of history in his own experience. Since, in prophetic thought, that reality is determined by Yahweh's part in what happens, history derives its meaning and finds its center in religion. Yahweh "maintains his covenant," apart from which Israel, as Israel, could have neither history nor continuing existence. He is her "Maker" now, as in the beginning.

Thus the meaning of all history is manifest to those who really *know* the history-making God. Repeatedly Hosea declares that the root of the nation's trouble is that she does not know God: "My

[59] E.g., Am. 4:11, 12.
[60] Am. 6:13, 14; 8:1–10.
[61] Is. 22:1–5; 7:10–16; Jer. 1:11 ff.

people are being destroyed for lack of knowledge"; "they did not understand that it was I who healed them." Amos affirms that Yahweh admits the prophets to his confidence, in order that they perceive the movement and direction of events. In an overwhelming experience Isaiah learns that the present reality of God rather than human leagues must be the object of the fear in which, and the confidence by which, men live. Amos and Micah know Yahweh as one who comes out from his sanctuary into the welter of events. To Zephaniah Yahweh *is* righteousness, an unfailing fount of justice welling up within the actual corrupt community. To Jeremiah he is the strength of the believing heart, against which no adversary can prevail; the undefeated God of the covenant, whose will it is that all shall know as a living presence him whose law is written on their heart.[62]

THE CONSUMMATION OF HISTORY

The unity and meaning of history are found in the knowledge of God. The Creator of man and of man's world is the author of his spiritual life and moral consciousness, the fount of justice in the judge and of valor in the soldier.[63] He has made man free, and is seeking to create in man through the instrument of free obedience a quality of life that reflects his own. The forces of overriding importance in human society are therefore not the economic and political, but the psychological, moral and spiritual. The moral law enshrined in the "Covenant" is universally applicable: "For three transgressions of Damascus, of Tyre, of Edom, of *Israel*, yea for four, I will not withdraw it" (i.e., the sentence of doom).[64]

The history of Israel, says Dodd, "is in form the history of a single people; but in intention it is universal history."[65] Jeremiah's commission was to affect the fortunes of nations. Whereas the people

---

[62] Hos. 4:6; 11:3; Am. 3:7; Is. 8:11–13; Am. 1:2; Mic. 1:2–4; Zeph. 3:5; Jer. 1:19; 31:31–34.
[63] Is. 28:6.
[64] Am. 1:3—2:8.
[65] C. H. Dodd, in *The Kingdom of God and History*, p. 18.

scheme to determine their own history by armies and political alliances, Yahweh's power, which is of another sort, overrules them and rebukes their pride. "I will once more do a marvellous work among this people, . . . and the wisdom of their wise men shall perish"; "Woe to those who go down to Egypt for help, and rely on horses, and trust in chariots, . . . but they look not to the Holy One of Israel; . . . yet he also is wise."[66] Nations, like men, can be Yahweh's instruments, wittingly or not. "Assyria, rod of my anger . . . against a godless people will I send him; . . . but not so does he think nor plan; . . . wherefore . . . when Yahweh has finished all that he has to do against Zion . . . I will punish the arrogance of the king of Assyria." Nebuchadrezzar is designated the servant of Yahweh, not as his worshipper but as his agent in international affairs.[67] Yahweh is the fount of all sovereignty, and allots earthly rule as he sees fit. He directs the movements of peoples, and his purpose "is purposed concerning the whole earth."[68]

When the prophets considered Yahweh's sovereignty in history and his ethical purpose, inevitably they were led to the thought of a consummation. For the divine purpose was contradicted by Israel's present life. The divine anger was not a temporary reaction to a particular episode; it must be related to Yahweh's ultimate goal. The sovereign God "must reign until he has put all enemies under his feet." Further, this would be an historical event, in accordance with this God's characteristic way of manifesting his power. That which had broken through here and there from time to time must come in fullness, sweeping all history before it. Short of final victory, judgment is not judgment and salvation is not salvation.

This final self-revelation of God in power will not be the bursting in of sheer supernatural forces, unrelated morally to man's actual

---

[66] Is. 29:14; 31:1, 2.
[67] Is. 10:5–12; Jer. 43:10. Cf. Am. 6:14; Hab. 1:6, and the literary prophecy of Is. 45:1–6.
[68] Jer. 27:4 ff.; Am. 9:7; Is. 14:26, 27.

life. Rather, it is the freeing of life from the contradiction of its essential nature. "Even the stork in the heavens knows her appointed times, . . . but my people know not the law of Yahweh."[69] Israel's disobedience had been unnatural, perverted. Amos tells us how Yahweh had withheld previous judgments at his intercession, but that now "I am about to set a plumb-line in the midst of my people Israel; I will not pass by them any more." That which has always been at work in history must show itself as history's final, all-resolving principle. The "Day" will disclose in power the full reality of that with which men have to do. It will mark the doom of the man-made world which has not taken God into account. "Neither their silver nor their gold shall be able to deliver them in the day of Yahweh's wrath . . . for he will make a terrible annihilation of all that dwell in the earth."[70]

So the historical process will have its summing up. The judgment and the salvation which have been always at hand in Yahweh's presence, but which have become actual only occasionally and in part, now are to appear in full and final form. That which has been affirmed in tradition and is known by faith but which has been obscured by man's self-will and self-assurance, will be manifest in a way that no one can ignore. "Men shall go into the caves of the rock . . . from before the terror of Yahweh and from the glory of his majesty, when he arises to terrify the earth."[71]

The moral urgency of their situation, linked in consciousness with the approach of actual enemies, led the prophets, in the first instance, to speak as if the end were immediately at hand. History seemed at its bursting point. The nearness of the divine reality has the semblance of imminence in time. The climax is impending. "Against this family I am planning evil, . . . for it is an evil time"; "the great Day of Yahweh is near at hand"; "wherefore would you have the Day of Yahweh? It will be darkness, and not light."

[69] Jer. 8:7.
[70] Am. 7:8; Zeph. 1:18.
[71] Is. 2:19.

"The noise shall reach to the ends of the earth, for Yahweh has an issue to settle with the nations."[72]

As noted in the concluding section of the previous chapter, Amos and Zephaniah apparently did not look beyond an immediately impending climax. For them it would be the end of their familiar world. But others of the prophets, though no less certain of the drastic nature of the judgment that was at hand, looked past it to the vindication of Yahweh's ultimate purpose of salvation. In Isaiah we read that Yahweh will "smelt out your dross in the furnace; . . . then will I restore your rulers as at the first, . . . and *afterwards* you shall be called, 'The stronghold of justice, the faithful city.' "[73] Hosea and Jeremiah sensed, beyond the darkness, a new dawn when the *intent* of Israel's history and of the wilderness covenant will become actual, and the salvation of Yahweh be manifest.

This salvation would not be in political terms of national success, but instead in religious terms of the authentic knowledge of God, and the realization of his presence in social righteousness, justice and love.[74] Yet this is no other-worldly, "spiritual" consummation. It belongs to the actual known world, and will have social and economic consequences. Man will find the security he has always lacked and always longed for (and has looked for in the wrong direction), security from hunger, from oppression, from unequal justice and from war.[75] These things, which man has sought in his own wilful way but has failed to find, will, "in that day," be added unto him.

In later writings the *material* blessings of the "Messianic Age" are over-emphasized. But in essence they belong, like the hope of a king of the Davidic family who would be a true vice-gerent of

[72] Mic. 2:3; Zeph. 1:14; Am. 5:18; Jer. 25:31.
[73] Is. 10:22, 20; 1:25, 26, *The Old Testament, an American Translation.*
[74] Hos. 2:18–20; Jer. 31:33, 34.
[75] Mic. 4:1–4; Is. 9:6, 7; 11:1–9; Jer. 23:5, 6; 29:10, 11; 31:4, 5; Hos. 2:18. Some of these passages in their present form may be later than the classical prophets, but the point illustrated is not affected.

Yahweh, to the conception that God's final salvation is to be achieved *within* history. It will not be different in kind from Yahweh's historic acts—his self-manifestation in the election, the deliverances and the judgments which his people had known. Rather, it will be but the completion of what he had begun—a consummation assured by Yahweh's sovereignty, by the consistency of his ethical will and the tireless goodness of his purpose.

8

THE PROPHETS
AND THE SOCIAL ORDER

The prophets were deeply concerned with the nature of the social order in which they lived because of their theology, particularly their doctrine of man and of Yahweh's historic purpose to create for himself a people.[1] The form of its social organization largely determines a people's way of living and even the pattern of its thought. The nature and purposes of political authority, economic and class interests, social institutions of many kinds, the way in which the individual finds his place in the community and adjusts his relations with his fellows, the physical conditions under which the community must maintain its existence—all these (and other) factors profoundly affect the quality of personal relationships and the worth of life itself. With this quality and worth the prophets were deeply concerned.[2] It was for them a religious imperative that society be so ordered as to make possible and to support a way of life which is *good* in the eyes of Yahweh.[3]

This good and right way of life is the *mishpaṭ*, of which Amos says: "Hate evil, but love good and establish justice (*mishpaṭ*) in

---

[1] On this see above, chap. 6, p. 130 ff., and chap. 7, p. 153 ff.
[2] "In the O.T. the central motive of moral life is the sense of community." Th. C. Vriezen, *Outline of O.T. Theology*, 1958, p. 320.
[3] Cf. Jer. 7:3–7; Is. 1:16, 17.

the gate."[4] For a just decision in a particular case helps to define the social good and confirm in social usage the standards which Yahweh upholds. "Woe to those who call evil good, and good evil," says Isaiah.[5] The particular evils which deface society reflect, from the prophets' standpoint, accepted standards which are wrong. The standards are wrong because, in turn, the real object of men's fear and reverence is not Yahweh, God of Israel, but the gods of the material civilization of Canaan.[6]

With the gods of Canaan and the way of life sanctioned by their worship there could be no compromise. As Elijah saw clearly, the nation must choose. It was impossible really to worship Yahweh while adopting the mode of life, the customs and institutions proper to servants of Baal.[7] Israel's national consciousness had been formed by the tradition of Moses and the deliverance from Egypt, the tradition of a covenant with Yahweh which prescribed the *mishpaṭ* of his people.[8] Yahweh was Israel's "Maker"; the foundations of any life which was her own were laid in his *righteousness*, which was the nature and quality of Yahweh's being expressed in his *righteous acts*.[9] A corresponding quality of common life and purpose must characterize his people if they were to be *his* people. His justice (*mishpat*) and his righteousness must flow among them like an unceasing stream; or (changing the metaphor) these were the fruits of their social life he expected to see, as a man in return for his care looks for good grapes from his vineyard.[10] It was the unhappy task of the prophets to declare that the national life could not meet that test. Since the fruit was bad something must be wrong with the vines. The nation had not ordered its ways so as to produce the fruit in life, character and action, which the nature of its pro-

[4] Am. 5:15.
[5] Is. 5:20; cf. Am. 6:12.
[6] Is. 2:7, 8; 8:12, 13.
[7] 1 Kg. 18:21; 21:17 ff., cf. Hos. 8:14.
[8] Jer. 7:21–26; cf. Am. 3:1, 2; Hos. 11:1 ff.; 13:4.
[9] Cf. Pedersen: *Israel*, I II, pp. 336 ff., and Is. 1:21–26; 28:16, 17.
[10] Hos. 1:9; Am. 5:24; Is. 5:1, 2, 7.

fessed religion demanded. With the clear insight and courage of their own faith the prophets proceeded to make plain what had gone wrong.

It is perhaps unnecessary to stress the fact that the prophets were denouncing the evils of the social order under which they themselves lived, and not that of modern Western civilization. It is consequently illegitimate to over-simplify the comparison of their situation and ours, and to transfer their individual sayings from one cultural and religious context to another which is very different, without recognizing the differences. Only as we understand the nature and form of the society the prophets knew, can we properly discern the import of their social message and its relevance today.

THE SOCIAL ORDER OF JUDAH AND ISRAEL

Like every social order, that of the twin kingdoms of Judah and Israel was the joint product of their physical environment and their social history. Canaan was a land which had supported a settled population for centuries. It was on the edge of the desert and constantly subject to inroads from roving desert peoples with their lower standard of living. It formed a land-bridge and a high-road for commerce and war between Egypt and Arabia on the one hand, and Syria, Anatolia and Mesopotamia on the other. The population of Canaan was consequently mixed in race, and its civilization and culture an amalgam whose dominant features had marked resemblances to those of the greater, neighboring nations. Though to the hungry nomad it seemed "a land flowing with milk and honey," it was a small country, much of it was mountainous and arid, and the fertility of the remainder depended on the sufficiency of the rainfall. Often we read of famine following on the heels of drought. In addition to the constant danger of desert raids and conflicts with smaller neighboring peoples, the national existence was made precarious by Canaan's position astride the routes of conquest of the great powers.

Within this physical and cultural environment, the life of the

Hebrew kingdoms had been moulded by the forces and circumstances of their own history. They were a tribal and pastoral people
with a distinctive religion and a strong sense of their own identity,
who had come recently into a long-established community with
many ancient fortified towns. But, though the newcomers were able
after a period to establish political supremacy over the previous
inhabitants of Canaan, and to fight off the Philistines, their only
serious challengers for the power of the state, Israel was less successful in maintaining her own distinctive culture. The way-of-life
of her desert traditions and of her religion had to accommodate
itself to the new physical conditions of a settled land, and to the
more developed civilization of its inhabitants. The continuity of
the people "Israel" was maintained in the united and then in the
divided kingdoms, but only through an uneasy and (as the prophets
held) an unworkable accommodation of the true Israelite tradition
to the Canaanite way-of-life.[11] The unity and integrity of society
were strained in the transition from mobility to permanent settlement, from a simple to a more complex culture, from the small
kinship groups to the large political society comprising also many
not of Israelite blood; from a mainly pastoral economy of semi-
nomads[12] to one predominantly agricultural and commercial; from
a property system where possessions were held in common (or in
trust) to a system of private ownership where wealth gave power to
the individual, and to a stratified society. Most notable of all was the
incompatibility of the ethics of Mosaic Yahwism with the institutions of Canaanite religion.

In the prophetic period the population comprised free Israelites,
slaves, and resident aliens (*gerim*), descendants of the Canaanites,
and later immigrants.[13] Israelites might be enslaved temporarily

[11] See above, chap. 6, pp. 124–126.
[12] The Israelite tribes had doubtless engaged in cultivation in a small way during
halts at oases. Cf. de Vaux, *Ancient Israel*, pp. 3–4.
[13] The *gerim* had neither political nor property rights and are grouped with the
poor and defenceless in laws enjoining charity. Cf. Deut. 10:18–19; 24:14–21.

for debt,[14] but the permanent slave class was of foreign blood, men, women and their descendants acquired by purchase or in war. There were slaves of the state, and slaves in the possession of private families.[15] Differing little in condition from the slaves were the "hirelings," poor Israelites and *gerim* possessing nothing but their labor power.

The primary social unit remained the patriarchal family. The vivid kinship-sense inherited from the tribal past was characteristic of the Israelite people throughout their history. We see this in their pride of descent and their desire for sons to keep alight the lamp of the family's life. We see it in the duties required of kinsmen, in the laws designed to keep the family's inheritance intact, and in the respect for paternal authority and for the position of the elders.[16] A man's home was reckoned to be the locality where the ancestral property of his clan was situated, no matter where he himself might live; Elijah was a Tishbite from Tishbe in Gilead, Micah belonged to Moresheth Gath, Amos came from a shepherd family at Tekoa and Jeremiah from a priestly family of Anathoth. Isaiah, Hosea and Zephaniah are identified only by their paternal ancestry, probably because they were city dwellers, for ties with the larger clan were more easily maintained in the country districts than under the conditions of urban life.

The power of the old sense of kinship in the larger society showed itself, not only in prophetic appeals to "the whole family that I [Yahweh] brought up from the land of Egypt,"[17] but in certain religious and political institutions. Circumcision and the Passover festival were domestic ordinances, and in the country districts at least, the harvest festivals were family gatherings. "All Israel" when assembled for battle, for worship in the temple courts, or at

[14] Cf. Pedersen, *op. cit.*, pp. 43 ff.; de Vaux, *op. cit.*, pp. 80–90.
[15] 1 Kg. 9:21; Jer. 34:8 ff.
[16] See above, chap. 2, pp. 21–24; and Pedersen, *op. cit.*, pp. 46–96.
[17] Am. 3:1.

the coronation of a king was still ideally an assembly of the tribes.[18] Royal absolutism seldom went unchallenged, and repeatedly we hear of the king sharing responsibility with the elders.[19] The king was the fount of justice and the court of final appeal, but the general administration of justice was in the hands of local elders who heard argument and gave decision "in the gate" in the presence of the citizens.[20] We see in Jer. 26 how the people might participate in decisions of the temple authorities at Jerusalem. King Ahab himself hesitated before invading the traditional right of one of his subjects to retain his family property.[21]

The political structure was centered in the king, a "sacred person" in unique relation to the people and to the national god. He was the chief priest, the first soldier, the principal judge and administrator. His council of ministers or "princes" included the head priest of the royal sanctuary, the commander of the standing army, the chamberlain of the royal household, a personal adviser (the "king's friend"), an official recorder, together with adjutants and secretaries of lower rank. Eunuchs were personal servants who sometimes attained to a privileged position. The queen-mother after the death of her husband seems to have retained a position of prestige, and the king's near relatives to have enjoyed the bounty of the court.[22] Attached to the court, very often, were companies of professional prophets, and there was, of course, a military guard which, at Jerusalem, also stood watch over the adjacent Temple.[23]

The upkeep of the court, the army and the state officials was provided from the king's "privy purse," with revenue from taxation in money and in kind, from tolls levied on trade routes which crossed the land, from state commercial enterprises, and from the

---

[18] 2 Sam. 10:17; 1 Kg. 8:1, 22; Jer. 26:2; 1 Kg. 12:1, 16; 2 Kg. 11:17.
[19] 1 Kg. 12:1–16; 20:7; 2 Kg. 6:8.
[20] 2 Sam. 8:15; 15:2; 2 Kg. 6:26 ff.; Am. 5:10, 12, 15; Ruth 4:1 ff. Note also oaths of innocence administered by the priests, cf. Deut. 21:5 ff.
[21] 1 Kg. 21:1–4.
[22] 1 Kg. 1:11–21; 15:13; 2 Kg. 10:13.
[23] 1 Kg. 14:27, 28; 22:6; 2 Kg. 11:4–20.

booty of war and the tribute of subject peoples.[24] From the last source it is probable that the Hebrew kingdoms gained less than they lost when conditions were reversed, for we hear repeatedly of the payment of tribute to foreign conquerors. The Jerusalem temple had its own treasury, deriving its support from the compulsory and free-will offerings of its worshippers; from this treasury, in the later period of the monarchy, the priesthood was expected to maintain the temple fabric.[25]

In addition to the court and the army, and the professional groups of priests, prophets and perhaps of "wise men," there was in the community a distinct class of wealthy land-owners and merchants, concentrated particularly in the cities. There they lived in a degree of luxury which made a startling contrast to the poverty of their neighbors, and which separated them in spirit from the equalitarian, kinship tradition of old Israel. They were the leading men of the lay community in close relationship to the court circle, together with which they aped the "refinements" of civilization.[26]

The bulk of the people were farmers, fruit-growers, herdsmen, small merchants, artisans, unskilled wage-laborers and slaves. We hear of various trades and crafts—stone masons, carpenters, metal-workers, potters, bakers, fishermen, watchmen, weavers, cleaners and dyers, and so on.[27] The milling of grain was a domestic task, assigned, like those of spinning and the carrying of water, to women. Education of children was chiefly by their parents, but there appear to have been schools for the privileged few.[28] Literacy was largely confined to the upper classes and the professional scribes.

The stability of Israelite society was strained by the frequent onsets of storm and drought and occasional fires and earthquakes, together with the drain of many wars and raids, and the constant

[24] See above, chap. 2, p. 30 ff.; and cf. 1 Kg. 10:15, 25, 29; 20:34; 2 Kg. 3:4.
[25] 2 Kg. 12:4 ff.; 22:4 ff.; Lev. 27:2 ff.
[26] 1 Sam. 25:2; 2 Kg. 15:20; 4:8; Jer. 9:23; Is. 5:8; Am. 3:15.
[27] Cf. 2 Kg. 12:11, 12 (EVV); 24:14; Jer. 16:16; 18:3, 4; 37:21. Cf. de Vaux, *op. cit.*, pp. 76–78.
[28] 2 Sam. 1:18; 2 Kg. 12:2; Is. 28:9–10.

menace of more to come. Depredations by wild animals, such as lions, bears and leopards, witnessed to the proximity of the untamed frontier.[29] And disruptive forces were at work within society itself. The juxtaposition within narrow confines of luxury and destitution, judicial corruption and commercial dishonesty, debauchery among the wealthy and the mad struggle for private gain by the community's looked-for leaders—these undermined the integrity of the nation. At times the king was a weakling in the power of self-seeking courtiers, or was at the mercy of party strife. At such times crimes of violence and immorality were common, thieves infested the highways, and neither life nor property was safe.[30]

A word must be said about the civil laws under which Israel lived. Though justice was administered according to custom and right by the elders, the formulation of civil laws was largely the work of the priests, often, apparently, under prophetic influence. The tradition of Moses was in their keeping, and the *mishpat*, or code, of the community had its source in the righteous will of the national God, who spoke through them. In Judah at any rate, the king himself was in theory subject to the divine laws of the covenant constitution which he was pledged to uphold. De Vaux remarks that "the two 'laws of the king' make no allusion to any power of the king to lay down laws. On the contrary, the first warns the people against his arbitrary acts, and the second orders him to have a copy of the divine law and obey it to the last detail."[31] The oldest collection of civil laws, found in Exodus 21-23, is the surviving part of a larger code dating from the early kingdom, and related to the ancient Code of Hammurabi of Babylon (eighteenth century B.C.). The later codes found in Deuteronomy and Leviticus show more clearly the marks of the religious auspices under which they were formulated. The only code of laws decreed by royal as distinct from religious authority is ascribed to Omri in Mic. 6:16, where it is spoken of as an evil innovation.

[29] Am. 3:4, 12; 5:19; Hos. 13:7.
[30] Is. 3:13, 14; 5:8 ff.; Hos. 6:8, 9; 7:5; Am. 6:1-6.
[31] 1 Sam. 8:11-18; Deut. 17:14-20; de Vaux, *op. cit.*, p. 150.

RELIGION IN CONFLICT WITH CIVILIZATION

The actual social order, as already noted, was an uneasy accommodation of a native and distinct Israelite tradition to the Canaanite way-of-life. It had the weaknesses of a structure whose builders had disagreed on architectural principles and materials. The Canaanite civilization imitated that of the great powers of the Nile valley and Mesopotamia; it was particularly influenced by the commercialism of its immediate neighbor Phoenicia. It was an urban-centered, power-organized, commercial and agricultural society, under despotic monarchies, sustained by the sanctions of a polytheistic nature religion. This civilization, with its developed arts and techniques and its accumulated prestige, could only have been displaced (and then temporarily), through the complete annihilation of the Canaanites. And this, as we learn from Judges, was not the result of the Israelite conquest. Instead, the conquerors' more primitive culture was increasingly submerged.

There remained in Israel, however, those who recognized that early Yahwism had created the nation, and had given it the vigor and social cohesion necessary to establish its power in Canaan. The old Israelite ethic had a religious and patriotic imperative behind it, and now the continuance of the national identity depended upon the preservation of its essentials. If its uniqueness was to be obscured by assimilation to an alien culture, Yahweh would become merely the name of another local deity, and Israel, having lost its history, would be swallowed up among the nations.

The standpoint from which the prophets attacked the evils of the social order was that of the socially and historically self-conscious religion peculiar to Israel and its theocratic society. They tended to idealize the nomadic period of the past before Israel had been corrupted in religion and life by contact with the Canaanites;[32] though, unlike the Rechabites, the prophets did not try to turn history backward through a dogmatic and artificial reversion to pastoral conditions of life. "The days of her youth . . . when she

[32] Hos. 2:14, 15; 9:10; 11:1; Am. 5:25.

came up from the land of Egypt"[33] became a symbol of this people's health and unspoiled nature when they had been clearly aware of, and genuinely devoted to, Yahweh. Now the body politic was old and sick (though men seemed unaware of it), and the strength and special quality of Israel's culture were being destroyed by forces alien to her tradition and her religion. The artificial, leaking cisterns of the cities, says Jeremiah,[34] have not the clear running water of the desert fountain. For Israel to turn away from her heritage in search of a substitute satisfaction is a wrong done both to Yahweh and to herself. She has mistaken a more complex civilization for a higher way of life, and has preferred its immediate advantages to fundamental values.

The prophets' quarrel with their existing social order was that it did not enshrine and sustain the human and social values integral to Yahwism, but on the contrary destroyed them. "Seek [set your minds on] good and not evil, that you may survive," says Amos. "Cease to do evil, learn to do good, set your minds on justice," says Isaiah.[35] The foundations upon which the economic and political structure must be reared are ethical and religious—a *right-ness* of human relationships by Yahweh's standards, and the dependable *justice* which maintains this norm in social life. With justice and righteousness, good-will, love and integrity are necessary strands in the social bond.[36] They are the prerequisite conditions for what men immediately desire from their social order—"well being, calm, and abiding security."[37] But Israel, dazed by the glitter of a material civilization and seduced by its passions, had sought these fruits from a tree where they did not grow.

A TREE KNOWN BY ITS FRUIT

The prophets condemned with a passion amounting to fierceness the particular evils they saw about them in society—oppression,

---

[33] Hos. 2:15.
[34] Jer. 2:13.
[35] Am. 5:14; Is. 1:17.
[36] Hos. 2:19, 20; Mic. 6:8.
[37] Is. 32:17. Cf. AV, "peace, quietness and assurance."

violence, debauchery, greed, theft, dishonesty, lust for power, callous inhumanity, faithlessness to trust. These are sins of individual men and women, evils which, on the face of it, may appear in any form of society, and by which any society where they are prevalent and tolerated stands condemned. It is worth recalling some of the prophets' language: "Will you steal, murder, commit adultery, swear falsely . . . and then come and stand before me in this house?" "Her rulers give decision for a bribe, and her priests give instruction at a price, her prophets practise divination for cash." "There is no truth, no kindness, no knowledge of God in the land; cursing, lying, murder, theft, adultery break out, and crime follows crime." Merchants "make the ephah [measure] small and increase the price and use dishonest scales . . . and sell the sweepings of the grain."[38]

One should observe the vivid realism with which the prophets describe the situation. They do not make vague accusations in general terms; they are concrete and specific as to what men do or leave undone, and they link the sin directly with its consequences. With a merciless candor which recalls Jesus' castigation of pious men who "devour widows' houses," they tear away the veil of custom and pretence to show social conditions and practices for what they really are. Behavior that has appeared respectable turns out to be robbery with violence (Amos 3:10), murder (Hosea 6:8, 9), the trapping of men like birds (Jeremiah 5:26), commerce in human life (Amos 2:6), a declaration of war against one's own people (Micah 2:8). The ruling classes are actually cannibals, for they have devoured the flesh of those who are undernourished because of their rapacity (Micah 3:1–3).

The weight of denunciation falls upon the chief beneficiaries of the existing system: the king and those who exercise authority; fat priests, greedy professional prophets and parasitic "wise men"; those who live in luxury heedless of the destitute at their door, and especially rich women, vain and irresponsible; venal judges, heartless creditors, sumptuous householders, greedy land-owners.[39] "Yahweh

[38] Jer. 7:9, 10; Mic. 3:11; Hos. 4:1, 2; Am. 8:5, 6.
[39] Hos. 4:4–6; 5:1; Mic. 3:5, 6, 11; Am. 4:1; 6:1–7; Is. 3:1–3, 13–15.

indicts the elders and rulers of his people: "It is you who have consumed [all the fruit of] the vineyard; what is in your houses has been plundered from the poor."[40] But with anger against the oppressors and pity for the victims the prophets combine rebuke of popular apathy and degeneracy. It is a case of "like people, like priest," and if the rulers resemble the rulers of Sodom, the people are like the people of Gomorrah.[41]

The evils condemned are not fastened on as individual aberrations from the normal *mores* of the society, common but still exceptional. They are characteristic of the society as such, permeating its political structure, its economic activities, its culture and its accepted morality, and profoundly affecting its religion. They correspond in some way to the form and ends of the social order itself, to the principles upon which it operates and to the values it enshrines. "O priests, . . . you have been a snare; . . . the rulers of Judah have become like those who move a boundary mark; . . . Israel is defiled; their deeds will not permit them to return to their God."[42] The nation has made its covenant with the nature deities and has thus set its whole life upon a false basis, for the covenant with Yahweh is thereby in effect annulled.[43] The corruption and degeneracy of leaders and people are (to change the metaphor) symptoms of a disease deep-seated in the nation's life: "Ephraim wastes away among the peoples, . . . strangers consume his strength, . . . his gray hairs are many."[44]

The social order, as the prophets see it, is a corrupt tree which brings forth corrupt fruit. The tree is corrupt because it is not rooted in the worship of Yahweh (as Israel pretends), but in a false religion to which little more than the *name* of Yahweh could be attached. "This people . . . honour me with their lips, but their

[40] Is. 3:14.
[41] Hos. 4:9; Is. 1:10; cf. Is. 9:16.
[42] Hos. 5:1, 10, 3, 4.
[43] Is. 28:15–18.
[44] Hos. 7:8, 9.

thoughts are far from me." The Canaanite fertility religion sanctions what in Yahweh's community is vicious: "a man and his father go to the prostitute, thus *profaning my holy name*, . . . and wine which has been seized they drink in the houses of *their gods*."[45] Yahweh cannot tolerate these false principles and corrupting practices of the social order; they are alien to his nature and to the nature of the community he seeks to create among men. "Therefore . . . I will take satisfaction from my adversaries and avenge myself upon my foes, . . . I will smelt out thy dross in the furnace, . . . and I will make thy rulers what they were at first; . . . and after that, thou shalt be known as 'The City of Right,' a trustworthy city."[46]

The organizing principles of the social order thus condemned may be summarized as follows. Man lives in society because his life is under constant threat. In association with his fellows, and particularly by securing a favorable or dominant position among them, he is the better able to maintain his existence, increase his satisfactions and perpetuate his kind. The mysterious natural-supernatural environment is the source of his life and of his food supply, and also of dangers which threaten these. Therefore through a religious cult he seeks a prevailing influence over that environment, that there may be fertility among men, animals and crops, together with good fortune, and deliverance from natural and social catastrophe. The cult is thus not a special-interest association within society, but is essential to its existence. But the forces with which the cult deals are mysterious, and man's influence over them uncertain. So, in the world of the seen and tangible, also, man seeks additional security and satisfaction by possessing things, and by exercising power and influence over other men.

The desire for security and satisfaction, then, was the mainspring of social action, and determined most decisively the form of the social order and the quality of its human relationships.

[45] Is. 29:13; Am. 2:7, 8.
[46] Is. 1:24–26.

Within the Israelite society certain individuals, groups and classes
had attained a position of dominance and privilege through the
exercise of power, the influence of prestige and the possession of
wealth; and the latter means were continually being sought for the
former ends. The interests of society as a whole were, as in modern
times, too easily identified with the interests of the ruling classes in
maintaining their position and privileges. Those who were "com-
placent in Zion, and who felt secure in the hill of Samaria" were
not "sickened by the breaking up of Joseph" (i.e., the nation).[47]
They sought to maintain the nation's position, and their own, by
the same means that were used in their society's internal affairs—
power, through the exercise of military force, alliance with stronger
peoples and the subjugation of the weaker; and *possessions*, the land,
loot and tribute money obtained by conquest, and the wealth
accruing from foreign commerce and from the taxation and exploitation of their own people.[48]

The prophets had no patience with the nation's ways. "Israel
has forgotten his Maker, and built palaces, and Judah has made
many fortified cities." "Woe to those who go down to Egypt for
help, and depend upon horses, and trust in the weight of numbers
of chariots and charioteers."[49] For this meant that the final faith of
the nation was not in Yahweh; the pillars of its social structure did
not rest on the bed-rock of his righteousness.

It was, on the contrary, the religion of Baal and the other
nature gods that sanctioned this struggle for material satisfactions,
and led men to put their trust in power and possessions. That
religion was itself the fruit of the attempt to harness supernatural
forces to the chariot of human desire. "I will go after my lovers
(the Baals), who give me my bread and my water, my wool and my
flax, my oil and my drink." The land was filled with silver, gold,

---

[47] Am. 6:1, 6.
[48] Cf. Am. 6:13; Hos. 5:13; 7:11; Is. 30:1–5, 15, 16; 31:1; and see above, Chap.
2, p. 30 ff.
[49] Hos. 8:14; Is. 31:1.

untold wealth, with horses and chariots beyond number—*and with idols.*[50] Hence the social evils which the prophets denounced were not political and economic merely; they were at the same time *religious* evils. They were allied with a false religion which produced a false morality. And at the same time they contravened the ethics of community which were fundamental in the tradition of Yahwism. Jeremiah pointedly contrasts the selfish despotism of Jehoiakim with the just and benevolent rule of his father, Josiah; "Did not this show that he knew me [Yahweh]?"[51] Religion and the social order profoundly affect each other, and they must correspond if that which religion defines as holy is not to be distorted and defiled.

THE DOOM OF THE SOCIAL ORDER

The social order of the Hebrew kingdoms being what it was, the prophets in the name of Yahweh rejected outright the form of constituted society, its power and its purposes, just as emphatically as they rejected the form and purposes of the perverted religious cult. They did so because the social order embodied a wrong view of life in society, supported false values, and sought its security and satisfactions from wrong sources and by mistaken methods. Political forms, economic activities, legal and judicial practice, social institutions, public morals, culture and religion—all were deformed by a basic error as to the meaning, values and direction of life. The prophets' message concerning society was not evolutionist or reformist but revolutionary. *They were social revolutionaries because they were religious conservatives*, seeking to revive the essential ethics and social creativity of historic Yahwism. Yahweh himself, they declared, is in the struggle for social justice. He is the Great Ally of the wronged and dispossessed.[52] But he is more, for he is the protagonist in the vaster drama of creation, whose final purpose

---

[50] Hos. 2:5; Is. 2:7, 8.
[51] Jer. 22:16.
[52] "What do you mean that you crush *my people?*" demands Yahweh of the rulers, Is. 3:15.

is the making of a people for himself. His purpose is to create *community*, an order of relationships with and among men in which his righteousness can find fulfilment.

So, to the prophets, the existing social order was doomed. "Zion shall be ploughed like a field, and Jerusalem shall be a ruin"; "For Yahweh of hosts has a day (coming) against everything that is proud and lofty," cedars and oaks and mountains and hills and towers and ramparts and ships—and men. "I will annihilate your horses from your midst and destroy your chariots, and I will blot out the cities of your land and overthrow your fortresses." "At that time I will punish those who are at ease, . . . and their possessions shall be plunder and their houses a desolation; neither their silver nor their gold can save them in the day of Yahweh's wrath." "The people of Israel shall live long years without king or official, without sacrifice, sacred pillar, priestly ephod or household gods."[53]

The prophets' language is often such as would arouse resentment among the powerful, and class-feeling among the victims of injustice and exploitation. Isaiah indignantly declares to the elders and rulers that the plunder of the poor is in their houses. Hosea denounces the debauchery of the court and calls the priests highway robbers. Micah calls the rulers cannibals and the professional prophets rogues.[54] It is no wonder that the civil and religious authorities regarded such words as dangerously subversive. Amos was banished, Jeremiah was imprisoned and accused of treachery, and threatened with death. The latter's contemporary Uriah was put to death by royal command (a fate which Elijah had barely escaped and which many of his colleagues did not).[55] More would have suffered the same fate had it not been for the superstitious fear of laying hands upon a "holy man," and for the popular support which an appeal to ancient rights and liberties could still evoke. As Hempel remarks, from the fable of Jotham to Job's despairing

[53] Mic. 3:12; Is. 2:12–17; Mic. 5:10 (EVV); Zeph. 1:12, 13, 18; Hos. 3:4.
[54] Is. 3:14, 15; Hos. 7:1–7; 6:9; Mic. 3:1–3, 5, 11.
[55] Am. 7:12, 13; Jer. 37:11–15; 26:16–23; 1 Kg. 19:2, 3, 10.

outburst, there was in Israelite thought and feeling a constant "resentment against power."[56]

The impact of Yahweh's judgment, say the prophets, will be felt by every constituent element of the social order which Israel has erected, in neglect and defiance of the human values fundamental to her professed religion. The monarchy and the royal establishment, the temple priesthoods with all the paraphernalia of their cult-services, the cities and palaces which are the outward and visible sign of wealth and power, the judges and elders who have betrayed their trust, the army boastful of its prowess—each will be struck down in a way appropriate to rebuke its pride.[57] The arrogance of power and possession is most hateful in the eyes of Yahweh, for it is the mark of a spirit in individuals and society which neither fears God nor has regard for man. "Ephraim says, 'Now I have become rich, I have acquired power for myself' "; "The inhabitants of Samaria have said in pride and vast conceit, 'Bricks have fallen down, but we will rebuild with hewn stone' "; "They are haughty, the women of Zion, and walk with necks outstretched." Victors in battle cry, "Is it not by our own strength that we captured Karnaim?" The very splendor of the sanctuary worship exhibits human vanity rather than devotion.[58]

Society, as men knew it, then, was doomed. It was useless to seek frantically to prop up the collapsing structure by an acceleration of temple services ("sacrifices every morning, and tithes every third day"), by new superstitions and the service of additional gods, by increased armaments, frenzied appeals abroad for help, and by laying yet heavier burdens on the people.[59] Yahweh, the integrating force within Israelite society, had become a disintegrating force, "a moth" in the fabric of Ephraim, and "rot" at work in Judah. "I

[56] J. Hempel, *Gott und Mensch im Alten Testament*, 1926, p. 63.
[57] Am. 7:9; 8:3; 6:11; 2:14–16; Hos. 1:4; 5:1; Is. 32:14; 30:16, 17; Mic. 1:6; 3:5–12; Jer. 22:13–19.
[58] Hos. 12:8; Is. 3:16, 17; 9:9, 10 (EVV); Am. 6:13; 4:4, 5; 5:21–23.
[59] Am. 4:4; 5:26; Jer. 11:12, 13; Is. 8:19; 31:1–3; 30:1, 2; Hos. 5:13; Mic. 3:10.

am your destruction, O Israel; who can help you? Where now is your king, that he may save you?" "You have ploughed wickedness, you have harvested wrong . . . for you trusted in your chariots, in the numbers of your warriors. But there shall be an uproar among your people, and all your fortresses shall be destroyed."[60]

The prophets' syllogism is simple: "If you are responsive and obedient, you shall eat the best of the land; but if you refuse and are rebellious you shall taste the sword." "What Yahweh requires of you is that you should do justice, love kindness and order your life modestly with your God." But instead "there is no truth, no kindness, no knowledge of God in the land." Therefore "the eyes of the Lord Yahweh are upon the sinful kingdom, and I will blot it off the surface of the ground."[61]

THE DIVINE ALTERNATIVE

The Israelite society thus heard its sentence pronounced, and that sentence was soon to be carried out. If the righteousness of Yahweh could not find realization in a social order it must destroy the order of life men built in its defiance. Yet the prophets who uttered the divine judgment were not merely destructive critics of society, with no alternative to propose. They re-affirmed, as a basis for Israel's life, the *covenant*, whose denial had evoked their denunciations.

Their references to the true native tradition of the Israelite people, and to the period of Moses and the wilderness, exhibit the covenant with Yahweh as the Magna Carta which had brought *this* people into being and conditioned her distinctive historical existence. Yahweh had made for himself a people before he had given them the land where their present social order came into being. The real national life had begun and its self-conscious existence had taken root in the religion of those far-off days. This nation was not like other nations who shared the civilization of the settled lands; it had come into being through. Yahweh's choice and his acts of

[60] Hos. 5:12; 13:9, 10; 10:13, 14.
[61] Is. 1:19, 20; Mic. 6:8; Hos. 4:1; Am. 9:8.

deliverance and revelation. It was pledged to him and to a way-of-life that corresponded to his nature. Hence, in Hosea's figure, Yahweh is Israel's first and only real husband, the source and sustainer of her life.[62]

The Israelite nation, then, had its true existence apart from and prior to the erection of their political, social and economic order in Canaan. The people themselves and their community were primary; their religion and the ethical values it enshrines were paramount. These must be preserved genuine and undefiled. The distinctive ancestral faith, and not political and economic institutions alien to it, must define morality. The political and economic structure must subserve human and religious interests, as defined by the ancient and central tradition of Yahwism instead of by the fertility, nature religion of Canaan. Thus, in economic matters, Yahwism was concerned with the welfare of the people as a whole and with distribution in terms of justice and kindness, while the emphasis of Baalism was upon maximum production and the accumulation of private wealth. On the political side, the ethics of Yahwism would invest with authority rulers who are instruments of social justice, and who "maintain the right" in the community of their neighbors. As Jesus long afterwards expressed it: "The so-called rulers of the nations dominate them, and their great men tyrannize over them; but it is not to be so among you."[63]

The "covenant" was an institution by which kinship could be extended artificially to include those not of the kin by blood.[64] It involved a solemn agreement to accept the conditions and share the obligations of a common life. Those who were thus united formed a family or people, whose principle of association was expressed in the terms of the covenant. These terms were of the essence of the compact which united men in life, interest and purpose. So, with respect to the historic bond which bound Israel to her God, Jere-

[62] Hos. 2:7, 16 (EVV); cf. Jer. 2:2 ff.
[63] Mark 10:42, 43.
[64] See above, pp. 22–23, 130–133.

miah declares: "Thus says Yahweh, the God of Israel: Cursed be the man who heeds not the words (terms) of this covenant, which were given as commandments to your fathers at the time when I brought them out from the land of Egypt." If one party to the solemn compact fails to make it a reality by meeting his obligations, the covenant is disrupted and he must pay the penalty inherent in the original conditions. "So I carried out against them all the words (terms) of this covenant."[65]

Thus, in the light of their essentially theological view of Israel's history, the prophets hold that the nation is constituted not by its political structure centered in the king, his judges and officials, his army and his laws; nor by the official cult with its priesthood; nor yet by its economic organization and institutions. The nation is the people, constituted as such by the covenant and characterized by the social ethic "written in" to the covenant. The covenant was, in fact, not a single fixed and written code, but a living tradition which was formulated variously at different periods. It found expression in the different forms of the Decalogue used (as a threshold rite?) in the Yahweh temples; it was integral to the coronation ceremony of Yahwist kings; it was a major theme in prophetic teaching; and it moulded the codes of civil and ecclesiastical law so that at least two of them were known as "the words (or terms) of the covenant."[66]

Only by a return to this charter of the national existence could Israel renew her life in a transformed social order. Meanwhile the doom of the old order was at hand: "Near is Yahweh's great day, near, and coming fast."[67]

BEYOND THE DOOM

While undoubtedly the pictures and promises of restoration to follow punishment are chiefly the work of anonymous prophets from the period after the doom had fallen, the classical pre-exilic

[65] Jer. 11:3, 4, 8.
[66] Ex. 34:28; Deut. 29:1 (EVV); cf. chap. 4, p. 64.
[67] Zeph. 1:14.

prophets give more than a hint of what they would have said had their circumstances been different. Yahweh's historic purpose is to create a people after his heart, and the future is his. Amos, indeed, sees nothing but the approaching storm. But Hosea looks to the day when Yahweh's love, now spurned, will be triumphant, and Israel will be betrothed to him forever in righteousness and justice, in kindness, love and faithfulness. Isaiah particularly, but also Zephaniah (and Micah?),[68] speak of the *remnant*, the core through which the nation's real life will continue and from which a new nation will spring. Jeremiah declares that, just as Yahweh had set himself to root up and to pull down, so in days to come he would set himself to build and to plant under the terms of a *new covenant*, written in men's minds.[69] Only by recognizing the inescapable ethical demands of Yahweh upon a social order, only by understanding the bearing of real religion upon daily life, could the men of the future create a society which Yahweh would permit to endure.

The earlier prophets sometimes pictured the Israel of the future in colors drawn from the idealized tradition of the wilderness period of the past, with its social simplicity and enthusiastic loyalty. The later eschatology of blessing is primarily social rather than individual, for the community is the corollary of the covenant. It is not a heavenly existence but a real social order in this world that they contemplate, for Yahweh's purpose must triumph in the only world Israel knew as real. Later Messianic prophecy as it develops emphasizes (and sometimes over-emphasizes) the concrete effects of the triumph of righteousness in physical well-being and social security. Whatever else that triumph may mean, it must mean the end of oppression, injustice and helpless poverty, of inhumanity, and the hurt and destruction of war.[70]

---

[68] Is. 1:8–9; 8:16–17; 10:20–21; Zeph. 2:3, 9; Mic. 7:18.
[69] Jer. 31:31 ff.
[70] Mic. 4:3, 4; Is. 9:2–7 (EVV); 11:1–9; Hos. 2:21–23; cf. Is. 60:5–16; 61:4–9. The genuineness of ostensibly pre-exilic Messianic prophecies is much disputed; the Messianic hope certainly goes back to the pre-exilic period, though it was in the exilic and post-exilic period that it was most eagerly fostered.

The prophets do not and cannot prescribe political, economic and cultural forms and institutions; they can and do insist that, whatever may be the apparent necessities of social order, its methods and principles are to be judged by their human consequences. The spiritual fruit of a social order determines whether the tree is good or bad, and whether or not it will survive in a world where Yahweh's clamant righteousness is matched by his power. The prophets make plain to us that the onus rests on the defenders of any established social order, as it rests equally upon those who champion an alternative structure, to show that what they defend or propose is a society congenial to true religion, productive of human values, and which is the concrete expression of real community among men.

9

PROPHETIC RELIGION

In the Hebrew prophets is found the clearest expression of what was most distinctive and creative in ancient Israelite religion. It was a spirit, a dynamic and a clarification of the essence of true religion that is discernible also in the way the patriarchal stories are told, and in the accounts of the work of Moses. It shines somewhat fitfully through legends and historical narratives; it left its mark upon law, liturgy and wisdom; and in the end it created a religious community which could and did survive national destruction. Duhm's claim that "Prophecy marks the beginning of the spiritual history of the world"[1] may be exaggerated, particularly if this be taken to refer only to the classical prophets. But in these men the meaning of a religion which was a relationship with such a God as Yahweh becomes unmistakable.

We may describe the working of this spirit throughout the religious history of Israel in terms of a dialectic process. The original Hebrew tribes with their ancestral gods came under the influence of the prophetic work of Moses. When Moses made Yahweh known to them as the God of their fathers who had intervened to save them in order to create from them a people to

[1] B. Duhm, *Israels Propheten*, 2nd ed., 1922, p. 8.

worship him exclusively, something divinely new emerged in the world—the people of a covenant. Yet the actual religion of this people was a synthesis of this new faith with older beliefs and religious practices of the Semitic east. With the conquest of Canaan, Israel confronted in turn the whole paraphernalia of ancient shrines of gods and goddesses. Gradually a new form of syncretism evolved, in which Yahweh came to be worshipped after the fashion of a Canaanite god, and not always exclusively. This syncretism blurred the meaning of Yahwism, and engendered the emphatic protest by the prophets with which we are concerned in this chapter.

The work of the prophets was largely unheeded and resisted, but eventually it was to raise Israelite life and religion to a new plane. The Deuteronomic school of writers embodied much of the same prophetic spirit in their reformulation of religious laws and their re-writing of the national story from the Conquest to the Exile. Ancient forms of worship in Solomon's temple were modified and re-interpreted in the light of a revived piety and a new understanding. Yet, as Jeremiah had perceived, the laws of God must be written in men's hearts if they are to be freely obeyed. This meant that pure religion was to become essentially independent of traditional—or of *any*—required forms of worship. When post-exilic Judaism was reconstituted as a temple state around a reformed cultus and a developed corpus of "salvation history" and its laws, writers of books like Ruth and Jonah and certain of the Psalms were constrained to protest a new rigidity and exclusiveness in the name of a universal, prophetic faith.[2]

Nowhere in this long historical process are the religious insight, decisiveness and power that are ancient Israel's distinctive contribution to our religious heritage more marked than in the lives and words of the classical prophets. The fierce struggle against submergence by the Canaanite religion and civilization made what was essential in Yahwism stand out. The champions of Yahwism were

[2] Cf. Ru. 1:4; 4:13–17; Jon. 4:11; Ps. 51:15–17 (EVV).

forced to distinguish for themselves and for their people what it was that made Israel's own religion infinitely superior to the worship of the gods of Canaan, and why this religion was indispensable to the nation's heritage and historical mission. For the very life of the people who were Yahweh's people was dependent on the reality of the covenant bond which united them in a living relationship with a living God. Themselves vividly conscious of the presence and nature of God and of that in their people's life which contradicted it, keenly aware of the social tension created by injustice and of the dangers inherent in the political situation, the prophets saw more clearly than any of their predecessors what the service of such a God must mean. Thus they were able to bring to the front what was primary, to set aside as indifferent what was secondary, and then to challenge what was fundamentally opposed to their central faith.

CANAANITE RELIGION[3]

The official religion and popular religious practices of the Israelites were, in the mind of the prophets, fatally contaminated by the polytheistic nature religion of Canaan and its attendant pagan civilization. W. Robertson Smith once said that Israel had one religion for times of patriotic exaltation and another for daily life. Yahweh was indeed the unique God of the nation, worshipped not only at the royal sanctuaries of Jerusalem, Bethel and Dan, Gibeon and Shechem, but also at many other ancient sanctuaries up and down the land. But the distinctive characteristics of Yahweh were obscured by the fact that the forms of worship were similar to those of worship offered to other gods in Canaan and beyond. Since pagan shrines also dotted the land, Yahweh became to many little more than the head of an Israelite pantheon. "As many as your cities are your gods, O Judah!" (Jer. 2:28). The people, in adapting themselves to agricultural and

---

[3] On Canaanite religion cf. W. F. Albright, *From the Stone Age to Christianity*, 2nd ed., 1957, pp. 230–36; C. H. Gordon, in *Mythologies of the Ancient World*, ed. S. N. Kramer, 1961, pp. 181–217; J. Gray, *Archaeology and the Ancient World*, 1962, pp. 105–20.

urban life, were easily drawn to acknowledge in particular the great Syro-Palestinian rain-god Baal in his various manifestations,[4] and to superstitious beliefs of the pre-Israelite population, among whom (it must be remembered) they were at first a minority.

Such passages as Jer. 7:18; 44:17–19, supported by the finding of large numbers of 'Ashtarte figurines in Palestinian excavations, suggest that worship of the great Mother Goddess, "Queen of heaven," was widespread. Furthermore, the adoption by Israel of a monarchy, to be "like all the nations," brought into her state-religion myths and rituals associated with that institution among contemporary peoples.[5] The worship of foreign deities was deliberately introduced by certain of the kings: those of 'Ashtarte of Sidon, Chemosh of Moab, and Milcom of Ammon, by Solomon; of unspecified "idols" (i.e., foreign gods) by Abijam; of the Phoenician Baal and his consort Asherah or 'Ashtarte by Ahab; and of Assyrian astral deities by Manasseh.[6] We read also of a bronze serpent connected in tradition with Moses (but which also was a symbol of the Mother Goddess) that was reverenced in the Jerusalem temple until the time of Hezekiah; and of "horses and chariots of the sun" and of roof altars for worship of the heavenly bodies that were destroyed in Josiah's purge.[7]

The religious situation in the time of the great prophets was thus complex. The worship by many of these foreign deities was doubtless facilitated to some degree by the thought that they were subordinate to Yahweh, or operated in areas with which he was not directly concerned. He was the God of the nation as such, of its historic tradition, of its battles and its king. He did not seem to be concerned with the

[4] This seems to be the meaning of the plural baalim, although many scholars hold that the baalim were minor divinities or spirits thought of as resident in various localities. Cf. M. Noth, The Old Testament World, 1966, pp. 281–82.
[5] Cf. A. R. Johnson, Sacral Kingship in Ancient Israel, 2nd ed., 1967. See below, pp. 198–199.
[6] 1 Kg. 11:5, 7; 15:8, 12–13; 16:31–33; 2 Kg. 21:3–7. The "golden calves" of 2 Kg. 12:28 were doubtless wooden images of bulls covered with gold leaf. They were not idols, but were regarded as pedestals on which the unseen Yahweh was regarded as standing. Cf. W. F. Albright, op. cit., p. 299.
[7] 2 Kg. 18:4; 23:11–12.

problems of the individual cultivator. Israel *"did not know* that it was I who gave her the grain, the wine and the oil" (Hos. 2:8). So the farmer and the herdsman brought their offerings to the local shrine, but also made their appearance periodically at the temple of Yahweh.

The word "Baal," unlike the name "Yahweh," was not a proper name but an honorific title meaning "master, owner" (cf. "the Lord"). Sometimes it was combined with the name of the locality where Baal was worshipped, like "Baal-Peor." The proper name of the Baal of Canaan was "Hadad"; he was the god of storms and fertilizing rain. Alongside each Baal was his consort 'Ashtarte or Asherah.[8] The Baal cult in a great city like Tyre shared the city's importance, with the result that the Baal of Tyre assumed almost a distinct identity and was worshipped as such in Israel under Ahab.

The Baal religion was essentially worship of the reproductive powers of nature, through an operative cult which sought to influence these to serve man's interests. It was one of many forms taken by fertility religions among peoples dependent on the regularity of "seedtime and harvest." These forms had something of a common pattern throughout the ancient Near East. According to this pattern, the god represents the vegetation that dies in the heat of summer or autumn, or is cut down that man might have his harvests. He descends to the underworld, where his goddess-consort goes in search of him during the winter, struggles with the forces which hold him captive, and returns to earth with him in triumph in the Spring. Then the marriage of the divine pair is celebrated, to symbolize and ensure the renewal of vegetation and the fertility of man and beast.[9]

The Baal shrines were located either on "high places," open-air mounds or platforms on which were the altar, an upright stone pillar representing the god and a wooden pole or pillar representing the

[8] These were originally distinct goddesses, but they seem to be confused by the writers of the Old Testament. Cf. W. F. Albright, *From the Stone Age to Christianity*, pp. 231, 233.
[9] Cf. E. O. James, *Myth and Ritual in the Ancient Near East*, 1958, pp. 60–65, 122–28; A. S. Kapelrud, *The Ras Shamra Discoveries and the Old Testament*, 1963, pp. 37–51.

goddess; *or* in a temple enshrining an image, together with the other appurtenances of divine service.[10] To these shrines came worshippers with offerings to gain the favor or avert the displeasure of the deity. More important were the three agricultural seasonal festivals that were to be assimilated by Israel as the feasts of "Unleavened Bread," "Harvest" or "Weeks," and "Ingathering" or "Booths."[11] It is clear from such passages as Amos. 2:7–8 and Hos. 4:13–14 that many of the temple rites of (or influenced by) the Baal cult were occasions for dissipation and sexual licence. Sacred prostitutes, male and female, appear to have been regular functionaries of these temples; in the first instance, perhaps, as priestly actors in the sacred marriage drama, but also (as the above passages and Babylonian analogies suggest), participating with the worshippers in symbolic fertility rites.[12]

Temples of the greater Canaanite and foreign gods flourished in the cities, especially at times when the reigning monarch was not a strict Yahwist. Just as a large part of the Canaanite ritual (without its grosser features) was taken over by the Yahweh temples, so the myth-and-ritual pattern as related to the kingship, left its mark on Israelite royal rites. The king on the day of his accession and anointing became the *son* of Yahweh. As (almost) the incarnation among his people of their God, he had a unique role in the life of the community and in the national cultus. There is no evidence, however, that the kings of Judah or Israel engaged in a ritual representation of a divine death and resurrection, combat and sacred marriage, as in the ritual pattern elsewhere. The assimilation of Yahwism to Canaanite religion never went so far as to obliterate Yahweh's characteristics under the myth of the dying vegetation god. But it is noteworthy that another feature of the myth-and-ritual pattern, viz., the annual celebration of the god's victory at Creation over the forces of chaos,

---

[10] Cf. Deut. 12:2–3; Jer. 2:27–28; Hos. 4:11–14.
[11] Ex. 23:14–17; 34:18–23; Deut. 16:1–17. The last-named combines "Unleavened Bread" with the old "Passover" festival of the herdsmen. Lev. 23 prescribes the more elaborate festal calendar of the post-exilic temple.
[12] Albright, *op. cit.*, pp. 234–35.

is reflected in certain psalms which apparently belonged to a festival linking Yahweh's assumption of royal power with his creative work. On such an occasion Yahweh's anointed and adopted son, the king, in the ritual of the national sanctuary, must have had an outstanding role. It is most probable that at this point the royal ritual of Israel resembled the royal ritual pattern elsewhere.[13]

As already remarked, Canaanite religion was the worship of the productive powers in nature, through an operative cult by which man sought to harness these powers to the service of his own interests and desires. Thus, though the sexual licence associated with the ritual undoubtedly suggested to the prophets the description of idolatry as "fornication" with other gods,[14] it was not the sole reason for it. The whole purpose and object of the cult was the satisfaction of human desire, and the cult *was* the religion. The only ethic it sanctioned was man's own ethic of the struggle for life, security, satisfaction and power. Its fundamental difference from Yahwism lay in the belief that its gods had power superior to man's but not ethical character superior to his. It therefore did not carry with it *morality as an obligation*.[15] It was man's method of making himself secure, in relation to the mysterious powers of nature, rather than his submission to One greater, stronger and better than himself.

RELIGIOUS DEGENERATION IN ISRAEL

In the pages of the prophetic books we are given vivid glimpses of the popular religion which had little but the name of Yahweh to distinguish it from the many other cults of Canaan. It is, in fact, often difficult to tell whether the speaker is referring to Yahweh

[13] Cf. Ps. 2:6–9; 89:3, 4, 14, 18–37 (EVV); A. R. Johnson, *Sacral Kingship in Ancient Israel*, 2nd ed., 1967, pp. 106–23, 128–30.
[14] Ex. 34:15, 16; Hos. 4:11–14; Am. 2:7, 8.
[15] W. O. E. Oesterley and T. H. Robinson, *Hebrew Religion*, 1930, p. 166, speak of the "divorce of morality from religion. An act might be universally recognized as a vice or a crime; it did not follow that it was a sin. Except as religion insisted on the observance of certain primitive *taboos*, it was indifferent to the treatment accorded by a man to his neighbors."

shrines or to pagan temples, and it is quite plain that there was little discrimination so far as the people were concerned. The same men who prostrated themselves on the roof-tops to the (probably Assyrian) star-gods, prostrated themselves also before Yahweh and swore by Milcom, the Ammonite king-god. At the sanctuary of Beersheba oaths were taken by the name of Yahweh, but also by the name of the Baal of Beersheba, Dod or Hadad; at Dan by the god of that shrine, and at Samaria by a deity apparently the same as the Asham-Bethel of the Elephantine papyri.[16] Jeremiah states specifically that images of other gods were set up, and sacrifices offered to them in the Yahweh temple at Jerusalem,[17] and that child-sacrifice was practised by the same people at the near-by shrines of the Baal (in this case, Milcom). Micah implies that in this latter rite Milcom was confused with Yahweh. Amos infers that sacred processions in honor of the Assyrian star-god Sakkuth (Saturn) were held in the precincts of a Yahweh temple.[18]

"The Israelites," says Hosea, "turn to other gods and are lovers of raisin-cakes." Raisin-cakes, we are told, were dispensed by David on a festival occasion as part of the feast following sacrifice, while Jeremiah 44:19 refers to sacrificial cakes shaped or marked with the likeness of the Mother Goddess.[19] Hosea implies that the Israelites love sacrifice because of the feasting which accompanies it, and speaks of the round of religious occasions as times of merriment. Amos links the debauchery at the shrines with man's inhumanity to man in the world outside. Isaiah describes the drunkenness of priests and prophets (i.e., professional prophets attached to the temples) in the discharge of their functions. Jeremiah says that the priests care nothing for Yahweh, while the prophets prophesy by the Baal, and commit fornication.[20]

[16] Zeph. 1:4, 5; Am. 8:14; cf. A. Cowley: *Aramaic Papyri of the Fifth Century B.C.,* 1923, p. xviii.

[17] Jer. 7:30, 31; 19:4, 5; cf. notes 6 and 7 above.

[18] Mic. 6:7; Jer. 32:34–35; Am. 5:25–27.

[19] 2 Sam. 6:19; Hos. 3:1.

[20] Hos. 2:11; 4:11; Am. 2:6–8; Is. 28:7, 8; Jer. 23:14.

There is general testimony to the great number of temples, and to the frequency, abundance and expensiveness of sacrifice. Large numbers of priests and temple prophets were constantly occupied, and a considerable proportion of the community's time and resources was thus devoted to the operation of its religious cult.[21] In addition to this, the daily life of the cultivator was affected at every turn by animistic and fertility beliefs. The Hebrew verb meaning "to prune" suggestively means also "to chant." In Isaiah 65:8 we have the words of a ritual song of the vintage, the melody of which (as appears from their headings), continued to be used in the chanting of Psalms 57, 58, 59 and 75 in the Jerusalem temple. Hosea tells of fertility rites at threshing-floors, and of those who "wail upon couches for grain and wine, and cut themselves" (as the prophets of Baal did at Mount Carmel).[22] This weeping for the dead god of vegetation explains the language of Psalm 126:5: "They that *sow with tears* shall reap with the ritual shout of joy"; for sowing is the burial of seed that new life may come. St. Paul recalls an age-old belief when he says: "That which thou sowest is not quickened except it die."[23]

The attempt to assimilate the worship of Yahweh to this Canaanite religion debased the whole meaning of religion. It had plunged priests, prophets and people ever deeper in the mire of corruption. The practice of religion had actually become a cloak for evil. What should have healed the hurts of society was itself a source of further infection. "The inhabitants of the land, both small and great, all are engaged in plunder, while all the prophets and the priests practise fraud." Most serious of all was the divorce between ideas, words and "sacred" acts as *constituting religion*, on the one hand, and, on the other, the righteousness without which they lacked moral meaning. "Resort to *me*, that you may live," says Yahweh; "resort not to [worship at] Bethel, nor come to Gilgal, nor go on pilgrimage

[21] Am. 4:4, 5; 5:21–23; Hos. 8:11; 10:1; Is. 1:11; 2:8; Jer. 3:1; 11:13.
[22] Hos. 4:14; 9:1; 7:14; 1 Kg. 18:28.
[23] 1 Cor. 15:36 (AV). For *rinnah* as the ritual shout of joy, cf. Ps. 42:4 (EVV), 107:22.

to Beersheba." For "with their flocks and their herds they shall go to seek Yahweh but they shall not find him; he has withdrawn from them." Men profess to desire the Day of Yahweh's appearing, but their words convey no suggestion of the dread majesty of Yahweh's justice. Even when outstretched in prayer their hands are blood-stained, but they do not stop to think of that. In time of trouble they use the language of repentance: "Come, let us return unto Yahweh, for he has torn, but he will heal us!" But the veneer is all too thin; or, to use Hosea's more poetic metaphor: "Your goodness is like an early morning cloud, like dew that is soon gone."[24]

Such people may be hypocrites unconsciously, but they are hypocrites none the less. "What?" cries Jeremiah in terrible indignation, "having stolen, committed murder, adultery and perjury, having sacrificed to *the Baal* and gone after other gods—do you come and stand in my presence in this house bearing my name, and say 'We are *saved*'?—to go on doing all these abominable things?" When men become accustomed to keeping religion and morality in separate compartments, they lose all moral sense and can no longer distinguish good from evil; they "take darkness for light and light for darkness, they take bitter for sweet and sweet for bitter." And at the same time their religious perception is so dulled that they no longer recognize the presence and action of God, nor understand his word. Like wine thickening upon its dregs, "they say to themselves, 'Yahweh neither brings good nor brings evil.' "[25] They are dazed, blind, asleep, so that revelation is a sealed book to them. They continue to hear the prophet's word, but not to understand it; to see, but not to perceive. This is the "ultimately fatal effect on character of continued disobedience to the voice of God."[26]

Such a radical falsification and corruption of religion had come about because the real nature of *deity*, as defined in Yahweh's person, was unrecognized. Consequently the reason and purpose of worship

[24] Jer. 6:13; Am. 5:4, 5; Hos. 5:6; Am. 5:18–24; Is. 1:15; Hos. 6:1, 4.
[25] Jer. 7:9, 10; Is. 5:20; 6:9, 10; Zeph. 1:12.
[26] G. B. Gray, *Isaiah I*, 1912, p. 109; cf. Is. 6:9–10; 29:9–12.

were misconceived. Men deluded themselves with mere words when they reassured themselves by contemplating Yahweh's temple in their midst. And "the more prosperous his land became, the more splendid became the sacred pillars." Man's pride in himself, in his possessions and in his power showed itself in the way in which he lavished his resources on temple and sacrifice. But ostentatious pride is a complete denial of the loyal trust in Yahweh which is the first essential of prophetic religion. Man therefore gratifies himself, not God, by the "religious" performances which are his substitute for the ethical covenant with Yahweh.[27]

IMMEDIATE STIMULI OF THE PROPHETIC REFORMATION[28]

To speak of certain moral and religious conditions as having given rise to the prophetic movement and evoked its message, is not to suggest that these stimuli sufficiently *explain* the great prophets. The clarification and intensification of Israel's distinctive religious witness was an act of God and constituted a Divine revelation, while at the same time it was a genuine human response to a given situation. The point is that similar situations elsewhere did not inevitably produce the same result. We affirm that God spoke through these men because of the spiritual quality of their lives and of their message. That God did not do so mechanically, or under the compulsion of a necessity more ultimate than himself, we recognize by saying that God *chose* them as his spokesmen. Sovereign freedom, as well as sovereign power, consistency and goodness, is an essential attribute of the God of the prophets.

The prophetic reformation took place in two stages. The first was the challenge by Elijah of the worship within Israel and Judah of the Tyrian Baal, Melkarth, as Yahweh's rival for the chief place among the gods. The Tyrian cult was extirpated in consequence of the movement initiated by Elijah, through the massacres by Jehu

[27] Jer. 7:4; Hos. 10:1; Am. 4:4, 5; Is. 1:11–17; Jer. 5:30, 31.
[28] Cf. von Rad, *O.T. Theol.*, i, pp. 64 ff.

when he seized the throne of Israel, and by his disciple in violence, the Jerusalem priest Jehoiada, who led the palace revolution which put the child Joash on the Judaean throne.[29]

Clearly, it was only because Yahweh had come to be thought of almost as Israel's *Baal*, a god of the same *kind* as Melkarth, that the latter's worship could threaten to replace his in Israel. It was doubtless a matter of family pride with those strong-minded queens, Jezebel and her daughter (?) Athaliah, that it should do so. With this danger averted, the second and more fundamental stage of the prophetic revolution was carried through by the classical prophets. This was the reassertion and clarification of Yahweh's distinctive nature, which put him in an altogether different category from Melkarth and the other manifestations of Baal; together with the assertion that he was not merely the national god, the leader in battle, but was *superior* to the other gods in their own spheres. Yahweh was supreme because there was no other deity like him. In consequence, the service he required of those who worshipped him was different in kind and quality from the service of other gods. For this reason he could not tolerate the idolatry of polytheism. To include him in a pantheon, even as its head, was to deny his essential uniqueness and so to deny himself.

Classical prophecy was the reaction of Israel's native religion to the debased religion and morality that has been described. Speaking in religious terms, it was God's answer to man's desperate need. The primary stimulus of this spiritual outburst was the increasing pressure of sheer human distress, social tension, political instability and general moral deterioration. Amos was commissioned to summon distant pagan Assyria and Egypt to gaze in astonishment on the great confusion and oppression in Samaria, where men "do not *know how* to do right, but fill their castles with treasures got by violence and plunder."[30] The innocent were sold into slavery, the poor trampled on, the weak oppressed, and the wronged found no redress. Hosea could see no sign that true religion was producing lives trust-

[29] 1 Kg. 18:40; 19:15–17; 2 Kg. chaps. 9–11.
[30] Am. 3:10.

worthy and humane, but only sin and crime among people and leaders alike. Isaiah rebuked worshippers who cared nothing for the rights of the orphan and the widow, rulers who ground the face of the poor, men who acquired great estates by evicting the peasant from his land, heroes—of the wine cup! The other prophets give similar testimony. Human misery and social tension had reached a breaking point.[31]

The second factor was the recognition that the tradition of the covenant society and its righteousness had a peculiar relevance to the existing situation. In the revival and development of Mosaic Yahwism were moral resources to meet the social crisis, resources which the debased and debasing religious institutions of the time patently failed to provide. "I will bring her to the wilderness, . . . and she shall respond there as in the days of her youth, and as at the time when she came up from the land of Egypt." "And I will restore your rulers as they were at first, and your counsellors as in the beginning." "Hear the terms of this covenant and fulfil them! For I solemnly charged your fathers at the time I brought them up from the land of Egypt, [as I do] to this day, with the urgent charge: 'Obey my commands.' " The jealousy of Yahweh (which meant that he must be worshipped alone or he could not be worshipped at all), must be respected if the nation he had created long ago was now to be saved from disintegration. "I am Yahweh your God (who brought you up) from the land of Egypt, and no god apart from me shall you know, for there is no deliverer except me."[32]

In the third place, the prophets were not blind to the import of the blows under which the life and health of society had suffered already. The lion's roar in the forest, the sound of the war-trumpet in a city, make known to all who hear that something terrible is afoot; why then when trouble comes do men not sense that Yahweh's righteousness is reacting against their sin? Famine, drought, blight and the locust pest, epidemics, defeat and earthquake—why have these come to a people so corrupt, except as omens of Yahweh's

[31] Am. 3:9, 10; 5:10, 11; Hos. 4:2, 8, 9; Is. 3:14, 15; 5:8, 22.
[32] Hos. 2:14, 15; 13:4; Is. 1:26; Jer. 11:6, 7.

rising anger?[33] If disaster were to be traced to the displeasure of a god like the Baal, its meaning would be that he was offended at some cultic negligence. But since Israel's God was one known to reveal his presence in notable *events*, and since one catastrophe after another had shaken Israel's society; since, further, the flouting of justice and mercy, truth and faithfulness contradicted the very terms on which Yahweh had become the nation's God;—was it not plain that the two were connected? The series of events had a terrible meaning, when viewed by men sensitive alike to the ethical character of the living God of history, and to the spiritual and moral decadence of their contemporary society.

Linked with this reading of events, and confirming it, was the prophet's awareness of a gathering storm in the sea of peoples,[34] among whom Israel and Judah were politically insignificant and helpless. In these vast movements too, there was significance, to champions of a religion historically oriented and conditioned as was Yahwism. Amos does not name the nation which he declares Yahweh is raising up against Israel. But he says that the people will be carried into exile *beyond Damascus*, and this leaves little doubt that he has in mind the Assyrian menace. Hosea, who was much closer in time to the conquests of the Northern Kingdom by Tiglath-pileser and Sargon, is sure that his people will be carried away either to Assyria or to Egypt. Micah seems to have in mind, in his dirge over the Judaean countryside, the devastation wrought by Sargon in 711 B.C. Isaiah, who vividly pictures the coming invasion as a river in flood, undoubtedly is thinking of the Assyrian torrent which swept over Judah's northern neighbors in 734 B.C. Indeed, he identifies the conqueror in one of the oracles of his early period.[35] When, many

---

[33] Am. 3:4, 6, 8; 4:6–11; Is. 1:4–8.

[34] Am. 6:2–3; Is. 10:5–11; Jer. 4:5–18. The prophets were well informed as well as sensitive to the significance of international events. On this, see N. K. Gottwald, *All the Kingdoms of the Earth*, 1964.

[35] Am. 6:14; 5:27; Hos. 9:3; 11:5; Mic. 1:10–16; Is. 8:7, 8, cf. v. 4. A glossator has inserted the words "the king of Assyria and all his glory" in v. 7; the identification is correct, but it is intrusive in the metaphor, as similarly in 7:17, 20.

years later, the Assyrian armies stood outside the walls of Jerusalem, a still more daring historical insight was given to Isaiah—that the conqueror who had been Yahweh's instrument of chastisement was setting himself above the Lord of history, and would pay the penalty of his pride. Jeremiah, finally, lived to see the collapse of Assyrian world-mastery, and sensed as the working of Yahweh's will, in the struggle for world supremacy which followed it, the inevitable victory of Nebuchadrezzar's Babylon.[36]

A final stimulus to prophecy was the opposition it aroused. The forces which worked, whether deliberately or not, to stifle its voice, paradoxically helped to make that voice yet more penetrating. The very suggestion of change is resented by the beneficiaries of an established social order, just as the exposure and rebuke of sin is resented by sinners. But when this resentment attempts to silence criticism by deliberate pressure, the result, more often than not, is to concentrate its power. Amos' banishment by the king's chaplain at Bethel apparently became a *cause célèbre*, and the fact that Amos' prophecies were the first to be collected in written form is probably its consequence. The vested interests of the priesthoods and temple prophets were threatened by the work of those individuals we call the "classical prophets"; in the first place because the denunciation of their delinquencies undermined their prestige, but also because the prophetic religion was fundamentally opposed to the kind of religion for which they stood. It is not surprising that these religious functionaries again and again attempted to silence the voice of prophecy.[37]

There was opposition, too, from groups in the community whose economic interests or views on public policy were challenged. Courtiers do not like to be accused publicly of wickedness and treachery, nor the wealthy of having acquired their wealth by exploitation and dishonesty. Hosea and Isaiah for religious reasons intervened in political affairs, when they denounced the linking of

[36] Is. 10:5–15; 37:21–35; Jer. 46:2–12; 25:9, 11; 38:2, 3; 43:8–13.
[37] Am. 7:10–17; 2:12; Is. 28:9, 10; 30:10; Jer. 11:21; 26:8, 16.

their peoples' fortunes with those of Egypt or Assyria. Without a doubt, they incurred the animosity of the advocates of such a policy. The military leaders, not unnaturally, were furious when Jeremiah urged soldiers to desert because Yahweh had already decided on their defeat; they made it a capital charge.[38] But perhaps the most deep-rooted opposition of all resulted from the moral lassitude of the community as a whole. Men would not hear a message which demanded attention and response. They were sunk in a stupor induced by their false religion and its attendant way-of-life. "They refuse to listen to Yahweh's instruction, and they say to the Seers 'See nothing!', and to the speakers of oracles, 'Give us not straightforward oracles; tell us smooth [i.e., seductive] things . . . ; stop talking to us about the Holy One of Israel.' " Yahweh testifies: "The more I called them, the farther they went from me." Yet his prophets could be silenced neither by hostility nor by indifference, for "How can I give you up, Ephraim? How can I let you go, Israel?"[39] Thus spoke through them the divine compassion.

THE DEFINITION OF ESSENTIAL RELIGION

The essence and meaning of real religion is defined by the prophets in the first instance negatively, in their rejection of the form and quality of the religion practised by their compatriots. Religion is not a species of "religious" behavior independent of the moral life. It is not to be equated with a cult of ritual and sacrifice operated by a priesthood on behalf of the community, and expected to influence the deity in man's favor in proportion to the effort and expense involved. Its object is not the securing of physical vitality, power and protection, but the maintenance of a relationship with God which has as its primary consequence the people's spiritual and moral vitality. It means man's alignment with the divine will rather than his effort to obtain from heaven the objects of his desire. The changes which religion effects are not in God but in the motives

[38] Am. 3:10; Is. 30:1–5; 31:1–3; Jer. 38:1–4.
[39] Is. 30:10, 11; Hos. 11:2, 8.

and quality of man's life. The facts and conditions of man's existence are not altered, but he is enabled to face them in confidence and hope.

Two scholars of a previous generation spoke of the prophets in a way that is worth recalling. Marti wrote: "The God whom the prophets serve . . . is a spiritual personality of an entirely ethical character. . . . Henceforth the closest union between religion and ethics is of the very essence of prophetic religion. . . . Religion and ethics form a whole, religion being the roots and supplying the dynamic, and ethics the fruit and displaying the effects." Duhm ascribes to the prophets two supreme achievements; first, "they gave to the world, to the restless movements of the peoples and to the fate of individuals a center in God . . . who became a world God, the ruler of human history and finally also of the physical world"; second, "prophecy, by its very nature reaching out toward the new, toward ever new acts of God, founded the religion of hope."[40]

Doubtless, as von Rad says, these critics exaggerated the originality and uniqueness of classical prophecy, under the influence of "modern ideas of the freedom and spirituality enjoyed by religious genius." The prophets "were never as original or as individualistic . . . as they were then believed to be . . . but were in greater or lesser degree conditioned by old traditions." Yet the fact remains that the classical prophets *are* unique in the clarity and force with which they expressed a *new idea of religion* in the ancient world. Von Rad agrees that "there is a definite break between the message of the prophets and the ideas held by earlier Yahwism. . . . What is new is the verdict the prophets passed on the history (i.e., of Israel) up to their own time, namely, that it was one great failure. . . . They introduce a fundamentally new element, which is that only the acts (of God) which lie in the future are to be important for Israel's salvation. . . . Salvation comes in the shadow of judgment."[41]

---

[40] K. Marti, *The Religion of the Old Testament*, 1907, pp. 147–48; B. Duhm, *Israels Propheten*, 2nd ed., 1922, pp. 459–60.
[41] G. von Rad, *Old Testament Theology*, vol. ii, 1965, pp. 3, 181, 185.

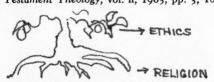
→ ETHICS

→ RELIGION

Prophetic religion, then, is the appropriate response, in loyalty, obedience, steadfastness and hope, to the spiritual reality of God the present Judge and the coming Savior. It means leaning the weight of life upon the Lord (Is. 10:20), in the conviction that he is goodness personified, and that he is working to realize his purpose in history and in the lives of individuals and of society.

True Religion:

1. The first element in true religion displayed by the great prophets is *Spiritual Perception*, the consciousness of God which includes aware-
(Level)
ness, discernment and responsiveness. Isaiah complains that Israel pays less attention to her God than a dumb ox pays to its owner. Jeremiah says that the people have turned their backs as on someone of no importance. Amos recalls the afflictions and disasters which they have been too obtuse to recognize as warnings. The grave words of the prophets appear as meaningless talk, and merely irritate men who have forgotten the meaning of Yahweh's mighty deeds of old. By every rejection of such testimony their minds become more impervious to the truth.[42]

A religious man, on the other hand, "will fix his attention on his Maker, and turn his eyes to the Holy One of Israel." He will recognize in momentous events the "strange acts" of Yahweh, who is the force in ethical reality, the Judge with power to punish. He will acknowledge him as the Master whose right it is to direct his life. The tokens of the presence and activity of a Divine Person will be evident to him, as to Jeremiah, as well in suggestive experiences of his own as in social crises. He will perceive that men and nations are confronted by a will of righteousness, with which they struggle, but that a heart of unquenchable kindness yearns over them in their waywardness.[43]

Spiritual sensitiveness, recognition of what is characteristic in God's acts and what those acts portend—these are both the source and the fruit of religious understanding. At its deepest level this

[42] Is. 1:2, 3; Jer. 2:27; Am. 4:6–11; Is. 28:9, 10; 6:9, 10; Hos. 13:6.
[43] Is. 17:7; 28:21; Mic. 6:1, 2; Is. 1:3; Jer. 1:11–14; 18:1–6; 24:1–10; 32:6–8; Is. 14:24–27; Hos. 11:8, 9.

is the understanding of the true nature of the "holiness" of God, i.e., of what alone is worthy of religious awe. "Yahweh of hosts, him shall you count holy; and let him be what you fear." The God manifest in the majesty of his ethical will can be served only as man aligns his own will with his. To honor him is not to ascribe to him honorific titles, but to accept as a sacred obligation the direction he gives to life; to trust in his goodness and to expect the triumph of his righteousness. This is to understand life and to have free access to the only unfailing fountain of vitality. Life's source and its support, its unity and meaning—and therefore its fulfilment—are found in the knowledge and consciousness of God.[44]

The second element in prophetic religion—separable from the first only for purposes of discussion—is _Moral Sensitivity,_ markedly 2. social in its reference. The familiar example from the story of Isaiah's call to be an apostle shows how the perception of God's presence is at the same time, and necessarily, the perception by the worshipper that he *and his people* are morally unclean. The converse of this is seen in Amos' picture of the greed and oppression which are natural to the debauched devotees of the fertility religion. Yahweh is outraged, says Jeremiah, that men in their social living should transgress his most elementary moral laws, and, with no thought of amendment, presume to stand before him in his house and expect his aid. Those who cannot distinguish between good and evil, who "turn justice into bitter poison," simply do not know the God they profess to worship. It is no wonder that they cannot discern the signs of his presence.[45]

On the other hand, the man who is sensitive to the supreme religious reality is in the same moment and for that reason sensitive to the iniquity which contradicts and flouts it. "My heart is broken . . . in the presence of Yahweh and of the majesty of his holiness, *for* the land is filled with adulterers." He is vividly aware of Yahweh's moral scrutiny, of his ethical requirements, and of his indig-

---

[44] Is. 8:13; Jer. 2:13.
[45] Is. 5:20; 6:1–5; Jer. 7:9–11; Am. 2:6–8; 5:7; Hos. 4:6; 6:4–6; Zeph. 1:12.

nation at man's failure to meet them.[46] His religious awe is radically
ethical in quality, because "the holy God *is* holy in virtue of [his]
righteousness." *To seek God* and *to seek goodness* are the same,
though this does not mean that religion is an ethical system and
nothing more. It means, rather, that the dedication of life to goodness is the way in which the devotion to God which *is* religion must
be expressed. And what is goodness? It is justice, kindness and
integrity, which are the reflected light of Yahweh's justice, his kindness and his faithfulness. "It has been told you, O man, what goodness is, and what it is that Yahweh expects of you: to do justice, and
to love kindness, and to behave humbly in the presence of your God."
The love of good means hatred of evil and the establishment of
justice in the seat of justice. It is to "seek out the right, restrain
violence, obtain justice for the orphan, take the part of the widow."
Goodness is the total response of man's moral nature, in the human
and social context of his conscious life, to a God who is *God* because
his power and his purpose are good.[47]

3.   In the third place, prophetic religion is *Knowledge of God through
Personal Relationship to him*, a meeting of wills, a knowing and
being known. This personal quality of religion is not confined to
individual piety as we see it in Jeremiah.[48] The people as a whole
was felt to have a *corporate personality*, so that its designation of
Yahweh as Master, Husband or Father of his people was something
more than a figure of speech.[49] To *know* him as he desires to be
known goes beyond the simple apprehension of his existence, and
even of his nature, historic purpose and imminent action as external
facts. It is knowledge which means response, a turning to him in
recognition of what his presence means, a glad meeting with another
for whom one has affection and respect. Hosea speaks of a personal
intimacy which grows through long experience of mutual trust and
faithful love, a concord of mind and heart for which the highest

[46] Jer. 23:9, 10; 11:20; 20:12; 25:31.
[47] Is. 5:16; Am. 5:4, 6, 14; Mic. 6:8; Am. 5:15; Is. 1:17.
[48] Jer. 1:4–19; 10:23, 24; 11:18–20; 12:3, etc.
[49] Is. 1:2, 3; Jer. 31:32; Hos. 2:16; 11:1; Jer. 31:9; cf. Mal. 1:6.

levels of spiritual union in marriage provide the closest analogy. This would be a covenant of hearts in a standing relationship, an enduring betrothal in terms of righteousness, justice, kindness, love and faithfulness. Those who know God in this way *know how* to do right; it is natural to them to do so. "Did not [Josiah], as he ate and drank, do what was just and right? He defended the cause of the poor and needy; then all was well. Was not *that* knowing me?" asks Yahweh.[50]

The fourth element to be distinguished is <u>Moral Obedience</u>. This *4.* must be understood in the light of the foregoing. It is not the obedience of one who *must* do what he neither cares about nor understands, but the ready response of heart and will to the "word" which utters the divine imperative. Obedience is not perfunctory when man waits for, heeds and understands the guidance given, and accepts correction humbly and penitently. Loyalty is confirmed and trust verified when conscience is quick to acknowledge the moral standards which religion has made holy. Again and again the prophets declare that moral obedience is the one thing essential to the worship and service of Yahweh. He is honored, not as are other gods nor in the way it may please men to praise him, but solely by the honoring of his law (i.e., instruction) and the heeding of his messengers.[51]

The defiant city which will not accept correction does not trust God nor fear him. They are rebels against him who will not hear the prophets' claims and protests in the name of love and justice, and will not acknowledge these as the *holy* requirements of religion. "The words of the covenant" provide a code of behavior of a specific kind, for to know Yahweh is to act as he does, to follow him in the good way which is *his* way. Jeremiah declares that when, in days to come, religion will be perfected and every man will know Yahweh as a familiar friend, Yahweh's law (the instruction and obligation of his way-of-life) will be written on men's minds so that obedience will be instinctive, spontaneous and complete.[52]

[50] Hos. 2:19, 20; Am. 3:10; Jer. 22:15, 16.
[51] Am. 7:14, 15; Is. 6:8; Jer. 7:23; 9:24 (EVV); 11:6–8; 23:18.
[52] Zeph. 3:1, 7; Is. 30:12; Jer. 7:5–7; 11:2–8; 31:31–34.

Religion results in action, in a quality of behavior among men which expresses obedience to God. It also produces in men a distinc-
5. tive *Quality of Spirit*. It gives them confidence and courage so that they can face frankly the hard facts of life and not be overwhelmed by them. Trust in the power of God's goodness and in the goodness of his power gives life an anchorage and man's spirit peace. "Take care, be calm, do not be afraid: ... if you do not believe you cannot be secure." Men "lean upon" Yahweh as upon a support they know will not give way. Because they trust in the divine wisdom their faith is patient; they know that God's judgment on unrighteousness is certain, and their knowledge of a Divine deliverer opens wide before their eyes the "door of hope." With attention centered upon God they serve him by faithful conformity to his commands, while their eyes are open to the future which holds the final triumph of his great design. "Turn thou to thy God, preserve kindness and right, and watch always for thy God with eager anticipation." This is the secret of spiritual strength and joy, of a vitality and quality of life undreamed of in the nature religions. "The people that walked in darkness have seen a great light."[53]

6. We must note, finally the *Meaning for Worship*, of the prophetic apprehension of religion. What is the use and value of the periodic assembling of the community for "religious exercises," and of the approach of the individual to the sanctuary? The most famous passage in the Book of Micah declares that what Yahweh desires of man is not the most costly imaginable ritual sacrifice, but justice, kindness and humble behavior before God. But the point of the passage is missed if it is taken as obviating the need for assembling to worship God. It declares that *this*, not the other, is the sacrifice which one must have to offer, *when* he comes before Yahweh and bows himself before the Most High God. Isaiah in Yahweh's name condemns the insincerity and unreal formality of those who "draw near" to utter Yahweh's praise; he rejects not only sacrifices but *prayers* by men

---

[53] Is. 7:4, 9; 10:20; Am. 2:6–16; Is. 30:15; Hos. 2:15; 12:6; Is. 9:2.

who will not cease to do evil. The religious axiom attributed by the prophetic historian to Samuel of old, sums up the prophetic view: "Has Yahweh as much delight in burnt-offerings and sacrifices as in obedience to Yahweh's voice?" Hosea has a similar antithesis: "I desire kindness rather than sacrifice, and knowledge of God more than burnt-offerings."[54]

True worship, then, is the sincere expression in words and symbols of the total response in life to what God is, and what he desires of men. Unless it utters the deep truth of how men really feel and act toward God and their fellow-men, men's praise and gifts are a mockery which adds sin to sin. Unless they perceive that, with such a God as Yahweh, it is justice, truth and kindness rather than priest, temple and ritual, that belong to the category of the *sacred*, they cannot offer acceptable worship. They must come into his presence, not to influence him by gifts and adulation to fulfil their wishes, but to learn what *he* desires and to express their loyal purpose to obey him. When in days to come the nations have learned of Israel's God, "Come," they will say, "let us go up to the hill of Yahweh, to the house of the God of Jacob, *that he may instruct us in his ways and that we may walk in his paths.*"[55]

[54] Mic. 6:6–8; Is. 29:13; 1:11–15; 1 Sam. 15:22; Hos. 6:6.
[55] Is. 2:3, a passage found also in Mic. 4:2; its authorship is uncertain, like that of many other oracles the spiritual value of which is not affected by the uncertainty.

IO

THE RELEVANCE OF THE PROPHETS

It may seem at first surprising that only part of the first chapter and the final chapter of this volume should be devoted to the subject of its title. The arrangement is deliberate, and the reasons for it may be quickly stated. In the first place, to declare that the prophets are or are not relevant for the modern world is a pretence, until one has a fairly clear grasp of the prophetic movement and literature as a phenomenon in itself. We must know the prophets before we can say that they have a message for us, and what it is. Again, it is the prophets themselves who are relevant, rather than their particular insights and predictions, and the total substance of their teaching. They speak, not *of* our age but *to* it, because the Word of God is in their mouth. Through their literary remains in the Old Testament we make contact with living men, rich and deep and powerful men, observant, sympathetic and in deadly earnest. They understand human nature and the human predicament. They feel the urgent meaning of history as the sphere of man's moral decisions and of God's participation in the conflict of human wills. They know God as the fount of meaning in the context of everyday life; and they find the reality of his presence in the inner world of their own spirits. Such men *must* be significant for religion in every age.

But the meaning and the moral imperative of religion for each person is for himself to recognize, and cannot be stated by another. The application to life of what we learn from the prophets requires ever new decisions as conditions change and experience grows. One cannot simply summarize and catalogue their insights, and consider them disposed of when their relevance to one set of circumstances has been suggested. The dynamic of their message is not so easily exhausted, nor can its intrinsic authority be claimed for all that seems to follow from the attempt to apply it at one particular point. What really counts is a first-hand knowledge of the prophetic records, the recognition of their formative influence in our religious tradition, and their potential spiritual power over men's minds today. Finally we need the capacity constantly to discern afresh their relevance to the human situation of this and every age.

The remarkable contemporaneousness of these ancient spokesmen of religion and the perennial freshness of their message, spring from their power to penetrate past the maze of appearances to underlying human and religious facts stated in universal terms, but with notable concreteness. "The Egyptians are men and not God, and their horses flesh and not spirit: and when Yahweh stretches out his hand both he that helps shall stumble and he that is helped shall fall."[1] Amid moral confusion they were able to define essential justice. Over against religious traditionalism, heathen and secular influences and man's stubborn waywardness, they were able to define essential religion. They assessed economic and social situations by their effect on the essential being of man, in his personal relationships with other men and with God. They knew that man is made for the shared life of community. Their intuitive apprehension of truth still commands the assent of the religious mind, for like Jesus Christ, they spoke with authority and not as the scribes.

The suggestions in the following pages as to areas of life and thought where the prophets of Israel have relevance today, are thus not to be taken as an attempted definitive statement. On the premises

---

[1] Is. 31:3.

laid down no such statement can be constructed, for in the last analysis each man must make his own decision in response to the prophetic Word. But it remains true that the prophets speak largely to the *collective* mind of society and of social groups, and each individual shares in the collective responsibility of hearing and responding. The writer can only say that here, and here, and here, the prophets seem to him to speak to our time and circumstances.

THE NATURE AND MEANING OF RELIGION

In chapter 9 the attempt was made to show how the essentials of true religion were clarified and defined through the work of the prophets. Religion was defined in the first place negatively. It cannot be indifferent to morality, nor be equated with the formal acts of worship which purport to give it utterance. Moreover, its end and object is not merely the satisfaction of the worshipper, but the establishment of a structure of living and authentic relationships among the members of a community of whom Yahweh is one. Positively, religion is the appropriate response by man as a person and in community, to the unique and all-embracing ethical reality of God.

What we learn about God and about religion through the prophets is not superseded (though it is illuminated) by the coming of God to man in Jesus Christ. Rather, it is an integral and essential element in the total Christian understanding of God and of his ways. The Bible is *one* literature, and we know more about the God of Christian faith than is found in the pages of the New Testament, when, like the evangelists and apostles, we read the prophetic writings with eyes opened by Jesus Christ. The relation between the Testaments is not simply one of succession and development, but one of interrelationship and vital continuity. The Bible comprises the family history and family archives of the Church, the new people of God.

There is thus every reason to feel that the timeless elements in the prophets' declarations on religion retain their urgent importance for Christians. What they say about *the ethical requirements* for man's acceptable service of a God whose moral character and action are the very constituents of his godhead, is, of course, underlined in the New Testament. But nowhere is this simple, primary fact of religion more forcefully stated than by the Old Testament prophets. At no time is its recognition more needed than today. The Church has the momentum of nineteen centuries behind it, and often its members are satisfied to subsist, mentally and morally, on what has been handed down to them, without any wish to hear and respond to the voice of the Spirit in the accents of their own time. Many are Christians rather by accident of birth, than from any conscious moral choice and spiritual aspiration affecting the quality and direction of their living. Others do not distinguish between things indifferent for religion and "the weightier matters of the law." Still others place first emphasis on correct belief and formal religious duties, rather than on conduct pleasing to God in the full range of human relationships. And those who invert the emphasis are often themselves remote from any deep sense that their conduct must be a *religious* response to the greatness and goodness of God. The prophets make it plain that religion and ethical behavior must form a vital unity.

Their further clear enunciation of man's social responsibility before God—a responsibility not only to the neighbor next door but to *all* his neighbors—is particularly important for the life of modern man, in the immense collective groups and activities of which he is a part. Since the group is now so large that its relationship to the individual becomes impersonal, he tends to restrict his acknowledgment of moral obligation to other individuals with whom he comes in contact. But his duty to his people, i.e., to all his neighbors, and to the common welfare, is inescapable. The recognition of this will transform the meaning of patriotism and galvanize democracy. The further recognition of collective responsibility before God for collective behavior toward other groups and peoples and the whole family of mankind, is the prime requisite for the ending of the ancient curse of war, and of the economic, racial and cultural conflicts which invoke it.

Turning to another aspect of religion, viz., its forms of worship and of corporate institutional life, we find that the prophets make certain things abundantly clear. The first is that religion is not to be equated with its operative mechanism and established organization, with a particular formulation of its theology or of its moral code, nor yet with the historic culture with which it has come to be associated. The second is that all of these themselves stand under its scrutiny. The third is that religion nevertheless requires some form of corporate expression in cult worship, pleasing to God because it genuinely serves the ends of religion in social life. The fourth is that conflict is eventually inevitable between religious institutions that are by nature conservative, and prophetic spirits alive to the demands of religion for a present that is always new. For religious like other institutions tend to develop a vested interest in their own survival, and this may oppose the very purpose of which they are meant to be the instruments. Another aspect of this is that the life of the religious community is chilled by the professionalism and corrupted by any moral laxity of its official spokesmen;—"like people, like priest."[2] "And it came to pass, when Jeremiah had made an end of speaking all that Yahweh had commanded him to speak unto all the people, that *the priests and the prophets and all the people* laid hold on him, saying, Thou shalt surely die."[3]

The application of what has been said to the organized life of the Church as we know it is so direct as to require little comment. Loyal churchmanship is a good thing which unconsciously may be a snare, for it can too easily become just a hobby. What is meant to be the instrument and occasion of religion becomes a substitute for it, and attention is diverted from faith's final object to lesser and more immediate goals. Emotional attachment to some venerable system of theology too often binds men to the fact that no attempt to state the truth has the permanent validity of the truth itself. A similar emotional reaction may prevent their recognizing that the obligations of

[2] Hos. 4:9.
[3] Jer. 26:8.

the Christian ethic too must constantly be re-examined, in the light of the changing conditions of personal life and the forms of human societies.

The deepest emotions of all find expression in worship, if it be true worship. The classical prophets[4] lay down no requirements as to the *forms* of worship (or the lack of them). They are concerned with the *ends* of worship, and with the effectiveness of any particular cult in serving those ends. Who is our God, and what kind of service and of praise does he desire, being what he is? This is the question we must ask ourselves, seriously and with as much detachment as is possible while we perform our accustomed religious exercises. What would his prophets say if they entered *our* church doors, having moved among the people where they live and heard their unspoken cry for justice and freedom, and for God? What are the ends our religious services are designed to achieve? Can the true ends of worship be kept in view when repetition creates routine, and the customary ordering of words and actions becomes in the end mechanical? How effectively do we guard against the supreme hypocrisy of uttering before God words of prayer and praise which have lost any urgent meaning; of professing a faith and a purpose that are not seriously related to our way of life? The offering which God requires is a life just, merciful and humble before him. Worship, to be acceptable, must be the token and occasion of such an offering.

We have the prophets to thank for the great insight that religion is not a specialized activity of man's life, but a quality and attitude in all his activities, a total way of living governed by the orientation of his spirit toward God. This total response demands, indeed, the specialized activities of prayer and worship, but it is not to be equated with them, still less with their conventional forms. Man's relationship to God must be a reality of his actual, conscious life in the present, while at the same time it is continuous with his spiritual heritage. This means that the ethical terms of his response to the

---

[4] See above, chap. 9, pp. 214–215. That Ezekiel does so is a mark of the difference of that book from those of the earlier "classical" prophets.

living God must correspond with the changed conditions of his life in the world, as compared to those of his fathers. It means, further, that the religious group which only carries on the momentum in belief and practice of an age which has passed away, and has not made its own the covenant of its fathers, will find that the covenant is no longer valid, and the living God has passed on to seek a new people for himself. "Therefore I will do unto the house which is called by my name, wherein you trust, . . . as I did to Shiloh." "Call his name 'Lo-'ammi'; for you are not my people and I do not belong to you."[5]

The relevance of the Hebrew seers for religion in its personal, as distinct from its corporate aspect, is to be found in what they were, rather than in what they said. In the framework of thought that they inherited, religion was the working relationship (through functionaries) of a people to its god. The prophets sought to transform this corporate religion, rather than to lead men into a radically different individual approach to God. Perhaps only Jeremiah among them passed far enough along this new road to sense that his own personal experience was a portent. But the religious experience of all the great prophets shared two outstanding characteristics of personal religion,—the sense of vocation to serve God in a life-time of witness, and the feeling of spiritual separation from those to whom one is bound by many human ties, but who do not share one's profound convictions.

There is no stimulant of personal religion more effective than the autobiographical witness of the authentic saints. The Hebrew prophet has a word for our corporate religious life which we cannot choose but hear. He has also this to say, in the living epistle of his life if not in spoken words: "The Creator of the ends of the earth, the Lord of life and history, has spoken to *me*. He has met *my* need and taken *my* part, saying 'Be not afraid because of them, for I am with thee to deliver thee.' He knows me and sees me and tries my heart.

[5] Hos. 1:9.

He is stronger than I, and has prevailed."[6] However our modes of
religion change (as change they must), and however strongly we
emphasize (as the prophets teach us we must emphasize) the social
aspect and consequences of religion, we cannot dispense with the
witness of these dedicated lives, or forget the tryst which every soul
has with its Maker.

THE SUBJECT MATTER OF THEOLOGY

The claim should not be thought strange, that the oracles of these
ambassadors of the Word seven or eight hundred years before Christ
have immediate importance for Christian theological thinking in the
twentieth century after him, even though, as emphasized above, these
men were not themselves theologians. The importance is twofold:
first, that the thought of the prophets, as well as its development in
pre-Christian Judaism, is necessary to the understanding of New
Testament theology; and second, that the peculiar intensity of their
apprehension of the ways of God demands the direct attention of
the modern theologian.

To begin with, the experience of these men must be reckoned with
when consideration is given to the thought of God as a personal
Being. Their God is not the remote, dispassionate, abstract deity who
becomes a term of intellectual discussion. The God we meet in the
pages of Amos, Isaiah and Jeremiah can only be described as a
vigorous and vivid personality, majestic indeed, and divinely "other"
than man, and yet meeting him in the commerce of mind with mind
and of will with will. His holiness (i.e., his divine reality) is emphasized not less but more by the awareness of his towering ethical
presence in human affairs, of his commanding and puissant purpose,
and of the peremptory and inescapable summons of his moral demand on men. His goodness and his mercy, his righteousness and his
wrath are not dogmas received on authority, nor deductions from
one central doctrine. Neither are they inferences from immediate

[6] Cf. Jer. 4:8; 11:20 ff.; 20:7 ff.

experience. Rather they are elements of the experience itself. God is known as one man knows another, with the indescribable differences that the "other" is God.

It is nonsense to suggest that man has made God in his own image, because in speaking of (and *to*) God in personal terms he inevitably depends on the analogy of human relationships. If God can be known by man at all, it must be in terms of the life we live as persons. Perhaps we are not nearly bold enough in speaking of God as the Supreme *Person*, present to other persons (though in him we live, and have our being), his will confronting our wills, his mind and purpose our spiritual environment. The parallelism of the two greatest commandments—and indeed the whole life and teaching of Jesus Christ—declare that the relationship of man to God is *similarly personal* with that of a man to his neighbor, and that God can be known most directly when he is known in personal terms.

A second point of relevance is the doctrine of revelation. It is axiomatic that the God of Christianity had "of old time spoken unto the fathers in the prophets." That he spoke is not all; *what* he spoke has become part of the deposit of revelation. Nevertheless, the primary substance of Old Testament revelation, as of its Christian counterpart, is not knowledge *about* God but knowledge *of* God. It denotes his self-manifestation as a powerful and holy Presence, in the hearts of dedicated men and on the stage of history. He becomes known as the ultimate Meaning, expressing itself, not in mysteries, but in a *word*, the intelligible articulation of reality. His is the supreme Will which confronts man's present life, and gives importance to man's freedom of moral decision, the condition of his spiritual existence. Such revelation is conditioned by man's capacity to understand and his readiness to respond. It is *pertinent* truth, deriving its immediate significance from the moment and circumstance of its utterance, and from the corresponding and right response it demands of men. It not only reveals God to man but also reveals man to himself. From such moments of revelation there remain deposits (so far as these have been preserved) to be added to the sum total of the knowledge of God and man. This latter is revelation in its objective, but secondary and derivative form.

The deeper understanding in prophetic thought of what constitutes sin is another point of present significance.[7] Even today sin is too generally regarded as the transgression of certain arbitrary taboos established by religious custom. But particular acts or failures are sin because of their origin in the alienation of man's spirit from God, and of their consequences in harm done to human personalities and to the common spiritual life. Sin is evil in the soul which rejects God's goodness and his mercy. In his proud isolation man refuses to yield himself to the life of community. Sin introduces a chaotic element into the divinely intended order of life. Where religion affirms and unites, sin denies and divides. Its awful power and dreadful responsibility are measured by the divine goodness it frustrates and the divine beauty it mars.

The world is ready for the declaration once more of the awful reality of human evil. The nineteenth-century myth of inevitable and perpetual progress has been exploded by the impact of world wars, with their demonstration that autonomous man cannot solve the vast problems of racial and cultural conflict, economic welfare and political order. He is overwhelmed by his own machinery, and by social torrents set loose through his unwillingness to affirm his solidarity with his fellowmen. The judgments of God are manifest in the world of today. The time has come to bring home to men that these are right judgments on human sin; that men bear these consequences inevitably, because they are morally responsible beings who have denied their own nature in denying their responsibility to their neighbors. This is so, even though they may have complied with the accepted ethics of their society; we must now "condemn as sin much that hitherto we have flattered as success."[8] For the reality of sin is present wherever a human spirit is denied its birthright of

[7] Cf. chap. 6, pp. 134–139.
[8] John Line in *Towards the Christian Revolution*, ed. R. B. Y. Scott and G. Vlastos, 1936, p. 47.

freedom in the life of full community with God and man. Every form of social order must be judged by its spiritual consequences, and according to that judgment it will stand or fall. Religion must concern itself with the solution of the clamant international, racial, political and economic problems of today in the light of their human consequences. It must examine by ultimate ethical standards the principles and goal of social order, and affirm the responsibility of those who wield power, to God and to the world-wide human family. And it must keep to the fore the awful destructiveness of the sin which denies this responsibility, for which no humanly devised controls can be finally effective, and for which the only remedy is the frank acceptance of the right ways of God.

Theology has always been aware of the fundamentally historical nature of the Christian revelation, and in recent years has renewed its interest in the meaning of history itself. In this area of thought the contribution of the Hebrew prophets is indispensable. It was they who first clearly discerned in history moral meaning, coherence, and movement in relation to an end transcending the experienced present. They knew the present not merely as the determined consequence of the past, but as a significant moment containing within itself something of both past and future, and vibrant with the presence of the living God. Time became for them something more than mere duration, and gained depth and meaning through events which marked God's presence and activity. Historical consciousness emerged in the recognized commerce of a divine will with the morally responsible decisions of men, and in the correlation of a divine purpose and human destiny.

The prophets had thus a morally adequate and constantly relevant frame of reference by which the multitudinous happenings of experience could be sorted out, and those isolated which were important and determinative. Men need no longer be enslaved by fate, their minds frustrated by meaninglessness or their spirits cowed by the tyranny of evil. Man has responsibility and freedom—if he will—to align himself with the divine purpose for his own and his people's life. In the interaction of wills, in man's response to or refusal of the initiative of the Maker and Lord of history, his own history is made.

The prophets in their smaller world had as great reason as we to quail before the tidal waves of society's upheavals, the rampant power of evil and the baffling, endless problem of human suffering and woe. They too faced social conflict and economic distress, and lived under threat of war. They can show us that the only way of sanity is to face the turmoil with the courage of faith. They can give us this faith for living in alignment with God's creative purpose, through the age-long historic process, to bring order out of chaos and good out of evil. They can deliver us from cynicism and moral impotence by giving value and direction to our present life, as the area of significant choices which carry with them the dignity of moral responsibility and personal freedom.

The clue to our historical experience is the truth grasped by Israel's prophets concerning the nature of God, his real presence in history and his intention for man's life. In the midst of the passions and moral confusion of war and social conflict, only this clue will enable us to see the finally important things in true proportion, and to learn what freedom is and why it must be found and kept as priceless. We may see in the terror and desolation of war, not only a revelation of God's judgment on the wrong choices and evil purposes of men, but also God's summons to man to repent, and to find life through losing it in devotion to the creative purpose which is life's meaning. Instead of being only an endless turmoil, our present history and all human history become personalized. That is, history acquires meaning to *persons* who make between good and evil real choices with historic consequences, who can distinguish morally momentous events, who can attain spiritual freedom, and live in confidence that history will not falsify their faith.

A final point of relevance of the Hebrew prophets for Christian theology is their eschatology. For obvious reasons their oracles have little bearing on the eschatology of the individual and of the Church, the two aspects of this matter to which Christian theology has given most attention. Their importance is that they introduce ethical and religious standards into the conviction of social destiny. Social eschatology may be the rationalization of a nation's will-to-power by the myth of a Herrenvolk, or the less vicious but equally fallacious liberal myth of perpetual progress, or the mind-picture of the inevitable triumph of the proletariat in the class struggle. In none of these is there the recognition, indispensable to the religion of the prophets, that *judgment must precede salvation*. A religious eschatology affirms that the real values of history must finally emerge from history's relativities and ambiguities. Because history has moral meaning, it moves toward an end in which the justice, the righteousness and the love of God shall have their full and final realization. In such a world as this the Day of the Lord will be darkness before it will be light. The truth of eschatology, like the truth of history, is the truth about God and about the spiritual structure of reality. That truth must inevitably work itself out in social history. It must realize itself in justice through judgment, and, beyond judgment, in the triumph in human life of God's goodness and his love.

This means, among other things, that the community must accept moral responsibility before God for the direction and goal of its common life. For it is the on-going community rather than the individual which is the carrier of history and the trustee of destiny. The individual tends to evade his share of this common responsibility because of the feeling that the community was before him and will be after him, and he himself is helpless. But the living historical consciousness, necessary to every vital and self-conscious community, can exist only through common awareness of social purpose and meaningful ends, as well as of meaningful beginnings and historical experience. There is the need for a religious eschatology of the community, to set beside its history.

In this eschatology principles and values which direct and motivate social life will be made clear and. vivid. But—as the prophets further insist—these are not to be relegated to a remote future for which responsibility can be shifted to generations yet unborn. They cannot be real unless they are real now. The judgment of eternity cannot be put off to the end of time, conceived as the end of a road beyond the horizon. We live and experience reality always in present time, an eternal present where the moral principles are already paramount which must emerge definitively in the End. Hence we must take our eschatology out of the air as Amos did, and apply it in particular socio-historical crises of experience. We must recognize that the harvest has begun while wheat and tares still grow together in the field. And so, as the justice and mercy of the Eternal work themselves out in experience, every day becomes Judgment Day.

THE WORK OF THE PREACHER

It has been emphasized earlier in this book that the prophets were something more than preachers. Nevertheless, their exposition of their own primary oracles had much in common with authentic preaching as serious exposition of Christian faith and responsibility. Their relevance for the preacher, in the first instance, is this serious and responsible attitude to their message. It contrasts painfully with the triviality or dull indifference, the exhibitionism or facile eloquence which counterfeits the clear and urgent pronouncement of a word of God. "My people are destroyed for lack of knowledge" (i.e., the true knowledge of God).[9] Hosea and his fellow messengers did not look for prominence or applause; they did not flatter men of wealth and position nor accommodate their message to what the people wanted them to say. They were the selfless mouthpieces of a word which possessed them and could not be contained, and they were conscious of its sublimity.

With respect to the subject matter of preaching we may turn to the prophetic scriptures for many illuminating and moving messages, notably for messages on social justice, national responsibility, the religious interpretation of historic events in our time, and on evangelism. Amos and Isaiah (to mention no others) are clamant voices

---

[9] Hos. 4:6.

demanding for the poor and disinherited the justice *and* the loving kindness of which they have been deprived. Their words are timeless. Their God and ours will put down the mighty from their seats and exalt them of low degree. But the man who proclaims this from a pulpit must do so in no lesser role than that of the spokesman of the Eternal. It must be the same, when the modern preacher speaks from a prophetic text on national responsibility before God for political decisions of grave importance, and for the principles and motives operative in our society. We can find in the writings of the prophets not only relevant messages for today, but understanding and wisdom for their presentation. They indicate the way to a theology of history which can give us that vision of God's purpose for the world, without which there may perish any civilization worthy of the name.

Today as in every age the message of the evangelist must begin with a call to repentance. From the prophets we learn that there must be corporate repentance for social sin and the defects of accepted morality, as well as personal repentance. We must go back of moral delinquency to the environment which promotes it, yet without ignoring the partial responsibility of the delinquent. Indeed, we must go back to the conventional *mores* and organizing principles of society itself—the selfish and internecine struggle for possessions and satisfactions, for position and power, and the materialism and practical atheism which predominate in so much of our modern life. This is the word of the Lord by Zechariah to Zerubbabel: "Not by might nor by power, but by my Spirit";[10] (literally) "not by material power or physical force," the twin pillars of the temple of this world.

Coupled with the call to repentance of a wrong way of life is the summons to believe and live in God's way, and the assurance of what God has done and will do to make this possible for man. This way corresponds to the moral and spiritual reality with which man supremely has to do, in a universe the Creator of which is not Baal or Marduk, Mammon or Mars, but the God of Moses and the prophets,

[10] Zech. 4:6.

the God and Father of Jesus Christ. For the corruption of man's life and the impotence of his spirit there is a divine remedy and a divine sufficiency: "The everlasting God, the Lord, the Creator of the ends of the earth fainteth not, neither is weary; there is no searching of his understanding."[11] From the standpoint of materialism and the self-centered pride of man, the religion of the prophets (and Christianity) is absurd. They call us to believe with their own passionate certainty that it is the world's way which is absurd, because it is not the way of the Eternal Justice and the Everlasting Mercy. "Do horses climb cliffs? Does one plough the sea with an ox?—you who turn justice into gall?"[12]

It is Hosea particularly who brings redeeming love into the prophetic message, and 2 Isaiah whose voice thrills with exultation at the "good news" of God. If we are to preach the gospel, we must love people for themselves with something of God's love for them: "How shall I give thee up, Ephraim? How can I cast thee off, Israel? My heart is turned within me; my compassion is kindled."[13] And we must be moved with the wonder of God's emancipating and renewing power: "O thou that tellest good tidings, . . . lift up thy voice with strength; lift it up, be not afraid; say unto the cities of Judah, Behold, your God!"[14]

THE CULTURAL CRISIS

It has been emphasized above[15] that the social evils denounced by the prophets were seen by them as concrete examples of a dominant spirit in their society, which contradicted the essential nature of man and ignored the commanding presence of God. This spirit and the culture it produced were the fruit of the nature religion, through which men then sought to make the unseen powers the servants of their self-interest. The magnitude of the prophets' achievement may

[11] Is. 40:28.
[12] Am. 6:12.
[13] Hos. 11:8.
[14] Is. 40:9.
[15] In chaps. 6 and 8.

be seen in the fact that their religion did much to create the unique spiritual culture of Judaism, a coherent and passionately-held structure of ideas which became normative in the on-going community.

To say that these men are relevant for the cultural crisis of today is thus, in the first place, to recognize their supreme importance in one of humanity's most notable spiritual traditions. It accords also with the recognition that a spiritual world-view, such as Judaism and Christianity offer, is indispensable to modern man. For only among a people who share deep ethical and religious convictions can a living and formative culture exist. We speak too often of the achievements of civilization as if these comprised primarily the social organizations, buildings, machinery and gadgets which men make and use, rather than the developed human quality of those who use them, and their accumulated intellectual, moral and spiritual resources. But it is men themselves who are or are not civilized. Their culture, the non-material achievements and possessions of their minds and spirits, their success in finding a way of living together according to the best that is in them—these are what really matter. All thoughtful men know that there is a lag here that may well prove fatal. Man has extended his controls over his environment but has not learned to control himself, his rulers, and the gods his own hands have made. He has taken into his hands terrific powers before he has attained the spiritual stature to insure his using them for good ends.

In this area of life the worth and effectiveness of religion in social life is of paramount importance. The basic atheism, materialism, irrationality, moral confusion and social tension of life today in the Western world are more than sufficient to explain our cultural poverty and impotence. Among the vast majority of our people there is little concern for, and less agreement on, the really important issues which should determine social policy: what life is for, and what are its abiding satisfactions; the priority of values; the proper motivating force of economic activity; the moral basis of civil rights and duties; individual liberty; the extent and limitations of state power; the essentials in the past and future of democracy. People are concerned with making a comfortable living rather than with living so that the world is better for their presence. In our wars we are so taken up with the business of organizing and achieving victory, that we give little thought to what we shall do with that victory that is at all commensurate with the cost of winning it.

Somehow or other the moral and political philosophers, the artists and poets, the writers and preachers who are the real architects of civilization must find and proclaim a spiritual understanding of life. It must be adequate for the new situation which industrialism, world communications and the emergence of new nations and forms of society have created for humanity. The *means* must be subordinated to the *right ends* of life. We must recognize that political and economic problems are basically *human* problems and demand a humane solution. We must see that the fundamental defect of any economic system which represses the human spirit and keeps many in poverty and insecurity, is its denial of moral values and of human brotherhood. This denial creates also the international anarchy which makes war from time to time inevitable. The social goal must be clarified; it is the establishment of the rights and duties of all men in a structure of social relationships, appropriate to the fact that they have been made by God to live as brothers. The principal mainspring of economic activity cannot rightly be self-interest, if the supreme commandments are that man should love God with his whole being and his neighbor as himself.

What Israel's prophets said long ago when they condemned the manner of this world and pointed men to the city of God, is directly and profoundly relevant for us. They concerned themselves with political and economic issues because of their human consequences. They laid bare the moral facts involved, in the light of Yahweh's will as the supreme fact with which man in this life has to do. They traced society's troubles to the inverted order of material and spiritual things, to man's self-interest and self-exaltation even against God, and to the denial of his own nature in denying human kinship.

The prophets' role was more than that of denunciation. The fruit of the religion they affirmed is equally pertinent to our situation. It offered a rock of security for men's spirits, and a coherent meaning and direction for life. It offered a moral motive in the sense of an absolute obligation for God's sake to realize in the community his justice, truth and love; and a creative faith that God's purpose for man's future was good. These things, again, religion can contribute to culture. Man craves security from want and fear, because without confidence he cannot live at all and retain his sanity. He must have something dependable to rest on, some shield against death. This is why he seeks to wall himself round with safeguards and possessions. But, as Jesus said of the man who thought he had found security in bigger barns, life has no final security at all apart from God. "Blessed is the man whose *confidence* is Yahweh," said Jeremiah[16]—life's foundation, its pivot, its integration. This is what modern man lacks and needs perhaps most of all.

Furthermore, Christianity offers to Western man, by recalling him to his heritage, an interpretation of the worth and meaning of life by which he may find again the bearings he knows he has lost. It can give him, as it gave to his fathers, the supreme motivating power of a conviction of absolute obligation to that which is right, because God is God. And in the goodness and historic purpose of the God of the prophets and of Jesus Christ, man can again find the faith that goodness is real and is to be realized on earth; and that it alone can overcome the rampant evil of which man is the partly consenting and partly rebellious victim. Only men who believe in God's goodness can discern his purpose and build for an unseen future, creating anew the cultural life of their people.

THE DEMOCRATIC STRUGGLE

Democracy as a system of government has assumed many forms, and various mechanisms have been devised in the attempt to give actuality to the democratic idea. At no time has the democratic idea

---

[16] Jer. 17:7.

been fully realized, from the days of the Athenian democracy resting on the backs of slaves to modern states where universal political rights are largely nullified by economic inequality. We speak of the democratic struggle because man's striving for fuller life is always the struggle for true personal freedom, in the spontaneous life of real community. Today there is visible and invisible war between the friends and foes of human freedom.

What is the democratic idea? It is the conviction that personal freedom is compatible with, and indeed can only be found in the ordered life of society, that the social order is good or bad according as it does or does not provide the opportunity of true freedom for all its citizens. It holds that the best government is self-government, that political authority is held in trust for the community. It affirms that the intrinsic equality of all citizens as human beings is more important than their differences in capacity, and is the right basis of political order. Democracy holds that the state is made for man and not man for the state, and therefore that the state has rightful authority only as it acts in the interests of all the people and of the people as a whole. It affirms that men can and should live together as neighbors, that they can work together for a common end and reconcile their differences—within limits set by the common ethic—without resort to violence. It declares that the only proper limit to personal freedom is what interferes with the equal rights of others, and that all rights are balanced by duties to others and to the social good.

As a matter of historical record, Christianity has contributed much to the development of the democratic idea and its institutions. Its doctrines of the equality of all men before God, of human brotherhood, of the emancipating power of the Gospel, of the subordination of all earthly authorities to God and his righteousness, and of property as held in trust—have given ever fresh impulses to the democratic movement. Much of this came into Christianity from the Hebrew prophets, whose spirit Christianity brought to a new fruition and whose words it retained in its sacred Scriptures. This is the first reason the prophets are relevant for modern democracy—that they belong to its spiritual ancestry, through the intermingling of the Hebrew-Christian and classical traditions.

Israelite society under the kingdoms was not, of course, a democracy—except in a very limited way, insofar as the king took counsel with the elders and on occasion came face to face with an assembly of the people. But the prophets did emphasize the concept of a society where all citizens were in essence kinsmen, where every man had an equal right to justice, and where social authority was subject to a divine law of righteousness whose purpose was the well-being or "salvation" of all. As we have seen before, they idealized the simpler, tribal society of the past, with its freedom, its sense of kinship, its system of common property and its representative administration of custom and right. In such a society Yahweh had been able to make known his right way of life. Again, they were the constant champions of the people against despotism and oppression. They did not ask for pity; they demanded justice in the name of God. Once more, they proclaimed the *covenant* society where Yahweh's way would be realized in the community of neighbors, where the king's heart would not be lifted up above his brethren but where he would rule according to the divine statutes which had been given the community.[17] And in their visions of Yahweh's purpose for their future, the prophets set before men's eyes the hope of a nobler and fairer day when the victory of Israel's faith among the nations would deliver all men from want and fear and war.[18]

Two other points may be added. The vivid realization in feeling of the individual's participation in the corporate life is something the prophets helped to revive, though it was their inheritance in Israel. Our excessive individualism has robbed us of this. But it is essential to cultural vitality and to patriotism that citizens of a democracy should be able—as sometimes the citizens of totalitarian states seem able—to realize with profound feeling their membership in the body politic, and so to find national unity of spirit.

[17] Cf. the formulation of prophetic teaching in Deut. 17:14–20.
[18] Cf. Micah 4:1–5.

Again, the essential thing in individual freedom is the responsible moral consciousness of a man or woman as a person. It was through the experience of men like Hosea and Jeremiah that there came into our tradition knowledge of the inner freedom of spirit, which creates the demand for civil and religious liberties. It is a matter of record that the struggle for freedom of conscience and of worship is part and parcel of the age-long fight for full democratic liberty, and with it stands or falls.

These impulses came into our liberal democratic tradition from the prophets of Israel and the apostles of Christ. But it is easier to see in a general way that the prophets are relevant to our modern social problems than it is to be more specific. Some suggestions, however, may be made. We may learn, for one thing, that the slogans of democracy and patriotism are no substitute for the costly service of these great ideals. If we really care about freedom and justice, we must judge the worth and effectiveness of our present institutions by their actual results in human terms for *all* people. We still have the hungry and deprived among us, though our economy could produce enough for all. The difference between them and the comfortable in benefits received is seldom due to the moral superiority or even the greater mental capacity of the latter. It is due, rather, to the acceptance of conditions and the operation of factors which an aroused democracy can alter. Divine justice demands that they be altered. Today as in the eighth century B.C. the economic system too often divides the people into groups with conflicting interests, and the nations of the "one world" into "haves" and "have-nots." It distributes its benefits according neither to men's needs nor to their deserts. It gives to many individuals social power without social responsibility, and sets men's hearts on a materialistic goal. Our political democracy is largely nullified by the absence of a corresponding economic democracy. For a man is not free unless he has the right to a livelihood, and participates in governing his economic life, as well as in choosing those who make and administer the laws. To read the prophetic books is to feel what only those whose selfish interests are served by so doing can ignore—that social and economic justice, within and between nations, *is* the concern of religion, and every man *is* his brother's keeper. In the modern age, this can only mean that those who direct the vast and impersonal industrial, financial and commercial enterprise must be primarily responsible to the community as a whole for serving the common welfare, and that rich and powerful nations must, in the name of God and of humanity, come to the aid of the less fortunate.

Finally, we may gain from the prophets that depth of moral earnestness which can gird the democratic idea with the conviction of eternal righteousness. God is at work in history to create for himself a people in whose hearts are his laws. Particular forms of society and government will prosper or perish according as they embody justice and right, sustain personal dignity and foster personal freedom and true community among men. God is not outside the world-wide human struggle but within it.

> *He shall judge between many peoples,*
>   *And shall decide for strong nations afar off;*
> *And they shall beat their swords into plowshares,*
>   *And their spears into pruning hooks;*
> *Nation shall not lift up sword against nation,*
>   *Neither shall they learn war any more;*
> *But they shall sit every man under his vine and under his fig tree,*
>   *And none shall make them afraid;*
> *For the mouth of the Lord of hosts has spoken.*
>
>   (MICAH 4:3–4.)

INDEX OF SUBJECTS

167, 227; sovereignty of, 167, 203; will of, 11, 13, 54, 56, 112–13, 118, 144, 152, 156–57, 163, 207; word of, 9, 43, 57, 90–113, 162; uniqueness of, 67, 81, 117–18, 121–22, 151, 194–95, 204, 211.

Zedekiah, 99.
Zephaniah, 86–87, 166.

INDEX OF AUTHORS

INDEX OF SCRIPTURE REFERENCES

Scripture References are separated from numbers referring to pages in *The Relevance of the Prophets* by a dash.